The Author

Nicholas van der Bijl, BEM

Nick van der Bijl spent a number of years in the Intelligence Corps, seeing active service in Northern Ireland and during the Falklands campaign – the latter with 3rd Commando Brigade. On leaving the Regular Army in 1989, he was commissioned into the 2nd Battalion Wessex Regiment (Volunteers) in Reading, serving nearly three years. Following a two-year post-graduate course at Loughborough University, he gained a diploma in security management, since when he has worked in the defence, logistics and healthcare professions in this field. He has also become a well-respected writer: in addition to articles in military and security period-icals, he is the author of *The Argentinean Forces in the Falklands* and *Royal Marines, 1939–1993,* as well as the best-selling *Nine Battles to Stanley.* Moving to Somerset in 1992, he now lives with his wife Penny and daughter Imogen in the village of Mark.

Other Hawk Editions' titles:

SOMERSET AT WAR, 1939-45
Mac Hawkins

THANKS FOR THE MEMORY
Mac Hawkins

THE SOMERSET & DORSET Then and Now
Mac Hawkins

THE GREAT CENTRAL Then and Now
Mac Hawkins

LSWR WEST COUNTRY LINES Then and Now
Mac Hawkins

IVO PETERS' FAREWELL TO NORTH-WEST STEAM
Edited by Mac Hawkins

IVO PETERS' CLASSIC STEAM
Mac Hawkins

THE RAILWAY PAINTINGS OF MALCOLM ROOT
Mac Hawkins

Air view of Brean Down from the sea, showing the fort. (Cambridge University)

Brean Down Fort

Its history and the defence of the Bristol Channel

Nicholas van der Bijl, BEM

Best wishes

Nicholas van der Bijl

Hawk Editions

DEDICATED TO THE MEN OF THE COAST REGIMENT,
ROYAL ARTILLERY
AND
THE MEN AND WOMEN WHO HAVE DEFENDED
THIS COUNTRY

First published in 2000 by HAWK EDITIONS
PO Box 184, Cossington, Somerset TA7 8YT

ISBN 0-9529081-7-4

Copy-edited by Gerard M-F Hill
Reprographics by Character Graphics, Taunton, Somerset
Printed and bound in Singapore

Contents

Foreword

By

Admiral of the Fleet Sir Benjamin Bathurst, GCB
Vice Lord Lieutenant of Somerset

The first duty of any government is to ensure the security of the United Kingdom. Over the centuries that has been the foundation stone on which successive defence policies have been built. Now in the 21st Century and with the end of the Cold War, in an increasingly interdependent and interconnected world, it is, perhaps, hard to imagine a territorial threat to this country. Yet 150 years ago, in the wake of the Napoleonic Wars and, notwithstanding Britain's dominance of the oceans and her ability to defend and sustain a worldwide empire, the possibility of invasion by France remained at the heart of the Government's concerns.

The manifestation of this was the series of fortifications around our coast that are still visible today, most obviously in the areas of the south coast naval bases. However, just as susceptible, was the Bristol Channel, the gateway to the trade of the Port of Bristol and the coal of South Wales. So, despite the fierce tides and many sandbars, which in themselves provided much natural protection against invasion, money was allocated to build a string of defensive positions across the Channel from Brean Down to Lavernock Point.

In this comprehensive book, Nick van der Bijl takes immense care to tell us the story of one such defensive position but at the same time manages to give a much wider perspective on the military, technical and social aspects of the Army as a whole. In a county where sadly the military presence, both regular and reserve, continues to reduce, this book is an excellent reminder of how Somerset men contributed to the defence of a strategically vital area. I hope it will also encourage those organisations that are trying to preserve some of these installations for posterity to stick to their task. A fascinating story is told here.

Sir Benjamin Bathurst

Preface

This book emerged from the investigation of Brean Down during the 1997 Heritage Lottery bid to restore Brean Down Fort. I had made it my task to find out as much as I possibly could about the fort so that, when it opened, visitors would have an accurate account of its history and its relationship to the defence of Great Britain and the Bristol Channel. When the bid failed, it seemed to me that its history was even more important because here was a story that needed to be told, particularly as many of those who served there left no record of life on Brean Down and those that do survive are elderly and their memories going back over fifty years deserve to be recorded.

When writing history, it is inevitable that some events will not be included or may have become embellished as time marches on. This is often when archaeologists step in and others speculate. History needs to be accurate, so far as is possible, so that when decisions are made about disposing of buildings, we know what we are destroying. This is surely the case with Brean Down Fort, about which little is known. It is interesting that while the ecology of Brean Down is cared for, the historic naval and military features have been ignored. Certainly the fort is not held in the same affection as the largely inaccessible Steep Holm, with its history lying around for no one to see. Perhaps Brean Down's isolation has meant that even the nearby towns of Weston-super-Mare and Burnham-on-Sea have tended to forget its existence. In telling the story of the fort and its 140-year life, I hope this book will show that, as well as its natural history, Brean Down has its human history too.

Nick van der Bijl
Mark, Somerset
May 2000

Glossary

AMPC	Auxiliary Military Pioneer Corps		*HQ*	Headquarters		*PAC*	Parachute and Cable	
AA	Anti Aircraft		*hr/hrs*	hour/hours		*PLUTO*	Pipe Line Under the Ocean	
			HRH	His (or Her) Royal Highness				
BA	Bachelor of Arts					*QF*	Quick Firing	
Bart	Baronet		*in/ins*	inch/inches				
BDH	Brean Down Harbour					*RA*	Royal Artillery	
B&E	Bristol and Exeter Railway Company		*JNCO*	Junior Non Commissioned Officer		*RAF*	Royal Air Force	
BL	Breech Loaded					*Rev*	Reverend	
			KCB	Knight Commander of the Bath		*RGA*	Royal Garrison Artillery	
CASE	Coast Artillery Sighting and Elevation		*Kg*	Kilogram		*RFA*	Royal Field Artillery	
			km	kilometre		*RIASC*	Royal Indian Army Service Corps	
CASL	Coast Artillery Search Light		*kph*	kilometres per hour		*RAMC*	Royal Army Medical Corps	
CD	Coast Defence		*kW*	kilowatt		*RBL*	Rifled Breech Loaded	
						RML	Rifled Muzzle Loaded	
DMWD	Department of Miscellaneous Weapons Development		*lb/lbs*	pound/pounds		*RMS*	Royal Mail Ship	
			LCT	Landing Craft Tank		*RN*	Royal Navy	
DRF	Depression Range Finder		*LDV*	Local Defence Volunteers		*RASC*	Royal Army Service Corps	
						RE	Royal Engineers	
ft	foot/feet		*M*	Metre/metres		*RDC*	Rural District Council	
g	gram		*MC*	Military Cross				
GOC	General Officer Commanding		*mm*	millimetre		*SS*	Steam Ship	
GCB	Grand Commander of the Bath		*MP*	Member of Parliament				
GEC	General Electric Company		*mph*	miles per hour		*TA*	Territorial Army	
GSO1	General Staff Officer Grade One		*MV*	Motor Vessel		*TLC*	Tank Landing Craft	
GW	Great Western Railway Company		*MVO*	Member of the Victorian Order		*TF*	Territorial Force	
			NAAFI	Navy, Army and Air Force Institute		*UP*	Unrotated Projectile	
ha	hectare		*NCO*	Non Commissioned Officer				
HMS	His (or Her) Majesty's Ship		*oz/ozs*	ounce/ounces		*yd/yds*	yard/yards	

List of Maps

ONE

Brean Down to 1860

View of Brean Down from Uphill showing Black Rock and possible route of ford. (H. Tempest, Cardiff)

Jutting out like a huge stranded whale into the Bristol Channel is the limestone headland of Brean Down, 1½ miles (2.5km) long but only ¼ mile (400m) wide and 320ft (98m) above the sea at its highest point. An extension of the Mendip ridge, it was once an island. To the north, south and west is the sea while to the east and south-east lies low-lying salt-marsh farmland. Two miles to the south, along a coast road now characterised by a parade of caravan sites and holiday camps, is the old village of Brean, from where the road continues through Berrow, past the golf course and into Burnham-on-

Sea. From Brean Down on a clear day there are fine views to Wales and across Somerset. To the north there are spectacular views of Weston-super-Mare, which at the beginning of the nineteenth century was a small fishing village about to be discovered. Rising sharply from the plain and jutting out into the sea are the three hills of (from north to south) Middle Hope, Worlebury and Brean Down, composed of hard carboniferous limestone, which was laid some 250 million years ago on the bed of a shallow, warm sea. In the recent geological past, the sea rose and the hills became islands, separated from the

Mendip Hills. To the south, sand dunes (now 50ft/15m high in places) built up and behind them the floodplain of the River Axe extended until the land joined up with Brean Down once more.

Brean Down is a Site of Special Scientific Interest. The combination of harsh conditions over much of the down, with damp south-westerly gales whipping in from the sea and across the Somerset Levels, and the calmer but colder conditions on the northern slopes, have led to floral habitats of lush grass and bracken and bramble, with a small area of wind-battered scrub above Brean Farm. Three species of rare plants have been identified, white rose, dwarf sedge and Somerset hair grass.

There have long been foxes and badgers on Brean Down. Warreners bred rabbits there between the fourteenth and eighteenth centuries, for food and skins; the warreners have gone but the rabbits are as numerous as ever. Cattle from Brean Farm graze on the slopes, which they share with feral goats, introduced in the 1970s. Brean Down is a designated bird sanctuary and is of particular importance to spring and autumn migrants. Peregrine falcons hunt rabbits and smaller mammals. Butterflies are in particular abundance on the southern slopes.

The name 'Brean' occurs in the Domesday Book (as *Brien*) but it is certainly much older. According to Ekwall's *Dictionary of English Place-names* it is an Anglo-Saxon name, which in turn came from the ancient British word *briga*, meaning a hill. It must have been the name of the down itself, long before there was a village of Brean. Newcomers should note that the name has two syllables: say 'Bree-un' rather than 'Breen'.

There is evidence of settlement in periods from the Neolithic to post-mediaeval, including well preserved Early Bronze Age round houses associated with salt production. At Sand Cliff, on the south side of the down, early evidence of Man was found between 1983 and 1987 by archaeologists unearthing well-preserved roundhouse walls at least 15,000 years old. In November 1983, Bristol University archaeologist and lecturer Dr Keith Crabtree and a student, Nicholas Waters of Bristol, each found 18-carat gold bracelets, dated 900–700 BC during an excavation. Both were considered to be treasure trove and handed to the Treasury.

An Iron Age hill-fort, dated between 300 and 100 BC, is unusual in that it was defended on only two sides and may have been abandoned before completion. A Romano-Celtic temple, dating from AD 340 to 367, was found next to a burial mound facing east, suggesting an early Christian presence. There are also remains of two field systems, one covering the eastern knoll and the other near the triangulation point on the highest part of the down.

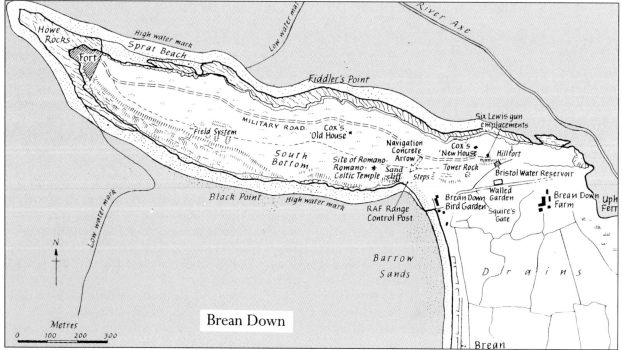

Map 1: *Brean Down*

Raids by the York and East Anglian Danes forced the Anglo-Saxons to strengthen Wessex and Mercia and, in November 914, to attack the Humberside Danes. French Danes, attempting to outflank the Anglo-Saxons, landed a party near Port Talbot but were defeated by the Welsh not far from Worcester. Returning to their ships, they established a base on Steep Holm and, although they raided the settlements at Watchet and Porlock, were largely contained by the West Saxons. Eventually hunger drove them to leave. Norwegian raids from bases in the Irish Sea continued to harass the west coast and then, in 988, 'The Black Host', sailing from Dublin, plundered Wales and attacked Watchet.

Brean Down was owned by Glastonbury Abbey until sold to the Wyndham family in the seventeenth century, who could see its use as a harbour. One of England's long-established families of landed gentry, they originally hailed from Norfolk. Their connection with Somerset began in 1561 when John Wyndham married Florence Wadham, who was a member of the Sydenham family and sister of Nicholas, who founded Wadham College, Oxford.

Brean Down appears to have been left largely undisturbed during the following centuries up until 1860. There is a warrener's lodge and post-mediaeval farm near the top of Sand Cliffs. However, from its shores would have been seen the trading and slaving ships that turned Bristol into a prosperous port. The first Bristol Channel fixed defences were at Battery Point in Portishead; they were built by the Royalists to defend Bristol. When the Parliamentarians besieged the city in 1642, the battery surrendered without a shot being fired. Several days later it opened fire on a Royalist ship intent on reaching Bristol.

In 1647 Colonel William Wyndham held Dunster Castle against Parliamentarian forces and gave the future King Charles II refuge. In 1671, anxious to bring government work to Somerset, Sir William Wyndham attempted, without success, to persuade the Navy Board to build warships at Bridgwater, possibly the first time that it was proposed to locate a defence industry in the West Country outside Bristol. It has been suggested that the Wyndhams planned, for purely personal reasons, to build a harbour at Brean Down in this period. At any rate, in the late 1680s, Sir William patronised the smuggling of wine, brandy and cloth under the cover of innocent cargoes through his harbour of Watchet, and grew rich. His friend Colonel Luttrell,

of another noted Somerset family, ran Minehead in a similar fashion. The Excise, with just thirteen officers, was barely able to cope. Even the stationing of a frigate between Bristol and Bideford was insufficient to deter the illicit trade.

The Threat from France

To Britain in 1789 the violence of the French Revolution was so horrifying that other events in Europe seemed secondary in importance. The storming of the Bastille was an unpleasant example of mob action, which hardened public opinion. By 1792 French zeal to broaden the Revolution was at its greatest but France's relations with the rest of Europe were at their lowest. Everywhere France looked, there was British meddling – reinforcing weak continental armies that cost French lives; supporting half-baked Royalist attempts to overthrow the Revolution; and, on the high seas, the Royal Navy ruled. Tired of this interference in her affairs, feelings against England ran high and the governing Directory decided it was time to deal their tiresome and long-standing enemy a crushing blow, once and for all.

After France defeated the Austrians in Belgium in November 1792, the new government declared that the River Scheldt, which historically had been closed to large foreign vessels, was now open to all ships of whatever nation. Britain regarded this as a threat to her commercial interests and she joined Prussia, Austria, Holland, Sardinia and Spain against France in hostilities that would last until 1815, apart from a few months of peaceful tension at the turn of the century. Financially weak after the rigours of the American War of Independence, politically isolated in Europe, threatened by Irish nationalists and at risk from rebellion in India and the West Indies, nevertheless Great Britain had been put on a sound war footing by Prime Minister William Pitt. There was civil unrest but this was not so much against the aristocracy as the destabilisation of the Industry Revolution. Her people watched, with horror, as the French Revolution developed into the vengeful bloodbath of the Terror. Most people wanted nothing to do with the turmoil in France.

Britain fears invasion

French agents reported the information that they believed that the Directory wanted – England and

Postcard view of Brean Sands from Brean Down, c.1920.
(Author's collection)

Wales were ripe for revolution. Lazar Carnot, who was appointed to the Directory in 1795, believed in *chouannerie* – whereby a few men could inspire the spreading of terror by a peasants' revolt – and Carnot and Hoche were behind French plans to start this in Cornwall. In Carnot's words, 'an expedition begun with so few men can succeed only by extraordinary means'.

With the emergence of the Belfast-born Protestant lawyer, Wolfe Tone, and (in 1791) the United Society of Irishmen, an organisation that stood for nationalist independence, the French also had hopes of rebellion in Ireland. So, while the obvious invasion beaches in Kent and Sussex were being carefully watched – and, within a few years, defended with Martello towers and the Royal Military Canal – and while the Royal Navy patrolled the Channel (no doubt recalling the landings in the West Country a century earlier of the Duke of Monmouth and then William of Orange), the French had plans to land further west. The Bristol Channel and the 'Celtic fringe' were the target of several enemy sorties and therefore were at greater risk, because they were largely undefended compared to the south coast of England.

General Lazar Hoche, a former grenadier sergeant in the elite French Guard, was the main influence on plans to invade Great Britain. He was a close associate of Bonaparte and was an advocate of the invasion of England throughout his career as a Bonapartist general, because "Ever since the beginning of the war, I have never ceased to believe that it is in their own country that we must attack the English" – that is, take the war to the English and not allow them to defend their country by fighting in Europe. Several ideas were discussed, including a raid by 100,000 men to destroy the London dockyards, and arming the merchant fleet to force a passage across the

Channel and land 40,000 men in southern England. Discreetly assembling such a large force in a country full of intrigue while concealing the transports seems to have been overlooked, such was the enthusiasm for such a venture. But the French Atlantic Fleet was no match for the blockading squadrons and main battle fleet at Portsmouth, which had recently been reformed after years of mismanagement.

Hoche had raised an invasion force but in February 1793 the troops earmarked for the invasion of England had to be rushed to La Vendée to quell a rebellion. British forces landed in Toulon to support the Royalists but were ejected by a young artilleryman, Napoleon Bonaparte. French conscripts then defeated the coalition regulars and soon Britain stood alone against a France seething with revolutionary zeal and determined to spread it throughout Europe. In English minds, the threat of invasion was immediate and alarming; in practice the likelihood of invasion was low. The French navy was then crippled at the Battle of the First of June in 1794.

The constant threat of invasion and the weak defences of Great Britain lay behind the passing of the 1794 Militia Act. Designed to 'augment the Militia' with volunteers, it legalised the raising of artillery volunteers, volunteer cavalry, and gentlemen and yeomanry cavalry. Raised by public-spirited members of the community, the volunteers were separate from the regular army and militia and bore no relation to any other military organisation previously raised in the British Army. In rural Somerset, landed gentry claimed that harm would be done to agriculture and the harvest if large numbers of yeomen and workers were expected to serve outside the county.

Nevertheless John Strode of Bath raised the Somerset Fencible Cavalry of six troops of dragoons. The word 'fencible' is a shortened form of 'defencible'. These were units raised to serve in Britain for the duration of hostilities. The first volunteer infantry to be formed was the Loyal Somersetshire Regiment of Fencible Infantry raised in West Somerset, by William Foster. Based in Taunton it was engaged on internal security duties in Ireland. Sea Fencibles were raised from lookouts, coastguards and fishermen at Pill, Minehead, Watchet and Bridgwater, and provided coast-watchers to look for enemy vessels.

In the wars between Great Britain and Europe, this was the first time the Bristol Channel had ever really been threatened. So, although Bristol was a major port and its approaches offered an alternative anchorage if the Royal Navy was unable to use Portsmouth and Plymouth, there were few fixed defences. There was no naval presence in the Bristol Channel, but the seas were busy with trading and smuggling between the many small harbours in the south-west, Wales and Ireland.

French invasion plans of 1796

The year 1796 brought the next upsurge of invasion fever. Ireland was in turmoil after the United Irishmen (an illegal organisation since 1794) had made a fatal bid for independence. Hoche planned landings in England and Ireland, with a diversion in Wales. The problem was that the French fleet was so ill equipped its ships in such a poor state of repair and the sailors so inexperienced that the delivery of the troops could only be piecemeal.

So far as the landings in England were concerned, the idea was for the 1st French Legion – a regiment composed of deserters of all nationalities and 600 convicts, – to land near Great Yarmouth, march north and destroy shipping on the River Tyne and then link up with Jacobean sympathisers perceived to be active in Lancashire. But the legion refused to board the flat-bottomed boats and when a storm sank several vessels, drowning many soldiers, the expedition was aborted. Hoche then planned to attach troops to the United Irishmen to attack British infrastructure and communications followed up by a landing in Galway of 16,000 troops. Much depended on evading the Royal Navy guarding the western approaches, the state of the British Army in Ireland and the support of Irish patriots.

Austria, Russia, Turkey and Great Britain then drove the French from Italy. Russia quarrelled with Pitt over Malta and withdrew from the coalition, leaving Britain again to stand alone. The Directory ordered that Ireland should be invaded at Bantry Bay.

Landings in the west

On 16 December 1796 Hoche and 14,000 men, in transports escorted by warships, left Brest but were scattered by storms. Over the next fortnight, ships arrived at Bantry Bay and landed a few patrols but the foul weather prevented their anchors from holding and General Emmanuel Grouchy, Hoche's deputy (who was later to dither at Waterloo), abandoned the enterprise. Ill from his failed expedition, Hoche then directed the 65-year-old American, Colonel William Tate, to land in England.

Tate was a gunner who was captured in the American War of Independence. When war broke out again in 1793 and America's neutrality was threatened, his plan for a motley group of adventurers to capture New Orleans failed and Tate fled to France. There he met Theobald Wolfe Tone and suggested that he raise a force to capture Jamaica. Hoche rejected this but gave him the 2nd Foreign Legion.

The 2nd Foreign Legion was a 1,300-strong irregular force of experienced soldiers recruited from French émigrés captured at Quiberon in 1795 and Irish prisoners-of-war, only too pleased to leave the drudgery and boredom of foetid prison camps. None knew what was entailed except they were told that the expedition was bound for the West Indies. Since they wore dyed dark brown British army uniforms captured at Quiberon, the army was known as the *Légion Noire* – the Black Legion.

Hoche believed the Welsh would rise against the English and he instructed Tate to stir up insurrection, interrupt commerce and divert the British government's attention to the West Country by destroying Bristol and then, under the inevitable confusion, capture Chester and Liverpool. Thereafter his orders were vague. If he was unable to land at Bristol, he was to land in Cardigan Bay and march north through Wales. The orders were optimistic, to say the least.

Sailing from Brest on 16 February 1779, the Black Legion was embarked on four ships commanded by Commodore Jean Castagnier. Flying false colours, he avoided the blockade and was sighted four days later, first by Revenue lookouts on Lundy Island. The French ships were beating with some difficulty against a strong north-easterly and could reach no further than Porlock. Alarm spread on both sides of the Bristol Channel and local commanders assembled their militia and volunteer forces. The Devonshire Volunteer Infantry Regiment marched to Bideford ready to deploy against the French.

Castagnier realised he could not reach Bristol and, although in favour of landing the legion in Swansea Bay, agreed to follow Hoche's instructions and landed Tate's men about two miles (3km) west of Fishguard, a small fishing town protected by a fort overlooking the harbour entrance. A corporal and two gunners from the Royal Artillery Invalid Company and 200 men of the Fishguard Fencibles manned its eight 9-pounder guns. Ammunition was in very short supply.

Some weeks prior to the raid, a ship loaded with wine had been wrecked nearby and many local families acquired a cask. The consequence was that many of the legion became drunk, and the discipline shown during the landings soon disappeared. After landing the legion and its equipment, next evening Castagnier weighed anchor to carry out his next phase of the operation, to intercept British reinforcements from Ireland.

By the time the news of the landing reached the Admiralty and naval commanders at Plymouth, Bristol and Milford, Castagnier's small squadron was reported to be several ships-of-the-line. Admiral Kingsmill, naval Commander-in-Chief Ireland, believed it was a feint to draw attention away from ports in Ireland and ordered ships to converge on the Bristol Channel and Wales.

Meanwhile on 23 February the 23-year-old Lieutenant-Colonel Thomas Knox assembled a force made up of infantry volunteers, the Pembrokeshire Militia, a troop from the Pembrokeshire Yeomanry, and 150 sailors with eight 9-pounder guns. However, when a prisoner said that the French numbered about 1,300 men, Knox – outnumbered – abandoned Fishguard and withdrew toward Haverfordwest. During the early afternoon the British, now about 600 strong, returned to Fishguard, where headquarters were set up in the Royal Oak Inn.

By the evening, Tate realised the raid was a shambles. Cut off in a foreign country, with the Irish threatening to desert after finding they were in Wales, and not the West Indies, and his advance guard in contact with a large force, it was enough to convince him to surrender. Tate's bold suggestion that the Black Legion be repatriated at the expense of the British Government was rejected and next morning they filed into captivity. Fifty-seven years later, when the volunteer movement was at its height, the Pembrokeshire Yeomanry was awarded the battle honour 'Fishguard' and is the only military unit to have been awarded such an honour for an engagement on British soil.

Britain was shaken by events in Ireland and Wales. Matters worsened when the Channel Fleet mutinied and conspiracies sympathetic to the French were discovered. The next threat was from 15,000 men of a Dutch fleet, the idea being to defeat the North Sea Fleet, sail to Scotland, seize Edinburgh, march on Glasgow and dominate the English northern counties. It was hoped this would force British troops to be withdrawn from Ireland

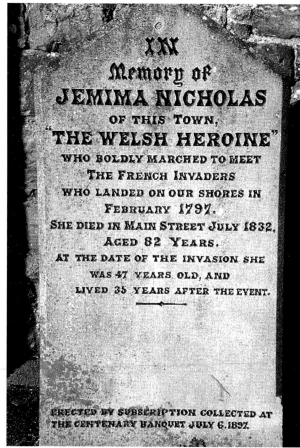

The grave of Jemima Nicholas who captured several prisoners of war during the invasion of Fishguard. (Author's collection)

and facilitate a French landing at Bantry Bay. In late September the Dutch were decisively defeated at Camperdown.

French calculations had been wide of the mark. But still the French persisted with plans to invade England. On 26 October 1797 the Directory formally issued a directive:

> There shall be assembled without delay, on the coasts of the ocean, an army which shall be called the Army of England. Citizen General Bonaparte is named commander-in-chief of that army.

Specially built shallow-draught gunboats, warships, transports, 70,000 infantry and 6,000 cavalry assembled in Channel ports from all over Europe.

But Napoleon hesitated, declaring that in spite of whatever efforts the French might make, without command of the sea, and the Channel in particular, invading England was the most dangerous operation that anyone could undertake. He continued:

If it is only possible by surprise, either by the squadron at Brest or the Texel slipping away, or by landing from small craft during the night in Kent or Sussex after a passage of seven to eight hours.

Napoleon was implying that at least the length of a winter's night was needed, if the British were to be taken by surprise. However, the weather in the English Channel is at its worst in winter. All invaders faced the same dilemma.

The Directory has second thoughts

The preparations were closely watched in Britain and the blockade reinforced. Bored soldiers are bad soldiers and Napoleon's army grumbled. Recognising that until the Royal Navy were defeated, there could be no invasion, the Directory decided that British interests in India should be threatened instead, by military operations in the Middle East, and instructed Napoleon to take the Army of England to Egypt where it was soundly defeated by forces under Admiral Nelson.

The French continued to attack Ireland as the soft underbelly of the United Kingdom. In August 1798 General Humbert and 1,150 Frenchmen landed at Killala Bay and after overwhelming the garrison at Castle Bay, surrendered to Lord Cornwallis at Ballinamuck on 6 September. Another expedition, which was intended to synchronise operations with Humbert, sailed from Brest on 17 September but were sighted. Shaking off their pursuers by a long track west and then north, the French squadron reached Lough Swilly but lost the engagement. Wolfe Tone was captured and later executed. It was a decisive victory and showed the French and, indeed, the Irish, how difficult it was to land troops in Britain and maintain a presence.

In spite of these reverses, the French continued to

The surrender of French-led forces on Goodwin Sands, Fishguard. (Author's collection)

plot invasions but, every time, their schemes foundered when the need to overcome the patrolling blockade remained unresolved. Britons, however, saw the threat as very real and, as we shall see in a later chapter, between 1800 and 1815 built a major system of coast defences.

As dusk crept across the sodden battlefield near Waterloo on 18 June 1815, Britain hoped that the long wars with the French were, at last, finished. However, while hostilities were over, the government was faced with the problems of increased political awareness among ordinary people, hardship and increased industrialisation. Demands for political representation induced civil disobedience and magistrates often turned to the yeomanry to suppress the unrest. War had ended but peace had not followed, and the militia was not disbanded.

De Joinville's Paper

It seemed there would always be suspicion between the two nations. A major contribution to peace was Prime Minister Sir Robert Peel's development of *entente*, culminating in a visit to France by Queen Victoria and Prince Albert in 1843, the first by a British monarch since Henry VIII. However, relations with France steadily deteriorated. When, in 1844 Prince de Joinville, the son of King Louis Philippe and a naval officer, wrote his visionary pamphlet, 'Notes on the state of the French Navy', he horrified British public opinion by suggesting that steam-powered French warships could cross the Channel and inflict a crippling defeat on the sailing ships of the Royal Navy. Just four years earlier the Admiralty had rejected the idea of using iron to build warships. The paper led to an invasion panic, with some volunteer units placing themselves at the disposal of the government.

In 1846, France's announcement of plans to modernise its navy and army was interpreted in Britain as a challenge to her traditional supremacy of the sea. A second invasion panic was induced when it was estimated that up to 200,000 Frenchmen could be landed. In February 1848 Louis Philippe was deposed as revolutions toppled monarchies and governments across Europe, and Britain breathed a sigh of relief.

A year later Admiral Dupetit-Thouars claimed that the French could land forces on British soil, anywhere and at any time, and again raised the spectre of a steam-driven French fleet outsailing the Royal Navy. When the foreign secretary Lord Palmerston, recognising that sail was obsolescent, declared in Parliament that "Steam navigation has rendered that which was before impassable by a military force nothing more than a river passable by a steam bridge", he accepted that Britain was under threat from her traditional enemy twenty-two priceless miles away, across the Channel.

By now Henry John Temple Palmerston, 3rd Viscount Palmerston (1784–1865), was two years into his second term as foreign secretary. He had been a Tory MP and minister, joined the Whigs and was three times foreign secretary. Brusque and assertive, his robust defence of British interests by 'gunboat diplomacy' won substantial popular support in Britain. As prime minister from 1855, he went on to make the fort strategy central to Britain's defence against invasion.

The military establishment, many of whom had fought in the Napoleonic wars, were pessimistic that an invasion could be defeated. A letter that the 77-year-old Duke of Wellington wrote to the Inspector-General of Fortifications, General Sir John Fox Burgoyne, was published in the *Morning Chronicle* and contained the words "we are not safe from invasion". But the reality was that France had no designs on Great Britain. The threat suggested by Dupetit-Thouars had been simply an attempt to push his government into building more ships.

Sir Francis Hart's 1850 publication *The State of the Defences of Great Britain* found that the fixed defences erected in the era of Napoleon Bonaparte were puny, the only credible addition being the arc of Martello towers from East Anglia to Kent and Sussex. With most of the army overseas, defence now rested with the militia but this was vulnerable to the social changes of the period. Many of the navy's ships had seen service against Napoleon.

The *coup d'état* by Louis Napoleon on 2 December 1851 induced another invasion panic. The mere mention of the name 'Napoleon' and a revolutionary France was sufficient to cause dread to the Victorian British, schooled in centuries of wars against the French who, they thought, had been finally defeated at Waterloo. The government refurbished fixed defences, particularly on Alderney, which was to be converted into a fortress akin to Gibraltar. One of those involved was Captain William Drummond Jervois of the Royal Engineers, who was responsible for the design of Brean Down Fort.

The 1852 Militia Act strengthened the militia to 80,000 men, put it for the first time under central control and instituted reforms to improve its operational ability, including voluntary enlistment to replace the traditional parish ballot. This had been used only when invasion seemed to threaten, and the militia had long been essentially voluntary. Its three principal functions remained:

- to provide a trained body for the defence of the nation
- to provide men to take over garrisons and fixed defences from the regular army, thereby freeing them for front-line duty elsewhere
- to act as a 'nursery' for the regular army.

In 1854 Britain and France, the *entente* still holding, marched to the Crimean War as allies and in 1857 British reinforcements *en route* to combat the Indian Mutiny embarked at French Mediterranean ports. The improvement in relations was damaged in January 1858 when evidence emerged that a bomb used by the Italian revolutionary Felice Orsini, in an attempt to assassinate Napoleon, had been made in Birmingham. French anglophobes promised retribution. French activities in Europe, Africa and Mexico emulated the expansionism and national glory of Napoleon I, but this time not in Europe but in competing for an overseas empire. All that needed was a fuse to set Great Britain alight.

During a visit to the heavily defended port of Cherbourg in August 1858, Queen Victoria and Prince Albert were impressed by the modernity of the French Navy. The following year the French launched the 5,600-ton ironclad *La Gloire*. Built of oak and with 4.7-inch (120mm) armoured sides, *La Gloire's* single-shaft 2,500-horsepower engine could produce a top speed of 13 knots (15mph/24kph), which was significantly faster than most ships of her weight and size. She carried thirty-six breech-loading 66-pounder guns. To the Victorians this major technical advance was another threat to the Royal Navy's command of the sea.

La Gloire altered the strategic balance in the Channel and challenged the conduct of naval warfare. No one could plan with any certainty any more, and no one had experience of a steam-driven battlefleet. For a time, the ironclads were a sign of the arms race on the high seas in much the same manner that the machine-gun would soon rule the battlefield. It is against this background of the maritime threat, on one hand, and paranoia about the state of home defence that the development of coastal defence must be seen.

As a deterrent against *La Gloire*, the British launched HMS *Warrior*, now docked at the Royal

THE IRON-COATED FRENCH FRIGATE LA GLOIRE.—SEE NEXT PAGE.

La Gloire. (National Maritime Museum)

Navy Museum in Portsmouth. Much larger than *La Gloire*, she had a single-shaft 5,720bhp engine which drove her at nearly 15 knots (17.3mph/27.8kph) and she carried forty 68-pounder guns. However, her armour was only four inches (102mm) thick. Palmerston was not terribly concerned when he was advised that the French were gathering information on her. The French built several more, bigger ironclads but in comparison the British response was piecemeal.

The French ejected the Austrians from Italy in 1859 and annexed Savoy and Nice in 1860. Napoleon also attempted to suppress the Italian revolutionary Garibaldi's bid for freedom. These acts were interpreted as French expansion, and Britons feared being "prostrate before hordes of Chasseurs de Vincennes and blackmuzzled African legions". As Howell-Everson colourfully put it:

It was as though the Iron Curtain lay in the middle of the English Channel – only ten miles from Dover and 100 from the outskirts of London. The growing bellicosity of France under the third Napoleon,

inflamed by the cult of the first of that name, lead to menacing threats of avenging Waterloo.

The influential journal *Vanity Fair* stated that "No nation has ever hated another more than France hates England, since the days of the Peloponnesian War". To the British, it was clear the French wished to avenge the centuries of military humiliation and that they had everything to fear from French technical and military achievement.

Appalled by France's threatening advance, the public demanded improved home defence and forced the resignation of the prime minister, Lord Palmerston, in favour of Lord Derby. His plans to modernise the Royal Navy were soon put in the shade by Secretary of State for War General Jonathan Peel who, in May 1858, established a committee to examine home defence and transferred the militia from the Home Office to the War Office. The deliberations of senior generals had concluded that volunteers could be only a partial remedy to the deficiencies in home defence; but their expert opinion did not seem to weigh with the public, who saw the

HMS *Warrior*. (National Maritime Museum)

militia as more cost-effective than regulars and far more likely to induce military awareness in the nation.

The campaign intensified and resulted in the government authorising in May 1859 the formation of a corps of rifle volunteers. The mood of the time was caught in the patriotic poem 'The War' by the Poet Laureate Alfred, Lord Tennyson, published in *The Times* of 9 May 1859:

> Form, form, riflemen, form!
> Ready, be ready to meet the storm!
> Riflemen, riflemen, riflemen, form!

Thus when Lord Elgin, on his way to India, accepted an invitation to dine with Napoleon, the latter outlined, with some pride, French achievements. When he had finished, Elgin suggested to Napoleon that he had forgotten one thing. "What was that?" asked a puzzled Napoleon, to which Elgin replied, "Your Majesty has made the British a military nation!"

Derby realised that, although a French invasion was most unlikely, concessions needed to be made, particularly as he had been brought to power on an anti-French ticket. Learning from the Indian Mutiny – when the European and Eurasian volunteers gave valuable service to the army – the government, acknowledging that arming the public was not a threat to the authority of Parliament, in May 1859 made use of the powers in the unrepealed 1804 Yeomanry and Volunteer Consolidation Act, authorising lords-lieutenant to raise a force to be:

> liable to be called out in case of actual invasion or the appearance of an enemy in force on the coast or in case of a rebellion arising out of either of these emergencies.

Five arms of the Volunteer Corps were formed and are covered in Chapter 3.

The government also examined the national fixed defences of the nation. The Crimean War had shown that forts could still be made to withstand naval bombardment and thus, when Palmerston returned to power, he wrote to Chancellor of the Exchequer

William Gladstone, saying that the Royal Navy alone could not prevent a landing. On 20 August 1859 he appointed a Royal Commission, with Major William Jervois (whom we last met in 1852 on Alderney) as secretary, to examine

the state, sufficiency and condition of the Fortifications existing for the Defence of Our United Kingdom and an examination had into all works at present in progress for the improvement thereof, and consideration given to the most efficient means of rendering the same complete, especially all such Works of Defence as are provided for the protection of our Royal Arsenals and Dockyard.

Such suggestions as may seem to you meet as, regard being had to the works completed and in progress, and to the ordinary number of Our Royal Artillery voted by Parliament, will render Our United Kingdom in a complete state of defence.

We may note two things. First, the emphasis was on protecting the Royal Arsenal and the dockyards, most of which were located along the southern coast from Chatham to Plymouth. Secondly, there was to be no increase in the Royal Artillery establishment to man fortifications.

A strong anti-fortification lobby, which included Gladstone, forced through a commercial treaty with France, which reduced tariffs on some goods, including steel and machine parts, in exchange for brandy and wine. This induced considerable hostility from Windsor Castle. Supported by Queen Victoria, Albert suggested the treaty was tantamount to supplying the French with iron to protect their ships and machinery to make weapons. The treaty remained in force but the anti-fort lobby lost their battle to prevent fixed defences being built. One of those fixed defences was to be Brean Down.

TWO

Defending the Nation

With Napoleon continuing his expansionist activities, the Royal Commission published their report on 7 February 1860. The report defined the aim of fortifications as being to enable a small body of troops to resist a superior force and for partly trained bodies of men to deal with those more perfectly disciplined than themselves. Some 750 miles (1,200km) of the British coastline were considered vulnerable to enemy interdiction and about 300 beaches were assessed as suitable for enemy landings. The committee was

> of the opinion that the fortification of this country should be confined to those points at which an enemy would strike and of the harbours whose possession would give him sure bases for operations favourable to his designs.

The report noted that the fortification of a defended line was impossible and that the Royal Navy, the Army and Volunteer Force were inadequately equipped or insufficient in numbers to withstand an invasion. It concluded that a chain of coastal forts be built. To overcome the problem of not being able to increase the strength of the Royal Artillery, the Commission proposed that

> previously untrained men of average capacity can be taught the ordinary duties required for such service in about one month and that in about three months such men might be capable of performing the duties necessary for the efficient working of Garrison Artillery in the contemplated works, when supported by fully trained men and commanded by properly qualified officers.

Although there was still strong opposition in Parliament – particularly from Sir Samuel Morton Peto, MP for Finsbury, more noted as the builder of Nelson's Column – the Royal Engineers were made responsible for the siting and construction of the forts and the Royal Artillery for equipping them. Each fort was to be fitted with standardised guns, ammunition and equipment. Major Jervois was placed in charge of this mammoth project and given four years to complete it.

Within weeks, Royal Engineer survey parties were scouring the country for sites. Some were well known

Sir William Francis Drummond Jervois, GCMG, CB, FRS	
10 September 1821	Born Cowes. Educated Royal Military Academies Gosport and Woolwich. Commissioned into Royal Engineers
1842–51	South Africa. Took part in wars against Boers and Kaffirs
1852–54	Fortified Alderney
1854–55	Commander RE London District Special advisor to Prime Minister Lord Palmerston on fortification in Great Britain and Ireland. Missions to Canada, Bermuda and India
1875–77	Governor of Straits Settlements (Singapore)
1877–83	Governor New South Wales
1883–89	Governor New Zealand; also advisor to Australian government on defence
1890–91	Member of War Minister Stanhope's Committee of Military Defences
1893	Commandant-General Royal Engineers
17 August 1897	Died

and already had been used as defensive positions. Others, like Brean Down, were completely new. They varied in size from the small seven-battery position at Brean Down, by way of totally iron forts at Plymouth Breakwater Fort, Portland Breakwater Fort and in Spithead Roads, No Man's Land Fort and Horse Sands Fort, to those with several levels of gun batteries, as at Fort Nothe in Weymouth.

Major Jervois was a technician in an age when soldiers with technological expertise were rare. Aware that artillery was developing, with a limited budget and without an increase in Royal Artillery establishment, he was prevented from allowing his natural eccentricities to run wild. From a few academic articles about fixed defences and lessons learnt from Crimea, he concluded that the forts needed to be defensible from the sea and from the landside. Much of their effectiveness depended on their elevation above sea level.

Jervois had sufficient originality and independence to abandon the European classic designs of huge fortresses and opted for a simple five-sided structure, which could be adapted for any location. The general concept was for the seaward sector to be protected by a high wall about ten feet (3.05m) thick, backed by earthworks and a rampart. Overhead cover was erected for guns firing through enlarged firing slits known as 'embrasures', which were open at the rear. The landward sector was surrounded by a 30ft (9.14m) wide walled moat about 30ft deep, which, if the location and terrain allowed, would flood, thereby creating a major obstacle. Triangular walls jutted into the moat and were provided with more slits for the defenders to fire onto any enemy who managed to infiltrate into the moat.

The inside of the complex housed the parade ground, surrounded by offices, barrack accommodation and stables. Magazines, storerooms and water points were positioned so that they were immune from enemy bombardment and fire. In some forts, there was strongpoint into which the garrison could retire to continue the fight.

Thus 'Palmerston's Follies' of forts began to appear the length of the Channel coast and beyond, westwards to Milford Haven, to Cork and eastwards to the Thames and Medway. Closest to France, Dover was a designated strongpoint. Harwich protected the Thames Estuary and the southern sector of the North Sea. Army garrisons were placed at Chatham, Dover, Portsmouth and Devonport.

Artillery Developments

The arrival of steam-driven ironclad ships travelling faster induced a re-examination of artillery, which was undergoing significant changes, anyway. Although larger guns remained smoothbore, the theory of rifling had been applied to small arms for several decades. Sir John Moore's riflemen in Spain and Portugal in 1808 were issued with Baker rifles, although the weapons were still loaded down the muzzle.

It was not until 1854 that Mr William Armstrong, at the Royal Woolwich Arsenal research laboratories, began experiments with rifled artillery. But he found that the increased pressure caused by rifling, and the need for an elongated and heavier shell to fit snugly into the tube, caused the gases around the projectile to expand and split traditional cast-iron barrels. This he resolved by reinforcing the barrel with wrought iron hoops.

At the same time, a former toolmaker, Joseph Whitworth, developed a rifled breech-loader (RBL) which improved range and accuracy. He also strengthened barrels by forcing wrought iron hoops and then plugged an obturator in the breech to confine the gases. The obturator was removed for loading the projectile and charge bag but unless it was fitted correctly, it would blow out as the gun fired, damage the gun and injure the detachment.

The first field trials with a 3-pounder rifled breech-loader in December 1858 proved it to be more accurate and with a longer range, and orders were placed with the Elswick Ordnance Company in Newcastle-on-Tyne and the Royal Arsenal at Woolwich. 12-pounder RBLs saw action with the Royal Artillery in the 2nd China War (1857–62) and although dragged through the jungle and soaked by rain, which tended to rust the breech screw, they performed well, although several vent pieces blew out. Not for the first time did equipment tested and proved under laboratory conditions fail under active service.

Rifled Muzzle-Loading Artillery

The Elswick Ordnance Company of Sir William Armstrong successfully developed a rifled, breech-loading (BL) 6-inch gun, which led to a debate over the merits of muzzle-loading and breech-loading. In 1864 a committee conducted several experiments using Whitworth's and Armstrong's RML and Armstrong's RBL systems, using 12- and 70-pounders. In both instances the RMLs were deemed the winners and this sparked a controversy that lasted for several decades. On 3 October a War Office Circular laid down the specification of rifled guns. All new artillery was to be 7-inch (178mm) calibre, muzzle-loaded and to the Woolwich uniform design. Smaller-calibre guns were withdrawn from service and assigned to the Artillery Volunteer Corps for training, and those smoothbore guns under manufacture were converted to RMLs.

The 7-inch rifled muzzle-loaders that first entered service were manufactured to specifications

Muzzle of a 7-inch RML on Steep Holm showing rifling, and the studs on which the loading tray was placed by gun numbers 9 and 11 for numbers 2 and 3 to ram. (John Barrett)

laid down by Mr R.S. Fraser, Assistant Superintendent at the Royal Gun Foundry at Woolwich. In his study *A History of the Maritime Forts in the Bristol Channel, 1866–1900*, John Barrett describes the manufacturing process:

> They were based on a simplified method of Sir W. Armstrong's original design and consisted of a rifled tube and cascable. Over these ports was a breech coil

Trunnion markings from a 7-inch RML at Split Battery, Steep Holm. They signify 'Royal Gun Factory. Serial Number 86. Mark 3. Manufactured in 1868'. (John Barrett)

composed of treble and double coils welded to the trunnion to form a mass which was shrunk on in one operation, the muzzle being strengthened by a short tube formed of two united coils. The outer coils in the Fraser construction were of a less expensive wrought iron than the Armstrong design. Two 1-inch (25mm) diameter studs on the muzzle face were for locating the ammunition tray. Rifling was on the Woolwich uniform system, the twist being 1 in 35. Guns were proof-tested at the Proofing Butts, Woolwich.

Three years later the first of 500 Mark III RMLs were ready for land service. The introduction of these rifled muzzle-loaders outdated thousands of smoothbore guns but with an urgent need for artillery, in an age of inventions, some came from unexpected quarters. Captain Sir William Palliser, 18th Hussars, developed a rifled sleeve that could be slipped into a smoothbore tube and convert a 32-pounder smoothbore gun into a 64-pounder RML. Over 2,000 were converted, much to the relief of the government who had envisaged having to spend thousands of pounds purchasing rifled artillery.

Ammunition

In the forts, powder magazines were generally underground and the gunners had to wear special serge uniforms and boots to prevent sparks igniting the inevitable spillages of gunpowder dust that accumulated on the floor.

New types of ammunition were also being researched. Now promoted, Major Palliser developed a cored projectile. When a target was hit, the charge was exploded by the heat and flash produced during penetration. A fuse was therefore not required. Palliser shells were about twenty per cent cheaper than other comparable projectiles. The nose was chilled and hardened and acted as a hammer on the armour to drive the hardened point into the plate.

The interior of some shells was lacquered, which gave a smooth surface, thus preventing powder shock during acceleration in the firing sequence, which sometimes caused a premature explosion by the friction of powder against a rough internal surface. There was also a tendency for the powder to compact at the rear of the shell. Shells were later cast in sand, which gave a sounder casting at the base; the days of round-shot were over.

Lieutenant W.A. Noble RA proved it was a combination of shell weight and muzzle velocity that damaged the target, not just the weight of the shell, and that during a high-velocity strike, armour was unable

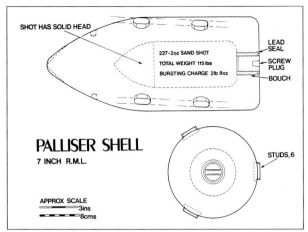

7-inch RML Palliser shell. (John Barrett)

to absorb the blow. This was contrary to artillery thinking of the day, which held that it was the weight of the projectile that counted. His calculation was based on the multiple of shell weight and muzzle velocity in feet per second, but his theories took time to be accepted.

Captain E.M. Boxer RA, of the Woolwich Arsenal Royal Laboratory, developed Captain Henry Shrapnel's 1804 roundshot and produced an anti-personnel projectile for dealing with boat landing parties. Mr Martin designed his Liquid Iron Shell, an incendiary shell. Battery commanders were apprehensive about having these shells, which required a ready-use locker full of red-hot coke near

the thin carpets of gunpowder that accumulated around the guns. With the demise of wooden ships, Martin's shell was obsolete by 1869. For close-quarter fighting, smoothbore case ammunition was considered sufficient against troops.

In 1870 Whitbread tested the first torpedo, which travelled 1,000yd (914m) at seven knots (8mph/13kph), and then the Admiralty developed the torpedo boat in 1880; but crews found the constant crashing into waves at speed very fatiguing. When their success inspired development in France and Russia, this presented problems for the Coast Brigade of how to sink low-silhouette fast vessels. 3-pounder and 6-pounder Quick Firing (QF) Nordenfelt and Hotchkiss guns firing from fixed pivots were the answer, but none of the Bristol Channel forts was equipped with them.

The advent of torpedo boats and the need for rapid firing led to the development of cartridge cases, enabling a fresh shell to be loaded without sponging the reside of bag charges. The cartridges also carried their ignition device. Guns so loaded were known as Quick Firing.

Gun Platforms

The heavier guns required new gun carriages, which led to the development of what was called the Carriage, Garrison, RML 7-inch Casemate or Dwarf

Torpedo Boat 1, HMS Lightning, *1877. The first torpedo boat to enter service with the Royal Navy.* (National Maritime Museum)

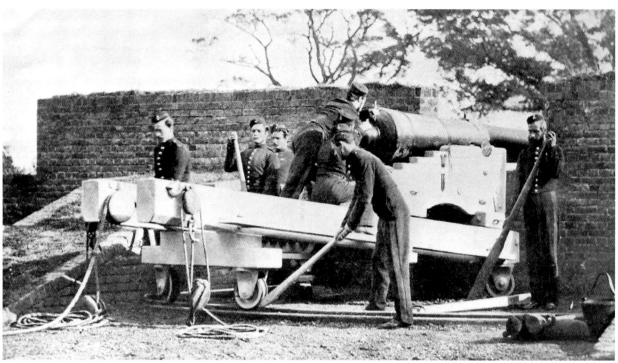

Dwarf Traversing Platform. The gun is a 64-pounder. (Ian Hogg)

Brean Down today: the George III 24-pounder gun at Number One Battery driven vertically into the ground, on which was mounted a 7-inch RML on a casemate C-Pivot Dwarf Traversing Platform. (Author's collection)

(Mark 1) Slide, usually known as a Dwarf Traversing Platform. This revolved around the muzzle of an obsolete, cast-iron, George III period, 24-pounder smoothbore cannon placed horizontally in a 3ft (0.9m) deep pit with its muzzle pointing upwards. Several variants were developed:

- Type A Pivot – under the muzzle of the gun in the run-out position
- Type B Pivot – just in front of the slide breast
- Type C Pivot – in the centre of the gun carriage
- Type D Pivot – about three feet behind the centre of the platform
- Type E Pivot – in front of the rear transom (crossbeam)
- Type F Pivot – at the rear of the slide

The platforms, 15ft (4.57m) long and weighing just over 4 tons, consisted of a rectangular wrought-iron frame mounted on small iron wheels, which ran on a circular iron track below the parapet. Elevation was achieved by driving a wooden wedge-packing piece between the gun and frame, giving a slope of 4 degrees. Block and tackle attached to two eyebolts in the gun

pits, and a preventer rope secured to a bollard on the platform at the rear of the transom, assisted in giving a controlled traverse and recoil. A hydraulic buffer connected to the gun carriage checked recoil and slowed because the gun travelled up a slope.

Gun positions also underwent significant developments. The idea of lowering a gun behind a high parapet was first conceived in 1835 by Colonel de Russy of the US Artillery. In 1863 Lieutenant-Colonel G. Shaw RA developed the Muzzle Pointing Carriage by placing the gun on a Type A pivot and proposed the axis for elevation and depression was no longer the trunnions but an imaginary line passing through the muzzle. A wheel turned the shaft, which operated two racks at the rear above its pivot. The casement only had to be wide enough to admit the muzzle. In effect the A pivot was elevated and depressed. Although a special committee assessed the design to be undesirable, the idea refused to lie down and Lieutenant-Colonel Inglis RA designed a small port carriage, which used a single hydraulic jack beneath the breech to lift and lower around muzzle pivot. This design is now used for coaxial

Summit Battery, Steep Holm: C-pivot with RML gun. In the background can be seen a 6-inch emplacement with plastic armour roof.
(John Barrett)

7-inch RML on Moncrieff's Disappearing Gun Carriage, as used on Flat Holm. (Ian Hogg)

door- and window-mounted machine-guns on military helicopters. In 1865 Captain Alexander Moncrieff of the Edinburgh Artillery Militia took Shaw's idea and designed the revolutionary Disappearing Gun Carriage specifically for the 7-inch RML. This allowed the gun to be served in a gunpit below ground level. When ready and the target identified, according to Barrett:

> A self-acting brake wheel on the platform held the elevators down and served to check them from rising unexpectedly when loading. When the brake was released the gun was quickly raised for firing.

The force of the recoil drove the gun back into the pit. The Ordnance Committee conservatively commented on the device:

> although somewhat ingenious, the arrangement is too complicated to be serviceable … incommensurate with the expense … recommend that no further encouragement be given to him.

But Moncrieff managed to inspire interest in his design and in 1869 a prototype was successfully trialled at Woolwich using a 7-inch RML. Armstrong's Elswick Ordnance Company later developed a similar system for larger guns. It was a particularly useful device for gun positions in flat areas.

Production of the Moncrieff gun carriage was soon underway, with twenty Pattern 1s made for 7-inch RML guns. Nine were deployed at Flat Holm, where the gunpits are still evident. An example of Moncrieff's system has been re-created at Crownhill Fort in Plymouth by the Landmark Trust. Most Pattern 2s were deployed overseas. Moncrieff's principle was eventually tested in 1885 when the frigate HMS *Hercules*, which machine-gunned, fired broadsides and tried independent fire, attacked a 6-inch (153mm) gun on a Disappearing Gun Carriage at Portland Bill whenever the gun appeared. Although there were several near misses, no hits were registered, which raised some questions about the standards of naval gunnery. A ship presented with a fort had a target. A ship presented with a disappearing gun had no target.

Moncrieff's Disappearing Gun Carriage remained in service until the last model in Mauritius was declared obsolete in 1926. By this time aeroplanes had arrived and could direct naval gunfire support onto below ground-level targets. Moncrieff later developed siege-howitzer carriages, some of which were used in siege trains.

Ranging and Sighting

RML guns were provided with a breech tangent sight and foresight on each side of the gun, with a hexagonal tangent scale graduated to 5° and a foresight on the top of the gun. The breech tangent sight fitted into sockets on the sides of the breech. Elevation and depression were obtained without using the sights by means of either the Spirit Level Quadrant or Gunner's Quadrant. To obtain elevation when using the Spirit Level Quadrant the long limb was inserted into the bore, the spirit level (bubble in centre of glass tube) attached to the graduated arc and the gun was then elevated until the spirit level was horizontal. With the Gunner's Quadrant the muzzle of the gun was raised until the plumb line cut the required angle on the graduated arc.

Difficulty had always been experienced in finding the range of ships underway. Registered marker sea-buoys, and at night kegs and barrels filled with burning tar, and a rangecard at Fire Command all helped. In 1886 'Hong Kong' targets came into service. These consisted of large chequered black-and-white canvas screens towed by a launch. Later, winches were installed which enabled the targets to be hauled in at speed, simulating a torpedo boat or destroyer attack. During the Second World War, the Hong Kong target became the uniform and vehicle insignia of the School of Coast Artillery.

The evolution in naval warfare meant that powered ships could maintain a higher speed in any direction and their guns had a longer range. The

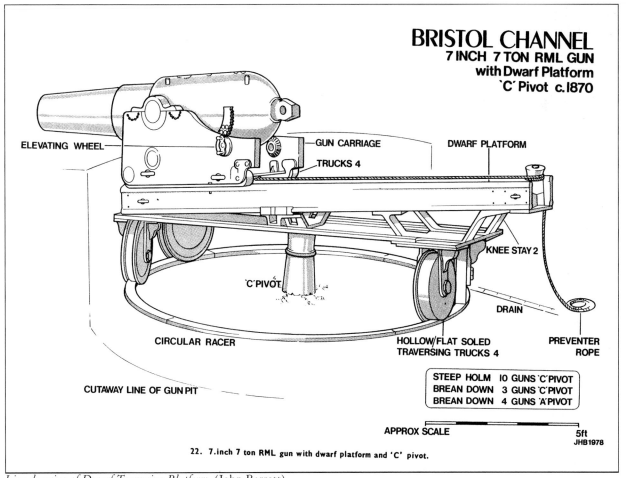

22. 7.inch 7 ton RML gun with dwarf platform and 'C' pivot.

Line drawing of Dwarf Traversing Platform. (John Barrett)

range of the RMLs also forced them further out to sea. Engaging the enemy at point-blank range was unlikely. Nevertheless coast artillery observers still had little more than a telescope until, in 1869, Captain Nolan developed a portable rangefinder. He accomplished target registration within $1^1/_4$ to $3^1/_4$ minutes of sighting the target by using two widely-spaced observers to calculate the range. But the distance between the two caused a communication problem and thus adjusting fall of shot was slow. The allocation of just three to four rounds of live firing per year also meant that expertise was lacking.

An experimental firing practice for a 9-inch (230mm) RML on a casemate slide at Shoeburyness in Essex gave some interesting rates of fire. A 5ft (1.5m) target moving at 3.5mph (5.6kph) was towed at a range of 1,000yd (914m). The target came under fire for 750yd (685m) for seven minutes. Initially, five rounds were fired in five minutes with the third round hitting the target. When the target moved at 7.5mph (12kph), five rounds were fired in $3^1/_2$ minutes, and the fourth round hit the target. If a warship had been used as the target every round would have been a hit. Bearing in mind the complicated gun drill, the rapid and accurate rate of fire was remarkable.

During the 1870s Captain H.S. Watkins RA, who was stationed in Gibraltar, solved the problem of clifftop observers' rangefinding. With one observer well above sea level laying onto the bow of the target ship and another reading the plot of the target's position in relation to time of flight of the shell, this formed a triangle, and a simple measurement of the angle of depression to the target automatically gave the range. The data could then be fed to the Gun Position Officer who calculated range, elevation and bearing. The gun detachment did nothing else except load, aim and fire. This system was known as the Depression Range Finder (DRF).

Manning

As part of the Royal Artillery reorganisation, the Coast Brigade was formed to man the artillery in the fixed defences and later took, as its insignia, a reproduction of a 7-inch RML. Numbering about 1,000 all ranks and controlled from HQ Coast Brigade at Sheerness, they were deployed throughout the United Kingdom and later overseas. They were formed into District Establishments of a sergeant Master Gunner and several gunners, usually veterans, with direct responsibility for the maintenance and serviceability of the guns, carriages, ammunition, instruments and associated stores in the forts.

The manning of the coastal forts was drawn from the militia and, later, the Artillery Volunteer Corps, who were recruited locally and taught "how to work a great gun mounted in their immediate neighbourhood". To ensure rapid mobilisation the gunners were expected to live close to their batteries and to be thoroughly familiar with the guns.

THREE

The Victorian Soldier

Members of 1st Gloucestershire Volunteer Artillery at Fort Efford in Plymouth on annual camp, 1898. Note the magnificent leather valises. (Bristol City Council)

The period 1859 to 1908 saw a major evolution of the British Army that set the foundations of today's army of professional and volunteer soldiers. Until 1859 the Army consisted of two major components: the regular army consisted of men who took the King's Shilling and enlisted for a set period as professional soldiers. The period of enlistment varied but was generally six years with the colours and they could be expected to serve in the United Kingdom or overseas. Evolving from Henry II's Assize of Arms was the Militia Corps, a conscripted force raised by the lord lieutenant of each county, to serve anywhere in the country.

Under the pressures of the Crimean War, the militia had been mobilised when there was no direct threat to the country and developed from an independent corps into a reservoir of men to replace front-line casualties. Enlistment into the militia was generally by parish although some men were exempt, such as those joining a volunteer unit. In times of great threat to the country, landed gentry would often form units of volunteers to defend their immediate locality. Like the Second World War Home Guard, they were disbanded when the threat had receded.

Contemporary records about the everyday life of Victorian soldiers at Brean Down either do not exist or have yet to be unearthed. However, it is possible to gain a view of soldiering from such books as *The Victorian Soldier*.

Secretary of State for War Edward Cardwell's 1870 Army Enlistment Act required enlisted men to serve six years with the colours and then, on discharge, six years with the reserve, which, for the first time, provided a mass of trained men available for active service. The 1871 Regulation of the Forces Act abolished the practice of officers purchasing commissions and transferred commissioning of officers, including those of volunteer units, to the Crown. From the Act sprang military institutions to train officer-cadets.

Cardwell's 1873 Localisation Act combined the two regular battalion-sized units (about 600 men), and similar-sized militia and volunteer units on a county basis, thereby enhancing the regimental traditions of the infantry and cavalry and creating a firm association between the regulars and their affiliated militia and volunteer corps. This idea of banding all elements met with resistance from both sides. Cardwell insisted that the Volunteers train annually, with a set minimum number expected to attend,

which counted towards the efficiency of the corps. An 'efficient' unit was often rewarded with better equipment, while the least satisfactory would be threatened with disbandment. These moves horrified most volunteers who perceived them as a gradual whittling away of the free spirit of their force until it would be no more than an unpaid militia.

The importation of younger officers, often former regulars and some with technical expertise, into the Volunteer Force introduced improved organisation, better training, logical discipline and greater commitment which, in turn, led to the study of the conduct of war and a fertile breeding ground for new ideas. Permanent staff and instructors were appointed from the parent 'line' regiments.

Cardwell's successor, Hugh Childers, resolved the brigading issue by converting the volunteers into the fourth battalion of each infantry regiment, the first two battalions being regular, one at home and one overseas, and the third militia. The first to be converted were the 1st, 2nd and 3rd Somerset Rifle

Corporal Joe Walford (left) *and Master-Gunner Sergeant Stepper* (rear centre) *with an army donkey and boatmen at the old boathouse, Anchor Head, Weston-super-Mare, 1902.* (Joe Walford)

Volunteer Corps into the 4th Volunteer Battalion, Somersetshire (Prince Albert's) Light Infantry. The old regimental facings were replaced by white for English and Welsh, yellow for Scottish, green for Irish and blue for Royal regiments. The move was widely appreciated throughout the army and gave the volunteers a regimental identity and tradition that formalised the basis of British Army philosophy.

Cardwell's radical reforms met with great opposition from the Commander-in-Chief, HRH the Duke of Cambridge, who for 25 years (and supported by his cousin Queen Victoria) resolutely refused to surrender his total control of the army to a mere politician, growing more cantankerous and stubborn against reform as the years passed. The volunteer gunners suffered from the long debate of whether they should be field or static artillery.

A key feature of all soldiers throughout the ages is their preoccupation with food. The first attempt to provide consistent rations was made in about 1580 when the Crown contracted out the provision of food on three provisos – it should not be penalising to the state; sufficient should be given to the soldier to prevent mutiny; and the cost of food above subsistence should be transferred to his unit. Inevitably, when a wealthy individual raised a regiment, and took responsibility for all that went with it, such as uniforms and equipment, rations were not high on their list of priorities and the system was open to corruption. The consequence was that the soldier at home, and even on campaign, could not be guaranteed varied and nutritional, nor even sufficient food.

In the eighteenth and early nineteenth centuries, the soldier's daily ration was ³/₄lb (340g) of meat, 1lb (453g) of either vegetable or potato, but not both, and 1lb of bread to be taken at breakfast between 7.30 to 8am and at lunch between 12.30pm and 1.30pm Between 1.30pm and 7.30am the soldier went hungry, purchased food elsewhere or filled his belly with beer. Some commanding officers introduced an evening meal but at a cost to the soldier through stoppages of pay until this meal was formally introduced in 1840.

Once the food had been prepared it was brought to the soldiers' barrack blocks in urns. Scandals of poor rations and badly trained cooks eventually led to a complete overhaul of the system of feeding soldiers. From 1863, commanding officers were expected to buy provisions from recognised traders, with profits ploughed back into newly formed can-

teen committees. However, as the army was reduced in size in the United Kingdom in order to reinforce units serving in the Empire, great emphasis was placed on feeding the thin young recruits. The problem of feeding soldiers was never really solved in the nineteenth century, with too few cooks, soldiers still expected to contribute towards a decent diet and modern kitchen equipment not available. Compared to his European colleagues, the diet of the British soldier was well below an acceptable level. Training was eventually introduced for regimental cooks and a commissariat corps of butchers and bakers was formed which, in 1941, became the Army Catering Corps.

Recreation is important to any soldier. Gambling was not permitted; however, card games such as 'Twenty-one' (or 'vingt-et-un'), the roll of the dice in brag and the forerunner of bingo, 'housey-housey', helped pass the time when the soldiers were not sprucing up their uniforms and equipment for 'spit-and-polish' inspections. One pair of boots, 'the best boots', was always kept highly polished.

Drink was a tradition closely associated with the army, largely because before the days of barracks, soldiers were accommodated in drinking houses. Nevertheless, drunkenness was always severely punished. Soldiers serving in Britain were more affected by changes in British society and were quickly exposed to the growth of temperance societies.

The temperance movement, promoting abstinence from alcohol, emerged during the expansion of the evangelical movement. Regimental temperance societies were first spawned in India by such officers as Lieutenant Henry Havelock of the 13th Foot (the 1st Somersetshire Regiment) who recognised that boredom, cheap drink and no organised recreation inevitably led to drunkenness and poor discipline. Havelock later became a hero of the Indian Mutiny. In 1860 the Temperance Rifle Volunteer Corps was formed in Southwark.

Temperance societies were formed unit by unit, and medals were awarded for abstinence. Eventually the Army Temperance Association became an accepted organisation in the army. The growth of temperance led to the establishment of the regimental and garrison institutes, which provided places of recreation and entertainment. These eventually developed into the Navy, Army and Air Force Institute – the NAAFI.

Many soldiers found that on being discharged, finding employment was difficult and consequently, in an age of social responsibility, such organisations

Master-Gunner Sergeant Stepper and Corporal Joe Walford with pets at Split Rock Battery, Steep Holm, 1902. (Joe Walford)

as the Corps of Commissionaires, founded in 1858 by Captain Edward Walter of the 8th Hussars, provided help and support.

Volunteer Force

When the government revived the unrepealed 1804 Yeomanry and Volunteer Consolidation Act on 12 May 1859, General Peel authorised lords-lieutenant, by a Royal Circular, to raise a force to be

> liable to be called out in case of actual invasion or an appearance of an enemy in force on the coast or in case of a rebellion arising out of either of these emergencies.

Five arms of the Volunteer Corps were formed, one for each branch of the army: infantry, mounted infantry, cavalry, artillery and engineers. Often based upon existing rifle and sporting clubs, recruiting was initially slow. Operationally, the volunteer infantry and cavalry were expected to avoid pitched battles in favour of using their local knowledge to skirmish, patrol and ambush enemy columns, and disrupt his lines of communications and supply chains. The Admiralty also encouraged dockyard management and mateys to raise naval volunteer units.

The Light Horse recruited in districts where there was no yeomanry. Their role was to provide a light cavalry screen and 22 regiments were founded, but their costs were so prohibitive that by the 1870s most regiments were disbanded. London had no Light Horse although the Honourable Artillery Company created a Light Cavalry Troop in April 1861, which was disbanded in 1890, resurfaced in 1979 and has sometimes been seen in the Lord Mayor's annual November parade.

It was not just the cavalry that needed horses: every officer would have one as personal transport, draught horses were needed for supply trains as well as field artillery. There were stables at Brean Down and they had to be kept supplied with feed and straw. Forage was limited to 10lb (4.5kg) of oats, 12lb (5.4kg) of hay and 8lb (3.6kg) of hay per horse with an extra 2lb (0.9kg) of oats for horses picketed in the open. 8lb of oats, 10lb of hay and 8lb of straw were given to draught horses.

The Mounted Rifles were a new innovation inspired by experiences in South Africa, where the Cape Mounted Rifles had been formed in 1827 from conventional British infantry in the so-called Kaffir Wars. Eventually, 26 regiments were formed but, as with the Light Horse, the expense of maintaining mounted troops, retaining good officers and finding sufficient men capable of riding horses was prohibitive. By 1880, all the Mounted Rifles had withered away, their role taken over by the Yeomanry.

Initially the Artillery Volunteer Corps had a field artillery role, but most were later converted into coast artillery. With the expansion of the fixed defences, they were organised into small detachments of ten to twelve men, all acquainted with each other, in charge of formation of a particular gun. They were numbered in order, with number one being the Northumberland Artillery Volunteer Corps and No. 64 that for Cardigan. A total establishment of 34,558 men was proposed although enlistment had reached only 18,833 effectives in 1863.

This was an age of new ideas and the Engineer Volunteers were much to the fore in developing communications, using railways and canals for military movements, and defending harbours with sub-surface and surface booms. For instance, the 32-strong and all-officer Engineer and Royal Transport Volunteer Corps was formed by eminent engineers, managers of railway companies and chief employers of labour to transport troops quickly to concentration areas and to maintain and expand the railways to support military operations. They worked very closely with the Railway Volunteer Staff Corps, whose members as civilians produced the complicated but accurate Bradshaw timetable. In the vicinity of the upper Bristol Channel, Engineer Volunteer Corps existed at Gloucester and Weston-super-Mare. Available to the Corps as sappers were about 15,000 navvies.

In the British Army the word 'rifleman' is synonymous with the tradition of light infantry. In May 1860 the Adjutant-General, General James Yorke Scarlett, who had led the charge of the Heavy Brigade at Balaclava in 1854, wrote a lengthy Circular to the Infantry directorate in which he encouraged the use of the Volunteer Rifles as light infantry:

> The nature of our country, with its numerous enclosures and other impediments gives peculiar importance to the service of Volunteer Riflemen, in which bodies each from his reliance on the support of his comrades – men whom he has known, and with whom he has lived from his youth up – intimately acquainted besides, with the country in which he would be called upon to act, would hang with the most telling effect upon the flanks and communications of a hostile army.

Light infantry were soldiers equipped, armed and trained to harass, delay and break up enemy infantry

The shooting team of B Company, 3rd Volunteer Battalion, Somerset Light Infantry, c.1890. This unit was based in Weston-super-Mare.
(Weston-super-Mare Library)

formations crossing the battlefield. They were trained to scout and use the ground, to be accurate shots and move fast. Hence their marching pace was at the double, that is, at a trot. British light infantry wore dark green uniforms and exist today as the Royal Greenjackets and Light Infantry battalions.

Until September 1870, the long- and short-barrelled versions of the Enfield rifle of 0.377in (9.56mm) calibre, dating from 1853, were the standard rifle until replaced by the Snyder. In 1884, this was replaced by the 0.450in (11.4mm) Martini-Henry single-shot, breech-loading rifle, which fired a heavy-calibre lead bullet. Sighted up to 1,450yd (1325m), its ideal battle range was up to 450yd (411m). It was normally equipped with a 21.5-inch (0.53m) socket triangular bayonet which, when added to the rifle's length of 4ft (1.22m), gave a total reach of nearly 6ft. In 1896 the 0.303in (7.7mm) Lee-Metford rifle was introduced.

A typical marching order load for the Rifle Volunteer Corps was:

- Head dress which varied from shakos, helmets, kepis, to Garibaldi-style brimmed hats
- waist belt, on to which were slipped ammunition pouches
- slung water bottle
- braces supporting both the belt and a haversack on the left hip.

On a wooden carrying frame were greatcoat, service cap, mess-tins with a cover, rolled cape and straps. The scale of field rations was $1\frac{1}{2}$lb (680g) of bread, 1lb (453g) of fresh meat, $\frac{1}{8}$oz (4g) of coffee, $\frac{1}{8}$oz (4g) of tea, 2oz (62g) of sugar, $\frac{1}{2}$oz (15.5g) of salt and $\frac{1}{36}$oz (0.87g) of pepper, with 3lb (1.36kg) of firewood and 1lb (453g) of coal for cooking and heating. A truss of 36lb (16.3kg) of straw was allowed sixteen days.

The terms under which the Volunteer Force operated were designed to be not especially attractive, with a view to keeping enlistment to the trusted middle and upper classes and not to those who would normally join the Army or Militia, namely, the vocal lower classes. Exemption from conscription into the Militia was permitted provided that volunteers attended drill parades eight times in four months or 24 in one year. Although the Act specifically decreed that the Government would supply arms, Peel's circular demanded that volunteers

> should provide their own arms and equipment and to defray all expenses attending the Corps except in the event of its being assembled for actual service.

This effectively ruled out a whole class of artisans and labourers who were unable to provide their own equipment. Consequently the Volunteer Force suffered from accusations that it was a middle-class organisation of individuals who enjoyed dressing up as soldiers and showing off to their wives and girlfriends at the weekend. Judging by the garish uniforms that soon appeared there might have been some justification to this assertion. There were, however, several examples of the less well off being helped by the wealthier. In North Somerset the 17th (Lyncombe) Rifle Volunteer Corps consisted of men without finance to equip themselves.

The collapse of Derby's administration on 6 June 1859 did not reduce the flow of people volunteering. The new Secretary of State for War, Sidney Herbert, responded to this public support for national defence, often at personal cost, and issued a third circular, which recognised that, because

> the very essence of a volunteer force consists in their undertaking to bear, without any cost to the country, the whole cost of their training and service previous to being called upon for actual service, Her Majesty's Government are of the opinion that it will be but fair to the Volunteers, as a just acknowledgement of the spirit in which their services are rendered, to relieve them, in some degree, of the expense their first outfit will entail them, and of which the purchase of arms is necessarily the heaviest item.

The circular also stated the Volunteer Force could expect to serve anywhere in the United Kingdom, which was a departure from their traditional operational role of serving in the county of origin under the command of the lord-lieutenant. Recruiting was swift and many smaller independent units, particularly in rural areas, were formed into administrative brigades. A feature of the force was that what they may have lacked in conventional military discipline, they made up for, with innovation and experimentation.

Some lords-lieutenant – who until 1880 had responsibility for reaching their quotas for the county Militia – opposed the Volunteer Force. At meetings, radicals and pacifists claimed that the concept would slow down political reform but were outweighed by the patriotic fervour and mood of the country. Crucially the Church supported the movement, as did the women of the country, who were active in fund raising for standards, bugles and tabletop silverware.

As with most all-volunteer units, the men did not subject themselves to the rigours of military discipline but introduced a relatively informal regime to run their unit. This seems to have worked reasonably well, although the frustrations of the Army adjutants and instructors can only be imagined. This culture extended to families. When, in April 1861, Private Alexander Robertson of the 4th Tower Hamlets Rifle Volunteer Corps died, after being knocked over by a van while returning from drill, a collection was made for his young wife and children.

In spite of the official criticism, the Volunteers took their responsibilities very seriously and exercised with imagination and novelty. It was a measure of the public paranoia about invasion that between May 1858 and May 1861 the strength of the force swelled from 15,000 to 161,239, divided into 747 separate corps. This was about 0.8 per cent of the population, in an era that was basically anti-militarist. The manual *The Drill and Rifle Instruction for the Corps of Rifle Volunteers*, known as 'The Green Book', was compiled with the specific purpose of reducing time spent on theoretical instruction. Shooting became an important aspect and laid the foundations for accuracy by British soldiers ever since.

The War Office insisted uniforms should be "as simple as possible", suitable for skirmishing, cheap and French-style, which was ironic since it was the French who were expected to be the enemy. Inevitably, most corps ignored the edict and a wide range of styles emerged. Members of the Prince of Wales's Own Civil Service Rifles of London designed their own uniforms but when Customs Company refused to accept the style of the belt agreed by the regimental council, it left the battalion *en masse*.

Corporal Joseph Walford of the Royal Garrison Artillery, c.1902. His son served as a sergeant at Brean Down during the Second World War. (Joe Walford)

Grey and green were the usual colours, although some corps adopted scarlet.

The Volunteer Force in Somerset

When the Volunteer Movement got underway in 1859, one of the first corps formed was at St Decuman's Cricket Club in Williton, but support was minimal. In Bath, proposals met with greater success and four Rifle Volunteer Corps were formed. The 3rd (Taunton) Somerset RVC was formed from those men who lived within twenty miles (32km) of the town. Otherwise the response in Somerset was generally apathetic.

Somerset was listed fiftieth in precedence in the Artillery Volunteer Corps and, although established at eighty all ranks, the average number of volunteer gunners between 1871 and 1880 was sixty-five. On 18 June 1860, 1st Artillery Volunteer Corps was formed at Clevedon and Portishead, and on 30 July 2nd Artillery Volunteer Corps at Weston-super-Mare, which suffered an immediate crisis when its captain initially refused to resign in favour of a more popular lieutenant.

Artillery Volunteer Corps covering the Bristol Channel included 1st Gloucestershire Artillery Volunteer Corps, which was formed at Bristol in 1859. On 21 July next year, it was issued with four 18-pounder smoothbore naval guns, which were placed on a position overlooking Avonmouth, known as The Butts, and exercised against sea targets and landing parties. Public concern at the age of the guns resulted in a bazaar being held to buy two Whitworth rifled mountain guns, which had a range of 8,000yd (7,315m) compared to the 2,000yd (1829m) of the 18-pounders. A company of Royal Naval Artillery Volunteers manned a battery at Avonmouth. Contributions were made by officers to help ratings pay the expense of enlistment, which in 1881 numbered 127 ratings. Covering the increasingly industrialised southern Welsh coast were the 1st and 2nd Glamorgan Artillery Volunteer Corps at Tenby and Cardiff respectively.

Under normal circumstances, the Volunteer Corps were not expected to become involved in internal security but, on 6 April 1861, the Weston-super-Mare Artillery Volunteer Corps was uniquely called out to restore order when some of its officers became involved in a domestic dispute.

Mr John Hugh Smyth-Piggot, a former officer of the Corps and Lord of the Manor (and a member of one of Weston-super-Mare's founding families), had a disagreement with his estate manager, Mr Robert Jones, about the role of the Artillery Volunteer Corps. In a letter read out to the unit on 14 March by the Captain Commandant, Major-General Murray Cox, Smyth-Piggot apologised for the disagreement and went on to mention that this agent had been dismissed. It then emerged that Mr Jones was lover to Mrs Smyth-Piggot. Her husband threatened divorce and refused to honour his wife's debts. In the meantime Smyth-Piggot appointed a Mr Harold Davies as estate manager and then left town, only to return a few days later to take up residence with his wife at the Manor House on Flagstaff Hill.

On 3 April, Jones arrived back in Weston-super-Mare and, accompanied by a solicitor and a private detective, met Smyth-Piggot. They agreed he should be reinstated as estate manager. Davies was about to leave for Bristol and put the letter of notice, unopened, to one side to deal with it later. That afternoon, Jones and several others entered Manor House. Returning from Bristol, Davies, believing himself still to be estate manager, was determined to eject him. Assembling a posse, at about 11pm, he entered the house and asked Jones to leave. When he refused, Davies had him unceremoniously dumped on the road. Jones then re-appeared with several men and a mêlée developed in which several men were hurt.

The incidents of the night were a topic of conversation in Weston-super-Mare and the following night a mob gathered outside 4 Birnbeck Terrace, the house of Mr Raymond Arundell, in the belief that Jones was inside. An uproar developed and stones and rocks were hurled, breaking several windows and causing damage. Shots were also fired. The police were powerless in controlling the mob although by midnight most had dispersed. The following evening fifty armed men of 2nd Corps assembled outside the Town Hall, where Captain Rockett, as Captain-Commandant and magistrate, ordered his men to help the police preserve the peace. Band playing, the gunners marched up Flagstaff Hill and cordoned Manor House. Apart from some townsfolk coming to see what was happening, there were no further riots and the affair ended when Smyth-Piggot offered Jones a public apology through the *Weston-super-Mare Gazette*.

The *Weston-super-Mare Gazette* dated 20 April 1860 reported on a 'Volunteer Artillery Spectacle' the previous Wednesday. With the town dressed overall with flags and bunting, it seemed that something was afoot. When the Bristol & Exeter Railway Company brought 100 men from the 1st

Sergeant Joe Walford of the Coast Regiment RA, 1943. (Joe Walford)

Gloucestershire (Bristol) Artillery Volunteer Corps and fifty men of Major Saville's 1st (Clevedon and Portishead) Artillery Volunteer Corps, and their accompanying bands, for the presentation of a silver trumpet to the 2nd Artillery Volunteer Corps, the military nature of the event became apparent. Forming up under Major Saville mounted on his grey charger, the two corps marched to Glossop's Field and joined the 2nd Corps, still commanded by Captain-Commandant Rockett, in front of the Town Hall. The Bristol volunteers were judged more soldierly having received busbies while the other two corps still wore forage caps.

The three contingents then marched to Roger's Royal Hotel along a road lined with cheering spectators and onto the lawn, where two 32-pounders had been placed on their arrival some months earlier. Forming the fourth side of a hollow square were the "beauty and fashion of the town". Then 2nd Corps were presented by Mrs Cox, wife of Major-General Cox, with the trumpet, which was inscribed:

'Vix Liber et Moriar'
Presented by the Ladies of Weston-super-Mare and the Neighbourhood
to the Second Somerset Artillery Volunteers.

Although, after the death of Prince Albert, court mourning dress was still universal for the upper classes, for this occasion the gay uniform of the gunners was matched by the pretty colours of the ladies' dresses. Several speeches were made and the two 32-pounders were placed on a wagon and hitched to six horses, lent by Mr J.C. Wall of Bristol. A baggage wagon, the bands and the three corps, followed by spectators, set off along the beach road, passed through Uphill and filed onto the sands where the trolley sank deeper at every turn of the wheels until bogged down, the axle resting on the sand.

The two horses from the baggage wagon were hitched to the trolley team but even their combined strength failed to extricate the wagon. One gun was removed from the trolley, which was then dragged by the gunners to the Battery, on land given to the 2nd Corps by Mr T.T. Knyfton, Lord of the Manor, and built under the supervision of a Royal Engineer NCO. The gun position faced Steep Holm with a commanding view of the Bristol Channel. Meanwhile the band played on. Those gunners not given orders to help were stood at ease in ranks but any semblance of a parade was abandoned as they adjourned to take refreshments.

The embarrassment soon forgotten, 2nd Corps took post and fired six volleys under the direction of the drill instructor, Sergeant Fairbairn. The three corps then marched back to a cold food reception at the Town Hall where there were yet more speeches, toasts and much self-congratulation about the efficiency of the British Army and the Volunteer Corps in particular before the party broke up shortly before 11pm.

In July the Somersetshire Artillery Volunteer Corps was brigaded into the Gloucestershire Artillery Volunteer Corps with six batteries in Bristol, by combining the 9th (Clevedon), 10th (Portishead) and 11th and 12th (Weston-super-Mare) Corps. It seems that the initial enthusiasm to join the Clevedon and Weston-super-Mare Artillery Volunteer Corps waned and by November 1863 both units had been transferred to the 1st Administrative Brigade, Gloucestershire Artillery Brigade, which took control of volunteer artillery units in Gloucestershire and Somerset. Four years later 2nd Artillery Volunteer Corps was disbanded through lack of volunteers and this meant that Volunteer gunners to man Brean Down Fort were brought from Bristol. At the same time the infantry 6th (Weston-super-Mare) Royal Volunteer Corps was raised, with its headquarters and depot at Wells.

In March 1880 there was further re-organisation of the Volunteer Force, and the 1st Administrative Brigade was retitled 1st Gloucestershire Artillery Volunteers (Gloucestershire and Somersetshire), who moved their ranges from Portishead to Clevedon and now had battery headquarters at Bristol, Newnham and Clevedon. Two years later the unit became part of the 4th Welsh Division Royal Artillery, which had responsibility for volunteer gunners in Gloucestershire, Worcestershire, Monmouthshire, Glamorgan and Somerset.

In July 1889 1st Gloucestershire Artillery Volunteers was retitled 1st Gloucestershire Volunteer Artillery (Gloucestershire and Somersetshire) with the same batteries in Bristol and others at Newnham, Cinderford, Lydney, Gloucester, Clevedon, Portishead and Weston-super-Mare. At about this time the Weston-super-Mare Volunteer Engineer Corps was formed. Upon the formation of the Royal Garrison Artillery in June 1899, 1st Gloucestershire Volunteer Artillery (Gloucestershire and Somersetshire) was absorbed into 1st (Gloucestershire and Somersetshire) Royal Garrison Artillery (Volunteers).

FOUR

Other Forts in the Bristol Channel, 1865–1902

Lundy

According to Barrett, there is evidence of a battery above Jenny's Cove anchorage; and the naming of Brazen Ward suggests a brass cannon may have covered the landing beach during the eighteenth century. A military surveyor visited the island in 1794, two years before Tate's landing at Fishguard, but nothing was done.

In June 1881, Vice-Admiral Henry Phillimore's committee considered that Lundy was an

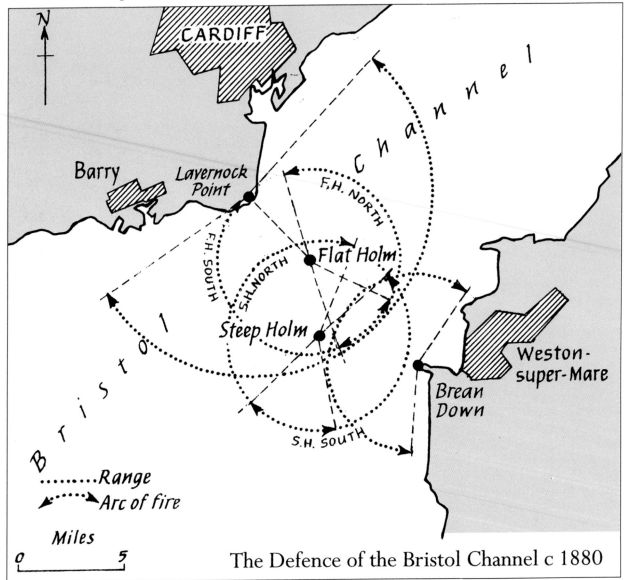

Map 2: *Defence of the Bristol Channel c.1880 — arcs of fire.*

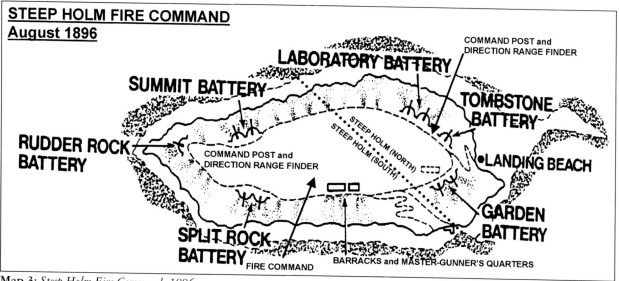

Map 3: *Steep Holm Fire Command, 1896.*

important outpost and should be included in the defence of the Bristol Channel to prevent enemy warships using the islands as a shelter, but his suggestion of a battery of three 9-inch (229mm) RML guns was not accepted. With the height of the cliffs, a Depression Range Finder would have been crucial.

Portishead

As mentioned in Chapter 1, there were cannon at Battery Point during the English Civil War. Following Tate's landing in 1796, four guns were installed to protect the mouth of the River Avon, in addition to the four warships patrolling the Bristol Channel. The guns were removed in 1815. In 1864 the War Office purchased the land from Mr Richard Bright for a battery, probably 32-pounder smoothbore guns, manned by the Bristol Naval Volunteer Corps to protect the River Avon; but they were not included in the defence of the Bristol Channel.

On 10 June 1881, Phillimore's committee visited Portishead, with Captain Parsons RN, Bristol's harbourmaster, and recommended that the battery should be equipped with three 7-inch (178mm) RMLs, to be removed from Flat Holm. Eight years later, in March 1889, the works committee of Colonel H.L. Geary, failed to support the recommendations, stating that the existing defence line across the Bristol Channel was quite sufficient.

Steep Holm

Rodney Legg has written comprehensively about Steep Holm, so here it is intended only to outline events that took place in its first military occupation. Mr John Perry of Weston-super-Mare was contracted to convert Steep Holm into a 'stone frigate' and began work on 19 February 1866. In 1861 Perry was listed as District Insurance Agent for the United Kingdom Temperance Provident, Life and Accidental insurance company in Oxford Street. By 1872 he is a builder and contractor with offices in Lington Villas, Walliscote Road so clearly his change of career was succesful. His employees were ferried over from Birnbeck Pier, near Weston-super-Mare, by steamer. One of them, David Reece, a mason, was charged by the Weston Pier Company of defrauding them of a toll, presumably by not buying a ticket, but the case was dismissed by Weston magistrates.

Although quarrying took place on Steep Holm for building material, a derrick was built on the south shore for materials brought from the mainland. It is not known how the 7-ton guns were lifted from the lighters but one possibility is that block-and-tackle was used. Another possibility is they were placed on sleds and hauled up Perimeter Path. The fort was equipped with ten 7-inch RMLs on Dwarf Traversing Platforms (Type-C), eight of them in two-gun positions at Priory Garden, Split Rock, the 250ft (76m) high Summit Battery and Laboratory, and two single-gun positions at Rudder

Breech markings from a 6-inch gun: BL signifies 'breech-loader'; 'WIRE' indicates the wire was wound around the barrel; VII notes its mark number; EOC is the manufacturer (Elswick Ordnance Company); the arrow is the War Office symbol; 1902 is the year of manufacture and No. 1575 the serial number. (Author's collection)

Rock and Tombstone. Officers from Horfield Barracks in Bristol regularly inspected the guns.

The soldiers' block, to house fifty men, and the Master-Gunner's quarters were built in sheltered positions. Gardening, farming and fishing were encouraged to supplement the stores brought by Mr Perry and help alleviate the boredom. As on Flat Holm, a small inn seems to be have been established on the island. Rainwater was stored in a 49,000-gallon (222,750l) tank.

In the 1871 census, only a labourer and Ann Harris, wife of the fisherman/boatman, are recorded as living on the island. By 1881 there was still no military presence, although ten years later Master-Gunner Levi Collins commanded the District Establishment of four Coast Artillery gunners. The 1st Administrative Brigade, Gloucestershire Artillery Brigade provided the bulk of the gunners. On 9 June 1881, Vice-Admiral Phillimore and a high-powered committee left Cardiff in a steamer, loaned by the Marquis of Bute's agent, Mr McConochie, and reported the guns were well placed to cover their approaches to the Bristol Channel. Later in the day the committee visited Flat Holm.

In July 1882 Lord Morley's committee suggested that the ten RMLs should be replaced by four 10.4-inch (264mm) breech-loaders but this was rejected.

At a special meeting two years later, after the Defence Committee had approved replacement of the RMLs by a smaller number of heavier guns, the Royal Artillery and Royal Engineer works committee concluded that the RMLs at Rudder Rock, Summit and Split Rock should be replaced with a single 6-inch breech loader and that Garden Battery should be equipped with two 9-inch RMLs for extended direct fire. None of these recommendations was implemented.

Then in December the Secretary of State for War provisionally approved the Ordnance Committee proposal that Steep Holm should be left with seven RMLs and reinforced with a battery of two 6-inch (152mm) breech-loaders, on a hydro-pneumatic gun carriage in a new position below Summit, with two machine-guns for local defence but, again, none of these improvements was carried out. Like Moncrieff's Disappearing Gun Carriage, the hydro-pneumatic gun carriage dropped below ground level. These proposals would have converted Steep Holm into a formidable fortress. Supported by the remaining three forts, penetration into the upper reaches of the Bristol Channel would have been near impossible. The same year another report recommended replacing all the existing guns with two 6-inch BLs and machine-guns. However, there is no evidence that any of the initiatives was put into effect.

In 1898 the War Office selected Steep Holm to test the placing of breech-loading guns in existing RML emplacements against the manoeuvrability and firepower of a modern warship. Rudder Rock Battery was chosen as the target and a dummy 9.2-inch (234mm) breech-loader, which had a range of 12 miles (19km), was placed in a 3-inch (76mm) nickel steel 'tortoise' shelter, the front of which was sloped to deflect shots and was on wheels running over a semi-circular racer that could be placed over the detachment working the gun.

In the early morning of 18 August, the 5,000-ton cruiser HMS *Arrogant* steamed to a position 1,880yd (1,720m) west of the target. Laid down in May 1896, she was armed with a 6-inch main armament, 4.7-inch (120mm) QFs and secondary armament. Members of the Ordnance Committee, led by General Sir Richard Harrison, watched from Flat Holm and the promenades at Weston-super-Mare and Lavernock were lined with spectators. Several paddle steamers set out from Cardiff but had to seek shelter when a rough sea sprang up before the cruiser had even fired.

HMS Arrogant *in 1896. It was this warship that shelled Steep Holm.* (National Maritime Museum)

At 8am the *Arrogant* carried out her first of six runs and opened fire with her starboard quick-firing main and secondary guns and Maxim machine-guns at near maximum elevation. The cruiser then opened fire with her 6-inch main armament but obscuration around the battery prevented hits being seen. The *Arrogant* then cruised around the island and as she passed Rudder Rock, her secondary armaments were brought to bear but again there was no apparent damage to the emplacement. Opening fire again with her 6-inch main armament, she, at last, began to hit the dummy gun position. At 12pm, cease-fire was called and when observers inspected the damage, they found 200 shells had landed, severely damaging the emplacement, blowing away parts of the iron shield and exposing the dummy gun. The test had proved the obsolescence and vulnerability of forts to sustained bombardment and effectively sealed their fate.

Flat Holm

The land to build a fort on Flat Holm was purchased from the Marquess of Bute in 1865 for £550. In 1869 additional land was leased for one shilling per annum from Trinity House, who operated the lighthouse. The only landing-place was below the lighthouse. Like the other Severn Defences forts, Flat Holm had a soldiers' accommodation block, which housed fifty men, and the Master-Gunner's quarters, completed in 1869.

Owing to the low terrain, the nine 7-inch (178mm) RMLs were all mounted on Moncrieff's Disappearing Gun Carriage in hardened pits below ground level. Castle Rock Battery and the Lighthouse Battery each had three guns, Farmhouse Battery two guns and Well Battery one RML. Lighthouse Battery is thought to have been the garrison keep. A hospital and isolation ward were later built on Flat Holm for cholera and infectious diseases, which may well have restricted frequent training by Artillery Volunteers.

No military were on the island in 1871, just two lighthouse keepers and their wives and two agricultural labourers working on the farm, but four years later there is evidence of military occupation. A commercial photographer wanted to photograph the new lighthouse and he managed to persuade a gunner to

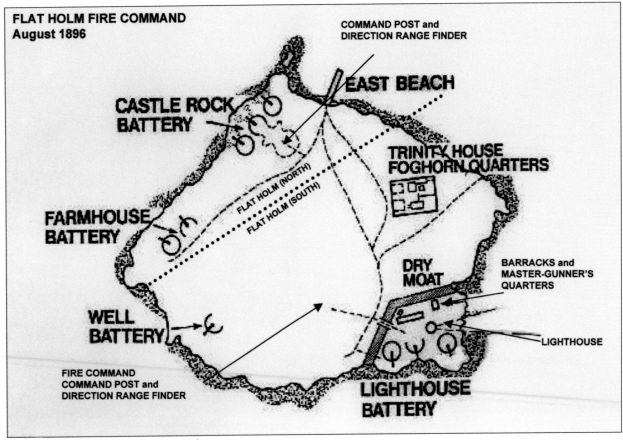

FLAT HOLM FIRE COMMAND
August 1896

COMMAND POST and
DIRECTION RANGE FINDER

EAST BEACH

CASTLE ROCK
BATTERY

TRINITY HOUSE
FOGHORN QUARTERS

FLAT HOLM (NORTH)
FLAT HOLM (SOUTH)

FARMHOUSE
BATTERY

DRY
MOAT

BARRACKS and
MASTER-GUNNER'S
QUARTERS

WELL
BATTERY

LIGHTHOUSE

FIRE COMMAND
COMMAND POST and
DIRECTION RANGE FINDER

LIGHTHOUSE
BATTERY

Map 4: *Flat Holm Fire Command, 1896.*

raise a Moncrieff Disappearing Carriage of Lighthouse Battery. When the photograph was printed, complete with lighthouse and raised 7-inch RML, the military authorities, in the interests of national security, took a dim view, had the photograph suppressed and reprimanded the unfortunate soldier.

Ten years later, Master-Gunner Thomas Barratt was at Flat Holm, accompanied by his wife and three children, and commanding three gunners. Manning the lighthouse was a principal lighthouse-keeper, with his wife and children, and an assistant lighthouse keeper. The Morgans occupied the farmhouse, with a niece and a servant: a total of twelve people. By 1891, Barratt had been replaced by Master-Gunner Ralph Somerville, with his wife and three children, and four gunners. Frederick Harris had retired from the sea and ran the pub at the farmhouse with his wife, four other adults and a child. In June Vice-Admiral Phillimore's committee inspected the battery and concluded it was in an efficient condition.

Life on the two holms must have been tedious. Mr Perry was contracted to supply Brean Down and the

two holms using his sailing-vessel, the *Spray*, and no doubt he took the gunners for short runs ashore. The round trip took about six hours in fair weather. Because they were in exposed positions in the middle of the Bristol Channel, the two islands suffered strong winds and wet weather all year round, but the garrison in late Victorian times also found them to be hotter in the summer, although colder and wetter in the winter, compared to the mainland.

The preoccupation of the garrisons was to keep the guns serviced and the ammunition in good condition, a particularly difficult job when the elements sometimes hurled sea-spray across the islands. Throughout the summer the magazines were ventilated from 9am to 2pm by opening the shafts. The guns were probably sponged out and cleaned daily, firing mechanisms tested, grease pumped into working parts and brass kept free of corrosion. The traversing platforms and disappearing carriages would have been tested to ensure trouble-free traverse and elevation. The magazines were checked frequently to ensure that bag charges were not leaking powder and that projectiles were in good condition. Secondary to these duties, the Master-Gunner ensured the accommodation was tidy, ablutions clean and personal weapons, which were usually stored in a rack by their beds, serviceable.

Lavernock

Completing the line-up across the Bristol Channel was Lavernock Fort at Lavernock Point, which had three, possibly five, 7-inch RMLs each on Moncrieff's Disappearing Carriage. The approaches to the fort were much more convenient and it was possible for the public to visit the battery with the permission of the Master-Gunner. The Penarth and Barry Dock companies of the 2nd Glamorgan Artillery Volunteer Corps provided the gunners and trained on 64-pounders.

In 1871 the only military presence was Sergeant James Howard RE, who appears to have been the military clerk of works for the construction of the fort. He was accompanied by his wife and lived in the barracks. In 1881 four gunners looked after the fort. The widow of Corporal Holloway, their five children and a sister also lived at the fort.

The 1875 photograph of the Moncrieff Disappearing Carriage in front of Lighthouse Battery, Flat Holm, which developed into a breach of national security. (John Barrett)

In 1888 Geary's committee suggested that the fort be equipped with two 6-inch breech-loaders on hydro-pneumatic gun carriages and two 3-pounder QFs on field-gun carriages but this was not supported.

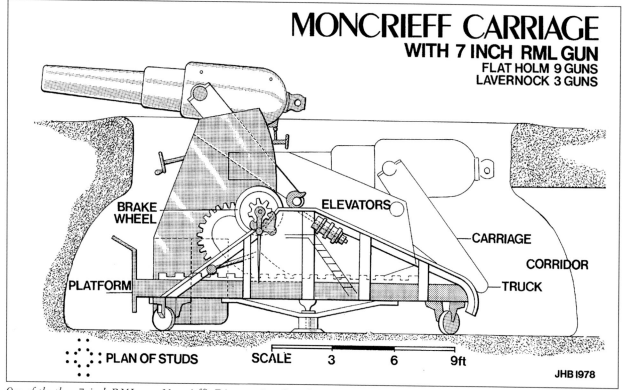

MONCRIEFF CARRIAGE
WITH 7 INCH RML GUN
FLAT HOLM 9 GUNS
LAVERNOCK 3 GUNS

BRAKE WHEEL

ELEVATORS

CARRIAGE

CORRIDOR

PLATFORM

TRUCK

PLAN OF STUDS   SCALE   3   6   9ft

JHB 1978

One of the three 7-inch RMLs, on Moncrieff's Disappearing Gun Carriage, at Lighthouse Battery on Flat Holm. (John Barrett)

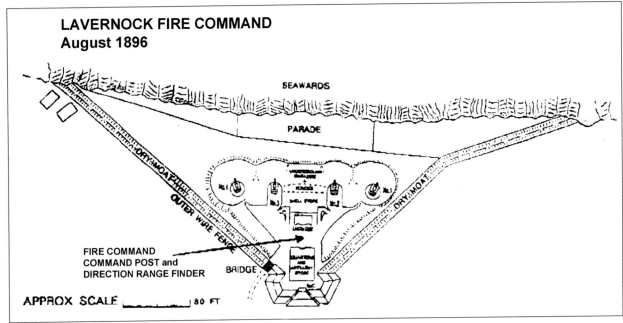

Map 5: *Lavernock Fire Command, August 1896.*

By 1891 Sergeant John Daly commanded the detachment of three gunners. His wife and nephew accompanied him. In July 1894, the volunteer establishment from 9 and 10 (Penarth) and (11) Barry Dock companies was listed as five officers, twelve sergeants and 196 junior NCOs and gunners, although it is thought the men from Penarth would have been deployed to Flat Holm.

Wireless telegraphy

When the Italian government rejected the wireless experiments of the Italo-Irish Guglielmo Marconi, he travelled to England in 1896 and persuaded Sir William Preece, then Engineer-in-Chief of the General Post Office, to take an interest. Marconi filed his first patent on wireless telegraphy after trials on Salisbury Plain between September 1896 and March 1897. Sir William was intrigued with Marconi's idea of using electromagnetic static to pass signals and announced that the Post Office would not spare any expense to develop wireless telegraphy. Assigned to Marconi as his senior engineer was the highly experienced George Kemp, a former member of the Royal Navy.

In early 1897 Lavernock was selected as a base to experiment with Marconi's invention, radiating to Flat Holm because there was line of sight over water. Several years earlier, Sir William Preece had success-fully trialled his Parallel Wire System between the two forts. On 6 May the research team travelled by train from Paddington to Cardiff, and Kemp went to Lavernock Point where he and his team hoisted a 110ft (33m) mast and repeated the exercise at Flat Holm the following day.

On 14 May, after a few problems had been resolved, Marconi at Lavernock, and Kemp on Flat Holm, tapped a few simple messages in Morse, which were countersigned by Captain Kennedy RE. The Post Office was delighted, although there was "still much to be desired in order to convert crude appliances into good working order".

The following day, Saturday 15 May, the success of the trials seems to have inspired the group to lengthen the distance of the transmissions and Brean Down, due south of Weston-super-Mare and eight miles (13km) across the Bristol Channel from Lavernock Point, was selected as the transmission point. Kemp dismantled the Flat Holm experiment and over the weekend assembled the transmitter on top of the cliffs at Lavernock Point. The weather was too rough on the Monday to cross by steamer to Brean Down but it does seem a party reached the area by Tuesday, possibly crossing by tugboat to Weston-super-Mare and then catching the ferry from Uphill to Brean Down. At the time a small Royal Artillery District Establishment was maintaining the guns at Brean Down fort and no doubt watched the trials with interest.

Kemp noted in his diary:

300ft *(91m)* of (four-strand) wire was laid from the top of the table (in the hut) through an insulated shackle, at the top of a 50ft *(15m)* pole and then onto a kite string by a plate of light aluminium with a hole in it. I then took the kite line to the top of a 107ft-*(32.5m)* pole, which gave a distance (height) of 200ft *(60m)* from the ground to the aluminium and transmitting wire.

Those at Brean Down had a similar arrangement. Kemp used six 2-volt accumulators but the team at Brean Down experienced some problems landing and could not work the kite, so a Marconi message was sent by cable from Brean Down to Steep Holm, to Flat Holm, and then by the Parallel Wire System to Lavernock Point, probably using the military communications connecting the four forts. Kemp noted in his diary, "Good signals to Brean Down *(from Lavernock Point)* using a kite and 300ft of 4-strand wire".

The following day the research team at Brean Down and Lavernock Point again flew kites, and in the afternoon the following messages were sent:

14.50 Vs to the right and left
14.55 How are you?
15.00 The kite is up
15.05 Send us news
15.30 Vs
15.45–16.00 Vs
16.10–16.20 Sky

Kemp heard on 19 May that the engineers at Brean Down had received his signals but the ink had run out. On Friday 28 May 1897, the trials were complete and the following day Marconi and the team returned to London, leaving Cardiff at 10.30am and arriving at London Paddington at 3.30pm. The apparatus was left secure in the cloakroom and transported by van on the Monday to the Post Office Works at Holloway.

A few weeks later Marconi registered the Wireless Telegraph & Signal Company but this led to a breakdown with the Post Office because the Secretary of the Post Office felt it would be improper

An artist's drawing, showing Marconi's tests between Brean Down, Flat Holm and Lavernock Point. Note that Steep Holm does not figure. (Author's collection)

for a public company to spend time and money developing a patent held in the public domain. Sir William Preece was instructed that "for the present Mr Marconi could not take part in any Post Office experiments whatever". The Post office then ceased all research into wireless telegraphy.

In 1898 Marconi successfully broadcast across the English Channel with a radio message and by 1899 with Kemp was consistently achieving ranges of sixty miles (96km). Two years later he had successfully transmitted across the Atlantic Ocean to St John's, Newfoundland, and proved that the curvature of the earth was no barrier to further developments in radio-telegraphy. The rift between Marconi and the Post Office simmered for many years but his continued success in developing wireless telegraphy forced the Post Office to re-examine radio communications and eventually led to a strong department dealing with wireless telegraphy.

The Post Office realised the commercial potential of wireless telegraphy and in the autumn of 1899 took advantage of the offer of an alternative receiver from the Hungarian inventor Bela Schaefer. Experiments between Lavernock Point and Brean Down proved the receiver to be inadequate and the Post Office again pursued radio communications some vigour. The isolation of Brean Down proved a nuisance and between October and the following April the experiments moved to Knightstone near Weston-super-Mare.

Marconi returned to Italy and established an experimental radio station at La Spezia and then returned to England where he founded the Wireless Telegraph & Signal Company, which in 1900 became the Marconi Wireless Telegraph Company, and is now part of the prosperous GEC Marconi Company. In 1907 Marconi and Karl Ferdinand Braun were jointly awarded the Nobel Prize for physics. Other scientists were experimenting in radiotelegraphy and for several years Marconi was plagued by patent suits in US courts until in 1915 the US federal judiciary ruled in his favour. In later years Marconi was created a member of the Italian senate and was appointed a member of the Fascist Grand Council by Benito Mussolini. He died in Rome on 20 July 1937.

By 1902 all the batteries protecting the Bristol Channel had been abandoned and most of guns and their carriages sold to a Cardiff firm, who cut them up. Most of the RMLs on the two holms were left when it became cost-ineffective to keep on transporting gas for the oxy-acetylene equipment to cut them up. Little evidence of Lavernock Fort now exists because a holiday camp was built over the site in the 1930s.

FIVE

Brean Down Harbour

Artist's impression of the proposed Weston-super-Mare harbour and Brean Down Fort. The fort is shown as six small houses, as opposed to the two main buildings that were constructed. Note the workmen's cottages. (John Tucker)

The Uphill Project

For several centuries the area to the leeward (northern) side of Brean Down was considered suitable for a harbour but the implementation of such proposals during the nineteenth century, when the greatest efforts were made, is a story of missed opportunity. The only existing port handling cargo in the vicinity was Uphill, but this was merely a narrow and winding creek off the estuary of the River Axe. At low tide it dried out, and inbound vessels had to wait off the mouth of the Axe in the lee of Brean Down, exactly where Brean Down Harbour was proposed.

In 1841, in giving evidence before a House of Commons Select Committee on the possibility of a port at Weston-super-Mare for the West Indies

mails, Captain Claxton RN, and Captain Richard Drew, one of the Elder Brethren of Trinity House, spoke of the difficulty in navigation above Steep Holm and pressed for the development of a deep-sea harbour at Brean Down. Captain Evans, of the Post Inquiry Commission, examining ports for the receipt and despatch of mail, reported that:

> To take England, Ireland and Scotland together there is no part of the Kingdom in my opinion so well suited for a packet station as Brean Down.

By the mid-1840s Uphill harbour was unloading annually about 16,400 tons of Welsh coal. In 1841 Mr John Harvey advertised in the local press:

> Steam navigation from Cardiff to Uphill to unite the Taff and Exeter Railways. The vast population with

an unproductive soil in Wales – the fertility of the Somersetshire coast – the market at Highbridge – the intended railway station at Uphill – the passage between Bristol and Cardiff and Bridgwater reduced by two hours – the demand for such accommodation by the population of South Wales and Somerset – and the establishment thereafter of a general carrying trade throughout the Channel afford almost certain success to the undertaking. Every possible encouragement short of a monopoly will be given to any party disposed to establish a regular steam packet as above.

There was no response to this forward-thinking plan to connect Wales and England via Somerset and the scheme died.

Meanwhile in 1845 the lands of the Somerset Wyndhams, including Brean Down, passed to their cousins, the Wyndhams of Dinton, Wiltshire.

The Uphill project was revived in 1854 when businessmen associated with the Weston Water Works and the Coleford, Monmouth, Usk & Pontypool Railway Company proposed a harbour and a railway to join the Bristol & Exeter Railway at Bleadon to transport coal to steamships plying the Atlantic Ocean from Southampton.

The Weston-super-Mare Steam Ferry and Railway Company was formed and the public invited to purchase shares. The 6 May 1854 *Weston Gazette* announced that:

> mutual benefits would flow ... particularly increasing the number of visitors who would avail themselves of the general air of our delightful watering place.

Claims were made that business and postal communications would improve and since the work would be at Uphill, this would not spoil Weston-super-Mare. According to the *Gazette* of 17 June 1854, the pier, railway warehouses and hydraulic cranes were estimated to cost £12,000 and Messrs Gaskell & Co. contracted to complete construction within six months.

In August 1854, to test the feasibility of a floating jetty, the *Taliesin*, skippered by Captain Stone, successfully steamed up the River Axe to Uphill while on a pleasure excursion from Cardiff. The *Weston Gazette* of 12 August 1854 called it the *Tabesin*, but in fact it was the wooden paddle-steamer *Taliesin* of 158 tons gross (85 net), built in 1842, which was owned and operated by the Cardiff Steam Navigation Company. It later provided a ferry service betwixt Burnham-on-Sea and Cardiff, between 1858 and 1860.

In September 1854, even though its operations would give them additional traffic, and therefore profit, at no major capital outlay, the directors of the Bristol & Exeter Railway declared they were not in favour of a harbour at Uphill. The fact that they were considering a station at Highbridge, itself a small port, and that connecting to both harbours would mean building new lines on both sides of the River Axe estuary, seems to have prejudiced their major investor, the Great Western Railway. However the Uphill proposal was well underway and after some negotiation, the directors decided to press ahead.

The following month a meeting was held at the Reeves Hotel to launch the rival scheme of the Weston-super-Mare and Uphill Pier & Railway Company, and notice was given to apply for an Act to enable the Company to construct:

- A pier jetty or Landing place in the Parish of Uphill at the junction of the Axe and a pill called Uphill Pill or Slimbridge Pill.
- To enable the Company to construct railways terminating with a junction with the B&E and another to Weston-super-Mare.
- A pier at the railway termination.
- Floating stages as necessary.
- To enable purchase of all lands, and bases required for the proposed works.
- To repeal or vary all existing rights which obstruct the Company's objects.

In October 1858, a press statement from the company revealed the intention to have a steam ferry from Cardiff to a pier at Brean Down, available at all states of the tide, with a railway running along the southern banks of the River Axe, either to join the Bristol & Exeter Railway or to go straight to Highbridge "and thence to Southampton", as the *Weston Gazette* of 20 Oct 1858 explained. Since coal traffic was the most important trade, slips were to be constructed so that railway wagons could be loaded straight on board in South Wales and off-loaded onto the tracks at Brean Down.

The direct line to Highbridge, was meant to link with the Somerset & Dorset Railway's line to the south coast, carrying bunker coal to ships using ports such as Southampton. The connection to the Bristol and Exeter Railway was to accommodate passenger traffic but perhaps the directors also had an eye to the deficiencies of the dock at Bridgwater. Besides handling locally made pottery products, this was by 1874 the fifth largest port in Britain for the

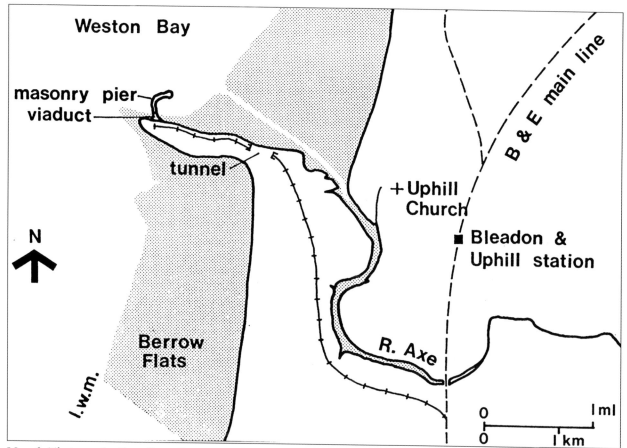

Map 6: *The proposed railway line to Brean Down harbour.*

importation of coal, but its trade was severely hampered by the difficult navigation of the River Parrett and its winding, tidal nature. The new harbour at Brean, available at all states of the tide, would end those problems.

The principal feature was a floating harbour measuring 100yd (90m) square with an entry of about 60yd (55m) to allow the largest ships to enter. Two sides of the harbour were to be constructed of solid masonry and would have the cranes and offices. The landward side would be left to allow for expansion and development, and a short railway line would run from Uphill and into Weston-super-Mare, along the back of Ellenborough Crescent, to join with the Bristol–Exeter line. The estimated cost was £35,000 and no engineering problems were envisaged. Concern was expressed that since the railway was needed, its directors might force the move of the project to Bridgwater.

The eminent marine engineer Sir John Coode published a feasibility study on a harbour at Brean Down. Calculating the distance between London

and Brean Down as 140 miles (225km), compared to 200 (320km) between Liverpool and London, he concluded that the route via Weston-super-Mare would save "nearly a whole day", a period not to be taken lightly in the Victorian era. He noted that the proposed site, on the northern shores of the down, was protected from southerly and south-westerly weather while the Mendips afforded protection from the chilly easterly and north-easterly winds. The depth, 28ft (8.5m) at low water, was adequate and, while noting that the bottom was tenacious clay underlaid by gravel and compacted sand, Coode concluded that a pier should prevent silting and wrote:

> The proposed harbour at Brean Down would have the advantage of being accessible to steamers and vessels of the largest class at all states of the tide, an advantage not possessed by any single port in the Bristol Channel; nor is it, I believe, attainable at any other site in this Channel at a practicable cost. The advantage is one, which in these days of rapid transport, cannot well be overrated, especially when taken

51

in connection with the important and increasing traffic of various kinds between South Wales, Ireland and Liverpool on the one hand and Bristol, London and the South of England on the other.

Referring to the evidence given by Claxton, Drew and Evans, Coode continued:

It is beyond question that the dangers lie above Brean Down and it is certain that there is no other on this Channel which can be compared with it; considering the facility of the approach, depth of water close to the shore and the economy with which steam coals may be delivered, the site of the proposed harbour being only 10 miles *(16km)* distant from the Cardiff docks, whence it is well known the best steam coals in the world are shipped.

There is one important advantage that would be afforded by the proposed works at Brean Down and their connection with the railway system of the south and west of England, viz the rapidity and certainty with which a supply of steam coals might be conveyed across the Bristol Channel within the batteries between Brean Down and Lavernock Point to the south of Cardiff, the steep Holm and Flat Holm, forming the immediate points of this line, the distances being 2 and 7/8 miles *(4.63km)*, 2 and 5/8 miles *(4.23km)* and 2 and 7/8 miles *(4.63km)* respectively. Guns placed at each of the points would cross fire and form a line of defence within which traffic might be carried on with the greatest despatch and economy and without interruption.

The 26 October edition of the *Weston Gazette* ran more details on Coode's proposals:

I propose to form the harbour and to acquire the necessary shelter by the construction of a pier from 800 to 850ft *(244–260m)* in length, run off from a point about 100yds *(90m)* from the west end of Brean Down, so designed that about 400ft *(122m)* of it will afford sheltered quayage from 21 to 25ft *(6.4–7.6m)* depth of Low Water Spring Tide.

It is a matter of importance in this locality to provide against the accumulation of silt, and on this point I would observe that there is an outset along the south shore of the bay, not only during the period of the ebb but also for the whole period of the flood, excepting the first 1 and a half hours.

Railway connection

Line to be laid from the outer end of the Landing Pier and thence along the north side of Brean Down, until within about 600yds *(550m)* of the eastern end

where the line would pass to the south side by a short tunnel of 200yds *(183m)* in length. The cost of the Harbour and a single line is estimated at £105,000.

The tunnel was to be built to avoid interfering with the proposed floating dock at Uphill.

First Brean Down Harbour Proposal

By December 1861, the Bristol & Exeter Railway Company had registered the Brean Down harbour scheme with Parliament. Directors for the project were nominated and included Sir John Eardley Wilmot as Chairman, Rear-Admiral Sir William Hall, director of the Peninsula & Orient Company, as Deputy Chairman, and William Lawrence Banks, Chairman of the Brecon & Merthyr Tydfil Junction Railway Company.

Investment for the scheme was sought by selling shares, the harbour share capital being listed as £125,000 with borrowing powers for £41,000. For the railway, the capital was provided by the Bristol & Exeter Railway Company. This may be compared with the Uphill docks' share capital, which was listed at £240,000 with borrowing powers for £80,000. Each share was sold for £2 on application and £2 for the first allotment.

To eliminate an expensive parliamentary contest between the Brean Down and Uphill schemes, the Brean Down company's proposal to construct a slip at Birnbeck Pier (near Weston) was withdrawn on the understanding that the Weston-super-Mare Steam Ferry & Railway Company would not compete for passenger traffic. In any case a new competitor was already planned: Birnbeck Pier, designed by the famous Eugenius Birch, was opened on 5 June 1867 to accommodate landing passengers. By this time the cult of the sea trip was becoming popular and since Weston had no jetty, and was only really accessible at high tide, it was losing valuable trade.

Coode's proposals undermined the Weston Bay Pier Harbour Company's plans for a port at Uphill and efforts to attract investors from home and abroad met without significant success. Uphill's importance as a commercial centre steadily waned, not just because of the distance from the Great Western: Welsh businessmen opened up Milford Haven for transatlantic traffic and shipping was also finding the approaches to the River Axe difficult to navigate and therefore inconvenient. A proposal to open up a canal from Uphill to the Somerset Levels

A different artist's impression of the proposed Weston-super-Mare harbour and Brean Down Fort. Clearly seen are the fortifications, and a railway train on the jetty. In the background are Kingsholme and Weston-super-Mare. (John Tucker)

to export and import cattle to and from the USA, as we shall briefly see, also came to nothing.

By 1862, as increasing mineral exploitation on the Mendips needed an outlet, support for the project grew. On 9 January Sir John Wilmot advised Mr William Wyndham that notice for the scheme had been deposited in the House of Commons. The Brean Down Bill was postponed but Mr Burnett, another director, sent the Bill and the parliamentary amendments to Wyndham explaining that not only would the Company's compulsory-purchase order lapse after three years, but they had no right of purchase beyond three furlongs (660yd or 600m) from the shore end of the pier. The only blot was the death on 7 March of William Wyndham; his son, also William, took over.

Work Begins on Brean Down Harbour

In contrast to the Uphill scheme, by October 1864 investment in Brean Down Harbour was doing well

and there was confidence that Weston-super-Mare would become one of the great ports of the Empire. The architect Mr Newton from London was awarded the contract and he engaged the engineering company Messrs Lomas and Hay, Abingdon Street, London to build it with economic use of material, with the emphasis on simplicity, practicality and rapidity, all for £86,000, to be completed by 1868. Mr R.W. Dowell was appointed contractor and Sir John Coode was engaged as the consulting engineer.

November the 5th, a glorious sunny Saturday, was selected as the day to lay the foundation stone of the jetty. At midday, buns were distributed from the Town Hall to children under ten years old but, since only £5 had been budgeted for this, many went home without one. At 2pm the official party and 200 invited guests grandly filed on board the 108-ton iron paddle steamer *Wye* at Knightstone and steamed to the site of Brean Down Harbour where a crane hoisted the 2ft 6in x 1ft square (0.76m x 0.3m) foundation stone, on which was inscribed:

Carved stones for the jetty stored on the Second World War hard standing. In the background is a worker's derelict cottage. (Somerset Archaeological and Natural History Society)

Brean Down Harbour
This Stone was laid on 5 November 1864 by
Lady Eardley Wilmot.
Sir J.E. Eardley Wilmot, Chairman.
Lomax and Hay, Engineers.
R.W. Dowell, Contractor.
The Rev W.W. Rowley, Incumbent of Emmanuel
Church.
God Bless This Undertaking.

Lady Eardley Wilmot then addressed the official party:

Here we find a vast promontory extending far out into the sea, well sheltered from gales prevalent in this district and with capabilities for a deep-water harbour at comparatively trifling cost. On the ground immediately in front of us, Her Majesty's Government propose to erect a powerful battery of artillery which with corresponding works on Steep and Flat Holms will constitute an effective defence of the Severn and the rich trading centres within its gates. May stone upon stone be placed at the bottom of the deep sea without delay or interruption and without injury from storm and tempest till the port of Brean Down appears above the waves in its full symmetry and strength, capable of accommodating the largest vessels, and being an emporium of commerce from every quarter of the globe.

Those on board then drank a toast of champagne and expressed the hope that the Prince of Wales, later Edward VII, would open the harbour when completed. The jib then lowered the stone into about 70ft (21m) of water and a small buoy with a flag with the letters 'BDH' marked its position. Accompanying boats hooted and those on shore cheered and waved flags. A volley was fired by the Weston-super-Mare Rifle Volunteer Corps.

To the sound of the first rocks being blasted by navvies on Brean Down, the *Wye* first steamed to Steep Holm and then returned to Weston-super-

Mare, where the official party landed and went to the Town Hall for lunch, more toasts, speeches and self-congratulation. *The Illustrated London News*, giving an account of the ceremony, emphasised that a harbour had long been required and Brean Down seemed to offer the best opportunity. Proposed artillery garrisons on Brean Down, Steep Holm, Flat Holm and Lavernock Point were deemed a valuable asset to protect the entrance of the Severn.

The following day there was consternation when the 'BDH' buoy and its flag were nowhere to be seen. That evening a fishing smack found it bobbing off Steep Holm, driven there by a swift current and high tide. This misfortune rather typified the story of Brean Down Harbour, as did the failure to provide the children with a bun.

In December the valuer Mr Dobson, acting for Mr Wyndham, arranged to sell four acres (1.6ha) of land adjoining the Fort for £200 per acre. Brean Down Harbour Company paid the fees. Plans for the Brean Down Harbour railway were deposited with the Board of Trade and a Mr Streeter of Bath, with his tender of £8,000, was declared the successful contractor to build the passenger railway station. Mr Dobson arranged for the sale of just over three acres (1.2ha) of land adjoining the fort for £775 for a workmen's club and cottages.

Three months later the Brean Down Dock Bill was given its second reading in the House of Lords, at which it was proposed to purchase compulsorily Brean Down Farm and additional land. Mr Dowell fenced the land but rumours began to circulate, in January 1865, that the engineers had resigned and work on the harbour ceased. Nevertheless by February the problem had been resolved and work began on constructing a slip at the north end of Brean Down. Work also began on the fort.

By mid-summer, construction of the jetty was well underway and more navvies were recruited to push the work during the favourable weather and long evenings. The directors agreed to open parts of the harbour as soon as they were ready, to relieve the pressure on Bristol. A meeting with engineers surveying the connecting railway line to Uphill concluded that 25 acres (10ha) of land would be required and the total cost of this project would be £275,000. Further impetus was given in March 1865 when the Transatlantic Steam Ship Company decided to use Brean Down Harbour for its steamers. Another major financial crisis was resolved and again the project was pushed forward.

As the slipway was nearing completion, the *Weston Gazette* on 24 November 1865 described it as

> built of solid masonry and extends 150 feet *(45.7m)* into the sea, the wall being 10 feet *(3.05m)* thick at the bases, 5 feet *(1.52m)* at the top, there is also an abutment of 40 feet *(12.2m)*. At the rear of this some 1000 tons of stone and shingles are thrown making the same one massive and impregnable structure.

A Mr Chaplin had taken over as the resident contractor. The same month the Company submitted an application for an Act confirming the docks at Brean Down.

Disaster struck in December 1868 when Mr Chaplin died after an accident and work was suspended pending an investigation. Worst of all, no one could be found to replace him. Sir John Wilmot applied for an extension of time but in September 1872 he formally acknowledged that the harbour scheme had failed because of a critical official report into Chaplin's death and the inability of the consortium to find a replacement. He advised Sir William Wyndham that he wished to revive the project but reroute the railway to join the Somerset & Dorset Railway at Burnham-on-Sea, as opposed to joining the Bristol & Exeter Railway at Bleadon, since they, he considered, had been obstructive throughout. This proposal was rejected.

The pier was lashed by winter storms and then wrecked in a particularly fierce gale in 1872. Today the only evidence of the project is a few dressed stones from the jetty, near the quarry site below the fort, on the northern shore of Brean Down.

Second Brean Down Harbour Proposal, 1887

In March 1887 Mr Vincent Lawson, an engineer, concerned that Weston-super-Mare was being left behind in the scramble to exploit the Wales–England and transatlantic trade routes, revived the Brean Down Harbour project. Sir John Wilmot again consented to be Chairman but, no doubt mindful of the 1868 failure, on condition "of being exempt from all personal financial liability", to which Lawson agreed. Sir William Wyndham declined to join the consortium as a director but agreed to support it.

Throughout 1887 Lawson attempted to secure investment and by August had convinced a Mr Edwin Lawrence to promise financial support for the

Group of coast gunners pose on the remains of the jetty, 1943. Gnr Patterson is on the extreme left. (Ray Patterson)

preliminary expenses. He again wrote to Sir William seeking his active support, as a landowner, so that his syndicate could have

> reasonable protection against other syndicates or companies from fore-stalling us in our undertaking and till we can comply with the requirement for plans to be deposited, which we hope to do by this coming 1st of November. Of course, this will have nothing to do with the terms of purchase of land that would be a matter for arrangements in the usual manner. We find the project being much talked of hence the reason for our request.

Sir William confirmed his support but then, hearing no more from Lawson, concluded that since no plans had been deposited, the project was defunct. However in October 1888 he heard from Sir John Wilmot that there was a proposal for Brean Down Harbour to be a terminus for American cattle and for a ship canal to the Somerset Levels from Uphill. Lawson then met with Sir William and, giving him a letter from Sir John offering to buy Brean Down, urged that he sell the whole down. By now Sir William was becoming impatient with the schemes and replied:

> Before you showed me Sir J. Wilmot's letter, I believe I told you that I was not disposed to sell more of Brean Down than was necessary for the Dock and harbour; of course, if any gentlemen open their mouths wide enough, they may swallow me.

Sir John was keen to place the Brean Down Harbour scheme before Parliament but was concerned that he had not seen a prospectus or probable financial outlay. At a meeting in November, in reply to Lawson's persistence that Sir William should join the syndicate, the latter said his solicitor, Mr Fletcher, would guide him. Lawson responded angrily, "If you don't join, we will take your land at its present price". Wyndham replied he would oppose and Lawson withdrew his threat. Sir Daniel Gooch of the Great Western Railway promised to make a short branch line, as outlined in 1861, from the proposed harbour to the main line.

Relations seemed to have deteriorated. On 9 November 1888 Sir John Wilmot met with Fletcher and gave a despondent account of the project. He had left a prospectus on which was written "Bleadon, say 2 and 1/2 miles from Harbour – line already arranged by GW Railway". Support for the project, even from within the syndicate, was not

total. Fletcher then advised Lawson that Sir William would not be joining the syndicate because time was too short for completing the arrangements, but held out a prospect of joining later on satisfactory terms.

Lawson continued to make every effort for a successful revival of the Brean Down Harbour and claimed "strong financial support". Another syndicate member, Mr Baxter, then wrote to Sir William that he had heard from Lawson that the former was willing to join the Company as a director. Sir William replied that Baxter was misinformed. On 16 December Lawson wrote to Sir William that he now had "very strong financial support … promise of all the funds for the Act promoting the company" and again asked him to join the syndicate and give a subscription for expenses. Baxter sent him a copy of the Bill and a draft agreement as follows:

Brean Down Harbour and Railway Bill 1889 Articles of Agreement

Between Sir J.E.E. Wilmot, Bart., J.H. de Rice, P.H. Stevens, T.B. Wilson and T.J. Perrett on one part and me on the other part.

Clause One If Bill becomes law and Company launched, Company shall pay £200 per acre for all land taken over including the Tunnel.

Clause Two Company shall take land required for the pier and railway only and not deviate inland from centre line marked on plan deposited, along north part of Down.

Clause Three Not to be any land within 100 feet (30m) of Pill near land numbered 11 and 12 on deposited plans; nor within 100 feet of Brean Down Farm buildings except for the purpose of a road to siding on railway.

Clause Four Company to take stone excavated in cutting or tunnelling free of cost but to pay £6 per ton for any stone they may take from my land. The tunnel to be 26 feet (7.9m) wide and 30 feet (9.1m) high and no larger. The Company to have no surface rights above the tunnel.

Clause Five Company to make before opening the railway a sufficient siding not more than 250 yards (229m) from Brean Down Farm with approaches from said road for loading goods and stock and until a proposal for station be made, allow tenants, their families and persons in charge of stock to travel in Guards' van or otherwise.

Clause Six Bridge over railway to be 16 feet *(4.9m)* high and 25 feet *(7.6m)* wide.

Clause Seven Company to make cattle creep under railway 10 feet *(3.05m)* high and 12 feet *(3.65m)* wide in position numbered 11 on the plan filed; also five gates and level crossings at places to be approved by me.

Clause Eight Company to make gates, gateways, watercourses, ponds and drinking places; and make and maintain all culvert to drains, archways and make a levelled communication between point No. 11 and road to Brean Down Farm, south west of railway.

Clause Nine Company to compensate me and tenants for temporary damage and within one month.

Clause Ten Company to build a similar wall for garden to that destroyed by them within 100 yards *(90m)* of the site of the old garden.

Clause Eleven Opposition by me to be withdrawn.

Clause Twelve The Agreement may be scheduled to Bill by Parliament and made binding on both parties hereto, but if Parliament make any material alterations therein, either party may withdraw therefrom.

The application to Parliament failed and with it Brean Down Harbour. Milford Haven, with its deep, well-defended inlet, opened in October 1889 and to the south Bridgwater, with easy access to the railway, was developing. In Worth's account of travels by rail and road in Somerset, the prospects held out by Uphill and Weston-super-Mare for international and commercial prosperity are not mentioned. They had missed the boat.

SIX

Brean Down Fort 1862–1900

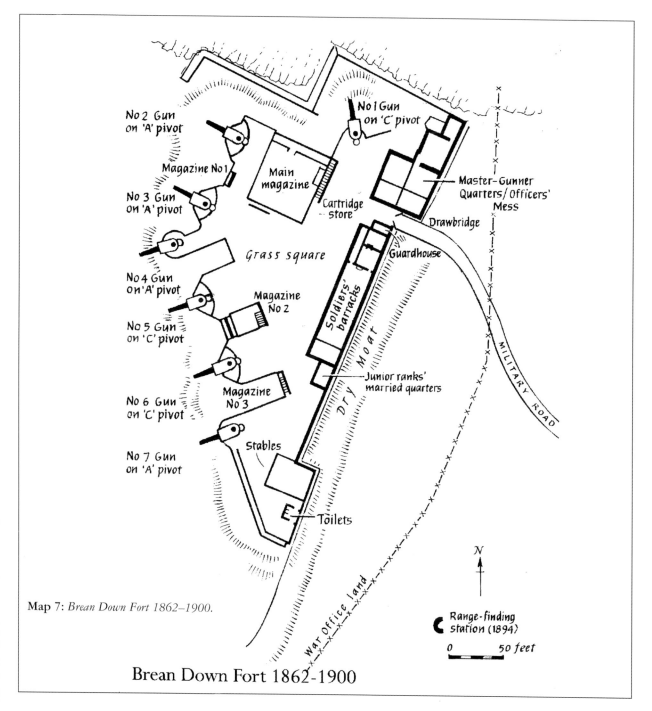

Map 7: *Brean Down Fort 1862–1900.*

Brean Down Fort 1862-1900

Howe Point Requisitioned

In the wake of the Royal Commission's report in February 1862, which recommended a chain of coastal forts based on a standard design and equipment, Royal Engineer surveyors were sent out scouring the country for suitable sites for fixed defences. They will have been aware of the proposed Brean Down Harbour (see Chapter 5). They will have seen the strategic value of a defensive screen across the Bristol Channel linking Brean Down to Penarth in Wales to protect its upper reaches, in particular Bristol, and the shipping routes from the Welsh coalfields. They may well have noted the concerns of Cardiff businessmen, who were decidedly jittery in 1861, the first year of the American Civil War, when the Union threatened, in the event of hostilities with Great Britain, to destroy ships in Cardiff and seize coal. At this time the port was largely undefended. The coal merchants Hill and Son wrote to the council:

> Permit us, as persons largely interested in the wellbeing of the port, to call your attention to its present totally defenceless condition. In the event of war we are liable to be attacked at any moment, and our property destroyed in a few hours, without even the means of returning a shot.

A solicitor, writing on behalf of Her Majesty's Principal Secretary of State for the War Department, sent a letter to Mr William Wyndham seeking a Requisition Agreement for four acres (1.6ha) of uncultivated land at Howe Rocks on the tip of Brean Down. The notice read:

> **To William Wyndham Esquire of Dinton near Salisbury in the County of Wiltshire or other the Owner or Owners of the Lands, Buildings, Hereditaments or Easements mentioned in the Schedule to this notice**
>
> On behalf of Her Majesty's Principal Secretary of State for the War Department, I HEREBY GIVE YOU NOTICE that he requires for the Public Service all lands, buildings and other hereditaments mentioned and set out in the Schedule hereto annexed, and delineated and verged with a brown line in the Map or plan herewith left, which premises are situated in the parish of Weston in the county of Somerset and that he is willing, and hereby offers, to pay you the sum of ten shillings as the consideration of the absolute purchase of such lands, buildings and other hereditaments; AND I FURTHER GIVE YOU NOTICE that if you refuse to accept such sum of ten shillings as the con-

sideration money aforesaid, during the space of fourteen days next after the delivery of this Notice to you, the said Principal Secretary will take all such meas ures as may be necessary, pursuant to the powers and provisions of one or all of the several Acts of Parliament hereinafter named, that is to say, the 5th and 6th Vict., c. 67, 18 and 19 Vict., c. 117 and 22 Vict., c. 12 for obtaining immediate possession of such lands, buildings and other hereditaments, and for causing a jury to be summoned to find compensation to be paid by the said Principal Secretary for the absolute purchase of such lands, buildings and other hereditaments.

Dated this twenty first day of February 1862.

The schedule reads: "A piece or parcel of uncultivated land situated at Breandown in the parish of Weston containing about four acres little more or less as shown on the plan hereto annexed". At the same time, the War Office also requisitioned Steep Holm, Flat Holm and Lavernock Point, near Penarth, and proposed the forts should all be equipped with 7-inch (178mm) RMLs. With mutually supporting fire, this would be a formidable

Colonel Robert Vetch. (Author's collection)

defensive barrier. In June, Lord Palmerston confirmed to Parliament that the Government had requisitioned land on Brean Down on which to build a fort.

In October 1864, Lieutenant Robert Vetch RE arrived back in Great Britain after a tour in the West Indies and, after being sent to Western Command in Cardiff, was placed in charge of the proposed defence

---

Robert Hamilton Vetch
1841–1916

6 January 1841	Born in Birmingham. Educated at Henley-on-Thames Grammar School and Hopkirk's School, Eltham.
23 Dec. 1857	After attendance at the Royal Military Academy, Woolwich, commissioned into the Royal Engineers. Posted to Chatham and Shorncliffe.
Nov. 1861	Barbados. Married Marion, daughter of Deputy Commissioner-General George Darnley; they had eight sons and six daughters. All, save one of each, survived into adulthood.
October 1864	Western District in charge of defence of the Bristol Channel. Resided in Weston-super-Mare.
October 1867	Plymouth and employed on naval base defences.
1872	Malta and employed on defences.
January 1877	Secretary of RE Institute. Promoted to major in February 1878.
Sept. 1884	Promoted lieutenant-colonel and commanded Submarine Mining Battalion RE. Posted to War Office as Assistant Director of Works for Fortifications/Inspector General of Fortifications.
July 1889	Deputy Inspector General of Fortifications. Secretary of Defence Committee and member of Naval and Army Committee on Defence.
Nov.1894	Chief Engineer in Ireland. Modernised many barracks.
6 Jan. 1899	Placed on Retired List.
28 Jan. 1916	Died at Kew, Richmond. Buried Highgate Cemetery.

---

works across the Bristol Channel. Living in Weston-super-Mare with his wife, Marion, he carried out a detailed survey of the proposed sites. For a subaltern, this was a demanding role but not unusual in a corps in which technically competent young officers were given complex tasks.

Colonel John Savage RE, formerly a captain in the Lanarkshire Engineer Volunteers, commented in 1882 on Vetch's tact, professional ability, common sense and charming manner. He also referred to Vetch's even temper, which must have been tested to the limit as he negotiated contracts. By late October 1864 work had begun, at last, on the construction of Brean Down Fort.

The Construction of Brean Down Fort

Although the first contract was awarded to Mr John Pollard of the Prudential Insurance Company, 10 Cromwell Terrace, Totterdown, Bristol, several local self-employed contractors were also engaged, one of whom was the haulier Solomon Boley. Using a horse-drawn tipper-cart, he hauled stone from the Uphill and Bleadon quarries to the fort. He met and married Eliza and the couple moved into a cottage built near the fort, where his wife gave birth to a daughter, Alice. She is believed to have been the first baby born on Brean Down and was one of ten children born to the Boleys. Boley prospered and bought two more tipper-trucks, two more horses and employed two drivers. When his contract was complete, Boley bought the Ship Inn at Uphill where Alice sometimes served behind the bar. He then he acquired a large dairy farm near Bleadon.

Meanwhile Alice, after working with her father, was, first, cook for a family at Keynsham Rectory and was then employed at Portman Mansions, Marylebone, in London. On 6 February 1906 she married James Poole at the Marylebone Registry Office. A former Regular soldier, who had served in the Boer War, he worked as a porter in the Mansions and was about ten years younger than her. Alice's age is uncertain because her date of birth on the marriage certificate is unclear; a tiny tear covers the year! In 1907 Solomon Boley died, aged 66, and was buried in Bleadon churchyard. The following year, Alice gave birth to Solomon James.

When the First World War broke out, James Poole enlisted and was cheered off to war, his young son Solomon running alongside him. Four years later, health shattered by wounds, gas and the

Eliza Boley at Brean Down. Wife of Solomon, she gave birth to Alice in a cottage on Brean Down. (Mrs Betty Poole)

strains of the Western Front, James set up a small business in Bristol, but he died in the early 1920s and is buried in Arno's Vale cemetery in Bristol. Alice was left to raise young Solomon and died in April 1951 aged about 85.

The workers at the fort, which relied upon muscle-power, were a mix of local men and navvies, mostly Irish, fresh from building the canals and railways. Most were illiterate. The majority had families and since the rule was – 'No work, no pay' – they worked in all weathers. If the weather was so bad that construction was impossible, they still received no pay. Sometimes the men were transferred, with little warning, to the islands and had to leave their families behind in their simple stone huts. Judging by archaeological finds on the two holms, these seem to have varied in size from a small family home to a community centre and were probably whitewashed.

Inevitably the navvies were soon in trouble. The ganger William Rose severely injured another navvy, Edward Grant, by knocking him to the ground and jumping on him. The magistrates noted that Rose had sixteen similar charges against him at his last place of employment on the railways and he was fined.

On 15 September 1866 work stopped when the new contractor, the Weston-super-Mare entrepreneur John Perry, felt unable to carry out the "extraordinary views of the Government representative". It seems he was frustrated by the frequent changes in the plans and his employees had become thoroughly disillusioned with buildings being put up and then dismantled. However Vetch seems to have settled the matter and work continued.

The increasing number of labourers on the Brean Down fort project led to the Brean Down Mission being set up, with the owner of Brean Down Farm, Mr Thomas Stevens, as its Scripture Reader. As was the custom of the day, he seems to have been accepted by the navvies and no doubt was a welcome, kindly face compared to the tough foremen and managers. Since there was no school for the children, he would often read to them.

In 1870 the capture of Napoleon III at Mézières by a newly-united Germany under Count Bismarck seemed to signal the end of France's influence as a continental power but not as an international player. Nevertheless Victorian Britain's paranoia with France remained and continued to govern home defence strategy. By September 1870 the four

Bristol Channel forts were complete but not equipped with artillery. By now Vetch had moved to Plymouth.

The 1871 census shows no military personnel at Brean Down, just the Foreman of Works George Goodwin, who was a stone-mason by profession, asphalt-maker John Lumsden and a gang of labourers, so presumably the Military Road was being built and the finishing touches were being made to the fort. Also shown on the 1871 census is the 54-year old Frederick Harris. This whole group lived in the cottages built near the fort.

Frederick Harris was an expert boatman and for forty years lived on Steep Holm with his wife, Ann, and their children, using his yacht the *Mystery* to supply the island. Frederick was listed at Brean Down, where he lived for some seven years, because a lady visitor to Steep Holm in 1857 had been mauled by a bear kept by Harris and, in order to escape paying compensation, he went to extraordinary lengths to appear homeless and penniless, including "arranging his arrest" for debt by a friendly fisherman, "disposing" of his assets and declaring himself "late of Steep Holm". He successfully persuaded the judge at Taunton Assizes to declare him insolvent. By all accounts Harris was a loveable rogue who developed Steep Holm, ran the pub there, smuggled and, by 1872, was owner of the Claremont Royal Pier Hotel in Weston-super-Mare.

The following year, records show that Brean Down was garrisoned by 51 soldiers from the Coast Brigade with 20 horses, but it was not until July 1877 that 6 Battery, 8 Artillery Brigade arrived to mount the guns. The fort was then manned by a Royal Artillery District Establishment supported by three officers and 50 Volunteer gunners from the 1st Administrative Brigade, Gloucestershire Artillery Brigade with its headquarters in Bristol.

Arming the fort often necessitated transfers and one occasion, on 8 December 1872, Harris was taking an officer and eleven gunners from Flat Holm to Brean Down in the *Mystery* when the wind forced him to run for shelter near Penarth Head, where she went aground. When the tide rose, the *Mystery* was swept into the Bristol Channel and collided with the schooner *John Pearce*. Its mate, Richard Jones, managed to rescue all the soldiers except for two, who fell into the sea. These he also pulled out and for his actions was awarded the RNLI Silver Medal.

Alice Boley, daughter of Solomon Boley, who was born on Brean Down. (Mrs Betty Poole)

The Fort

Brean Down conformed to Jervois's classic design of a five-sided complex with a relatively concealed seaward side, and the landward side protected by a moat. The Master-Gunner's quarters, which doubled as the Officers' Mess, consisted of a kitchen, ablutions and several large rooms, two of which had fires. A basement was probably used as the fort store. It is

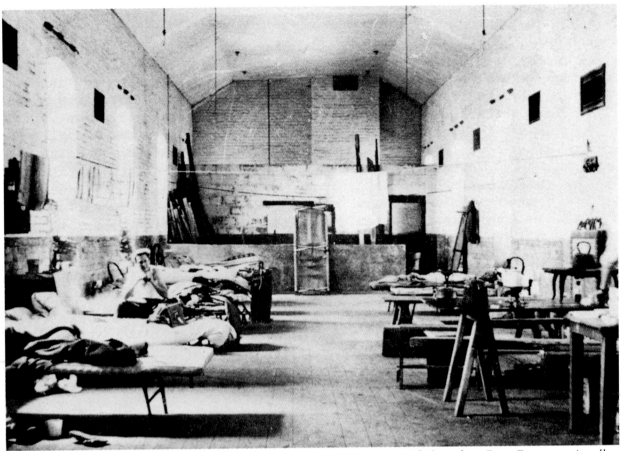

Interior view of the barracks at Steep Holm: a poor photograph but valuable for its rarity. The barracks at Brean Down were virtually identical except that the roof was much lower. (John Barrett)

of interest that in the 1881 and 1891 census, when the fort was occupied by the military, apart from a married Master-Gunner, an NCO also had a family with him and was probably accommodated in the same quarters as well.

The soldiers' barracks was built to accommodate 21 men and served as quarters and canteen, as was the custom of the day. Measuring 102ft by 24ft wide (31 x 7.3m), there were fireplaces at both ends. Three small rooms at the end of the building probably served as storerooms for such items as beds for the volunteer gunners. A small room nearest the gate was the guardhouse and others served as the pantry and kitchen. In this period, beds came in two basic types, a bed that folded into three, and doubled as an easy chair, and a standard folding bed. Each man was equipped with a straw mattress, woollen blankets and pillow. His uniform and equipment was stacked on a rack above his bed and his personal weapon kept in a rack near his bed. Also in the barracks would have been well-scrubbed

tables and benches on which to eat, write letters and otherwise relax, and a tin bath, although strip washing was the normal. For cooking there was a stove and sufficient pots, pans and ladles to prepare the food and take it to the tables to be served. A kettle was an important item, as was the coal scuttle.

Near No. 7 Gun Position were three lavatory cubicles. The seat was a wooden box with a lid. Some units may have had rudimentary flushing otherwise the waste dropped into a chemical compound and was eventually washed into the sea. Both blocks were built of local limestone and were flat-roofed to allow the blast of the guns to pass over without dislodging masonry and tiles. Presumably the windows were also fitted with wooden blinds.

When Staff Surgeon Rheilly, of the Army Medical Department, made a health and hygiene inspection, he found that "the barracks are built on the latest and most approved hygienic principles and afford cubic and superficial space". He found that visitors were welcome provided that permission was first sought from the Master-Gunner.

The landward side of Brean Down Fort was protected by a 12ft (3.66m) deep ditch, 33ft (10m) wide, and spanned by a timber drawbridge hauled up from inside the fort. A pair of inward-opening iron gates gave access, the right hand one being fitted with a pedestrian door for the sentry. Rifle slits in the walls covered the bridge and moat.

The Artillery

By the end of the 1870s, the Bristol Channel forts were armed with 7-inch (178mm) rifled muzzle-loaders giving excellent cross-fire, that made the approaches to Bristol and Cardiff almost impossible for enemy ships. No. 1 gun position covered Weston Bay and consisted of a single RML on a Type-C pivot in a semi-circular pit open to the rear. The pivot, a George III 24-pounder cannon muzzle facing skywards, is still jammed into the ground.

Aiming in the general direction of Flat Holm was

a battery of three RMLs, one on a Type-A Pivot firing over 4ft (1.2m) high concave-fronted parapets and two on Type-C Pivots. Still to be seen on No. 4 gun position is part of the rear race, retained by countersunk screws in the stone surround and an iron ring used for traversing. This battery is supported by a small underground magazine and fuse store.

Covering the channel to Steep Holm was another three-gun battery, two on Type-C pivots and one on a Type-A pivot, which was supported by No. 3 Magazine. This battery was destroyed in the 1900 explosion and the remains were built over during the Second World War. Part of Gun Position No. 5 remains, including a section of the parapet. Both these batteries were protected by deep earth bunds to absorb the impact of shells and to give some camouflage, cover and concealment.

Across the moat opposite the stables is a 3ft (0.9m) high concrete plinth, originally surrounded by a brick wall, which was most probably used as the mounting for the Depression Range Finder. According to Chris Webster's detailed architectural study, as late as 1891 Brean Down was equipped with a Mark 1a variant of the DRF.

Main gate about 1910, now advertising 'REFRESHMENTS – closed on Sundays'. Note the smaller sentries' gate. Above the window on the left is the inscription 'VR', meaning Victoria Regina. (Author's collection)

Gun position showing the George III cannon used as a pivot for the RMLs. (Somerset Archaeological and Natural History Society)

The Magazines

The main magazine is 15ft by 18ft and about 20ft high (4.57 x 5.48 x 6.1m). It is one of the largest in the Bristol Channel forts, and well protected with several feet of earth on the side facing the direction of enemy threat. A corridor leads into the magazine.

Every effort was made to prevent sparks. The floor was covered in wood and the space was well ventilated. Illumination was from oil lamps behind glass panels in the wall. A small changing area was used by soldiers working in the magazines to change into felt uniforms and shoes. Before entering they had to step over a 12-inch (300mm) board and brush off gravel and grit and anything else that could induce an explosion.

Near the bottom of the steps is a small room where the fuses were kept. This was designed to conform with recommendations made by the 1863 Royal Commission, examining the progress on the coast defences, that keeping fuses and ammunition together should be abandoned in favour of separated storage until they met at the gun for loading. This remained a basic principle of coastal gunnery until the disbandment of the Coast Regiment in 1965.

On the stairway to the magazine is the base support for the ammunition hoist.

A series of inspections of the Severn Defences began in 1881, so no doubt Master-Gunner Sergeant John Bond and his District Establishment spent much of their time ensuring that the artillery was in good working order, the magazines safe and the accommodation clean. The 40-year-old Master-Gunner had arrived – with his Canadian wife, Sarah, and their six children – from Steep Holm, where he had been since 1875. His establishment consisted of four gunners, one of whom, James Robinson, was accompanied by his Irish wife. For the professional soldiers of Queen Victoria's Army, families were important. They suffered the same rigours of overseas stations as their men – the long voyages, separation from family, facing the unknown in a foreign country, disease and the possibility of widowhood – but many were resilient and tough.

From a contemporary account, written by the new bride of a Master-Gunner on Flat Holm, life in the forts was pleasant and certainly different from the urban smog and grime in which many of the soldiers will have been brought up. As was expected, the women cooked and laundered although the soldiers were responsible for the cleanliness of their barracks. The children were probably educated at Brean School, possibly walking to the village or taken by the fort horse-and-cart, or possibly at Uphill. There was plenty of space for them to play and explore. With fresh air and guaranteed food, they were probably far healthier that than their contemporaries in South Wales.

In 1882 Lord Morley and his Defence of the Mercantile Ports Committee visited the Severn Defences and recommended that the seven RMLs at Brean Down should be replaced by three 10.4-inch (264mm) breech-loaders, to give an improved capability in hitting power and range, but the War Office Defence Committee agreed with the Inspector-General of Fortifications that there was no need to revise the existing armament.

The same year, garrison brigades of Coast Artillery were established and Brean Down and Steep Holm came under the operational and administrative command of HQ 7th Western District at Plymouth, while Flat Holm and Lavernock were placed under command of HQ 4th Welsh District at Pembroke Dock. HQ Bristol Channel Fortifications was commanded by a Royal Artillery officer, who also commanded the forts' District Establishments, which in accordance with War Department policy maintained them for 1st Gloucestershire Artillery Volunteer Corps on mobilisation and exercises. This officer lived locally, rather than in barracks.

Little is known about communications between the islands but it may be assumed that it would have been by light, flag and semaphore, weather permitting. The forts were probably equipped with $\frac{1}{2}$lb and 1lb (227/453g) emergency signal rockets, which produced a brilliant light. Certainly there was a telephone cable linking the four forts by 1897. In the absence of radios and telephones, co-ordinated fire control was generally not exercised; instead, each fort had arcs of fire and any ships encroaching into them were likely to be challenged.

In 1884 the Defence Committee approved strengthening Steep Holm and Flat Holm with larger guns, and on 23 August the Royal Artillery and Royal Engineer Works Committee visited Brean Down Fort. In Report No. 100 they recommended that the three 7-inch RMLs on C-pivots should be replaced with three 9-inch (229mm) RMLs, for long-range and direct fire, and that the remaining four 7-inch RML guns should be withdrawn. A

A poor-quality, but rare view of the soldiers' barracks c.1900.
(Somerset Archaeological and Natural History Society)

member of the committee was Robert Vetch, now a colonel and Assistant Inspector-General of Fortifications at the War Office. As a lieutenant, he had surveyed Brean Down in 1863.

A month later, the Inspector-General of Fortifications and the Director of Artillery referred the matter to the General Officer Commanding Western District, Major-General J.R.S. Sayer, who commented on 23 October:

> Although Breandown is overcrowded, I regret the reduction in the number of guns (which means reduction in the number of hits) unless the number is made good outside the present battery. The extraordinary strong tide and frequent fogs in the Severn render it particularly difficult to obtain hits and facilitates vessels running past the batteries.

On 1 December 1884, the Inspector-General of Fortifications and Director of Artillery proposed that the views of Western District could be met:

> Mount three 9-inch RML guns available for long range as well as direct fire and withdraw five 7-inch RMLs. The armament would then consist of three 9-inch and two 7-inch guns.

This plan was later revised to a proposal that all the RMLs should be replaced with 6-inch Quick Firing guns and machine guns but this was never enacted.

On 15 June 1889, Secretary of State for War Stanhope provisionally approved installing the 9-inch guns but the Ordnance Committee, in its Report No. 820, ordered that no more mounts for coastal artillery long-range fire were to be manufactured and since the recommended guns all needed new mounts, the existing ones being unsuitable, none of the proposals was implemented. This effectively ended any proposals to upgrade the defences of the Bristol Channel.

Postcard of the inside of the fort, showing the parade ground and tracker for the RML guns. (Author's collection)

Meanwhile, debates on national defence were reaching crisis point. British forces were then engaged in Afghanistan, in an effort to contain Russian expansion into India. Russia was an ally of France. Her nearest fleets to Great Britain were in the Baltic Sea and Murmansk, and she was involved in a naval building programme. Hostilities could mean a struggle against a powerful combined fleet with Russian attacks on the East Coast and French incursions in the South Coast. Chancellor Bismarck's expansionist aims for Germany were largely ignored, in spite of his massive naval building programme. In March 1889 Stanhope's Naval Defence Act set aside funds for improving the fixed defences and launching more ships. At last the Royal Navy could contribute effectively to the protection of the country but, as we shall see, there was confusion about the blockade. This strategy exploited the fact that onshore winds often kept the French in port. Fast frigates and smaller vessels monitored them, and dealt with any minor breakouts. On the horizon small line-of-battle ships were ready to support the frigates, and watched for blockade-runners. The main fleet swung at anchor in Spithead and the Nore, ready for action.

The defence strategy was also overhauled, which had a direct bearing on Palmerston's forts and the future of the Volunteer Forces. Stanhope believed that if the fortifications were modernised and properly manned, they could guard naval bases from attack by torpedo boats or amphibious raids. He also went on to say, "There are certain strategical positions round London, commanding roads and railways, which are essential to its defence". From this emerged the Lines of London, a defensive arc from East Anglia to the Home Counties.

A furious philosophical battle then developed between the Admiralty and War Office over the Army's assessment that, if the French could command the Channel for three weeks, an army of 150,000 could be shipped to England. The Admiralty scorned the idea that transports could be assembled without detection, and indeed it was unlikely the Channel Fleet would be off-station during periods of tension. So far as the naval strategists were concerned, with their bases protected by forts, there was no reason to change from the blockade strategy but that it should be adapted for steam-driven ships. Thus, if the French fleet broke out, it was to be brought to a decisive action while the Channel Fleet would intercept the amphibious forces as they neared any of the south-coast beaches.

This unimaginative and orthodox strategy was

soon discredited by the unreasonable behaviour of the French, not playing to the rules laid down by the Victorian naval strategists. Using steam-driven ships, they opted for the 'Hunting War', in which fleet actions were to be avoided and cruisers were to hunt down and sink British shipping anywhere in the world while torpedo-boats would raid Channel ports and anchorages. As one French strategist put it:

> Tomorrow, War breaks out. A torpedo-boat has sighted one of those ocean steamers ... will follow at a distance, keeping out of sight and, when night comes ... will send to the bottom cargo, crew and passengers not only without remorse, but proud of the achievement. Others may protest, for ourselves we accept, in these methods of destruction, the development of that law of progress in which we have such a firm faith.

Britannia was appalled by this outrageous revolution in naval warfare and was in great danger of losing its ruling the waves to the French. The policy adopted now demanded that the entire French fleet be blockaded. An exercise held in the Irish Sea to test the strategy was a disaster when the Royal Navy failed to prevent the enemy 'Achill Fleet', sailing from simulated French ports in Ireland, breaching the blockade in the Irish Sea (English Channel), 'shelling' West Coast towns (the South Coast) and generally causing havoc to merchant shipping throughout the area.

The exercise also showed the Royal Navy was in a sorry state. The annual estimates for the construction of ships had hardly changed since the 1840s and a committee examining its role in national defence concluded "the danger of invasion would be better met by increased naval expenditure than by costly shore defences". A programme to build iron ships got under way with great urgency and the fixed defences were revised to cope with torpedo boats rather than an invasion supported by a great fleet. Lower-sited batteries were built, booms constructed and thought was given to close-quarter night defence.

However, the influential 'Blue Water School' revived the blockade in a new guise, that of 'Command of the Sea' and a strategy in which invasion would never be attempted until an enemy had secured local control of the seas. Money spent, therefore on "Earth, Stone, Iron, Walls and a large army for Home Defence, was money wasted". A reasonable watch over enemy ports and a pre-emptive

destruction of naval forces would therefore preclude the necessity for fixed defences, other than to protect naval bases and commercial ports from bombarding cruisers. The Army agreed that the first line of defence lay with the Royal Navy but the issue was the second line of defence.

The Commander-in-Chief, Lord Wolseley, declared that a 100,000-strong army could capture London unless hampered by proper defences. He added:

> I know of nothing more liable to disaster and danger than anything that floats on water. We often find in peace and in the calmest weather, our best ironclads running into one another. We find great storms dispersing and almost destroying some of the finest fleets that ever sailed. Therefore it is essentially necessary for this country to defend our own shores.

He was referring to the extraordinary (and unexplained) collision between the ironclads HMS *Victoria* and HMS *Camperdown* in the Mediterranean in June 1893, which led to a heavy loss of life. The admirals resented the implications:

> Such a contingency as the landing of an enemy on these shores without interference on the part of our Navy is one which ... could not arise ... under these circumstances their Lordships do not consider it possible to make any calculations relating to the practicability of a scheme or undertaking when all the obstacles natural to its success are summarily removed.

The debate continued into the next century but culminated in Britain defending itself by fighting in Europe, as the country had always endeavoured to do.

Meanwhile, the needs of Brean Down, now a virtual backwater, continued. In 1891 Master-Gunner Sergeant William Stretton, accompanied by his wife and child, was in command with a bombardier and three gunners, one of whom was also with his wife. Rowland Perry in the 17-ton single-masted *Osprey* supplied the fort from Kingsholme Pier with all its needs, including ammunition, coal and the mail, which was carried in an official red box. Later the fisherman, John Watts, and his family took general supplies in handcarts along Military Road. Watts Boats still run trips today from Knightstone Pier at Weston-super-Mare.

On 8 July 1893, Major A. Heathcote RE, at the Western Command RE Divisional offices in Cardiff, wrote to Mr Benjamin Love, Springfield, Crewkerne, agent for the Wyndhams:

Sir,

For some time past the question of water supply to the Breandown Garrison on mobilisation has been before the War Dept. This proposal is to lay on water at the Point 7 on plan, some 300 yards *(275m)* west of Fiddlers Point. The water company will give permission to lay pipes from their mains at Uphill.

I have therefore now to ask whether you will give permission to lay the necessary 2-inch *(50mm)* from A to F along the dotted red line. It must be laid round the corner of the cliff to avoid rising too high for the head of water. I should be also be greatly obliged if you would let me know as early as possible what would be approximately the rent you would charge for this.

I only require now to know this approximately as the detailed calculation has not yet been called for. If therefore you could let me know this at once I should be greatly obliged.

In reply kindly address

The Divisional Officer,
RE Engineers
RE Office
Cardiff

Mr Love wrote a letter to Mr Edward Champion, who was farming Brean Down Farm, posing several questions:

To Mr Champion, the Tenant of Brean Down Farm, Property of W. Wyndham Esquire.

The War Department Propose Conveying Water from Uphill (Through Mr Wyndham's Property) To the Brean Down Fortifications.
Question: Can there be any objection to Mr Wyndham giving his permission?
Answer: I see no objection.
Question: The Engineer says "The Property will not be disturbed in any way beyond cutting a drain to receive the pipes about 2 feet *(0.6m)* in depth, but it may be found necessary to chip the rocks in a few places in order that the pipes may be made secure". What is your opinion?
Answer: If work carried as suggested, Property will not be disturbed but doubtless drain would be protected on wharf whilst the work in being done.
Question: Would it be any benefit to you, to get a share of the water supply, if it can be arranged?

Answer: It certainly would.
Question: Have you now a good supply from your well?
Answer: A scanty supply.
Question: Is the water good?
Answer: Very good.
Question: Have you a good supply for the cattle?
Answer: No
Question: Will there be any damage done to the Sheep shed in the Wharf in executing the Work?
Answer: Some.
Question: If so, how much should be claimed?

Love replied to Major Heathcote on 19 July and raised two issues:

Dear Sir

The Proposed Water Supply from Uphill to Brean Down Fortifications

The approximate rent will be Five Pounds per annum for conveying water through the Wyndhams Property at Brean from Uphill. If the tenant of Brean Down Farm can have a share of the water for his cattle (or Farm House) then the rent would be two shillings and sixpence per annum. A small compensation to be paid to the tenant for damage done to his sheep feed, on the lands, in executing the work, about One Pound.

The Proposed Brean Down Harbour and Railway

You are no doubt aware that a bill is before Parliament for carrying out the above. I enclose a sketch of the proposed railway for you to ascertain if it will in any way prejudice your water scheme. Please return the enclosed sketch, as it is the only one I have.

I remain etc.
Benjamin Love.

In the event the request by Champion to share the water supply was refused on the grounds that the cost of the work was to be borne by the War Office. On 3 October 1894, Major Heathcote again wrote to Benjamin Love, this time on a proposal to erect a rangefinding station to the rear of the Fort:

RE Office, Cardiff
3.10.94

B. Love Esquire.

Sir,

It is proposed to erect a Rangefinding Station in rear of the fort at Breandown. The attached plan shows the proposed site approximately.

I am to request that you will inform me whether you will be willing to grant permission for the erection of this structure and on what terms. It is a small semicircular parapet enclosing a space 6ft *(1.8m)* in diameter in which the instrument is placed. The exact position has not been determined as it depends on the height.

Perhaps you could say what your terms would be. A similar space under any circumstances would be required is about 24ft *(7.3m)* square. So will you kindly let me know whether you would be willing to let or sell the site and at what annual rental or price.

I must add that the site is not decided on and it may be decided that some site within the WD Boundary, coloured black, will be approved but it is considered by the OC *(Officer Commanding)* Royal Artillery that this is rather low considering that higher ground exists in rear.

I am Sir,
Yours Faithfully.
A. Heathcote
Maj. RE

B. Love Esquire
Springfield
West Crewkerne

The attached plan showed a 24ft square piece of ground enclosing a semi-circular pit, located roughly where the split-level Second World War Fire Command bunker is.

Upon the formation of the Royal Garrison Artillery in June 1899, the local militia and volunteer artillery units were amalgamated to form 1st Administrative Brigade, Gloucestershire Royal Garrison Artillery. By 1900, Brean Down Fort was occupied by a District Establishment commanded by a Master-Gunner, Sergeant James Withers, and several Royal Garrison Artillery gunners. In June 1900, men from Steep Holm and Flat Holm on an intensive gunnery course, using the now virtually obsolete 7-inch RMLs, augmented the garrison. Among those on the training course was Gunner William Haines from Bridgwater.

The Explosion

During the early evening of Tuesday 3 July 1900, Gunners George Johnson and William Haines walked to Burnham-on-Sea to collect two bicycles which they had left at the Commercial Hotel. At about 8.40pm, after three beers in the bar, they began to cycle back to Brean but Haines's bicycle

developed a puncture and they walked to the Wellington Arms where, over a glass of beer, they agreed that Johnson should continue to the fort to let the Master-Gunner know that Haines would arrive after lock-up, which was at 10pm Johnson arrived at the fort at 10.40pm and was followed by Haines at about midnight. Bombardier John Shillabeer asked him what time it was – about 11.45pm, was the answer. Shillabeer later said that Haines seemed sober.

At 5am the following morning Mr Harry Lewis, a road-sweeper employed by Weston-super-Mare Urban District Council, was cleaning Beach Road when he heard an explosion from the fort and then saw a black column of smoke rising into the dawn sky. Believing it to be an early morning gun practice, he was not unduly alarmed and continued sweeping. Edward Champion of Brean Down Farm also heard the explosion and sent his son Maurice to raise the alarm at Berrow Post Office.

At the fort, the explosion had ripped through the fort, destroying most of the Soldiers' Barracks. In the south-west corner, part of the 30ft (9m) moat wall had collapsed and two RML positions lay wrecked amid the debris. No. 3 Cartridge Store had collapsed, and zinc powder cases and twisted wreckage lay everywhere. Gunner Reed, a burly Irishman who had been sleeping in the barracks, lay moaning on the ground with blood seeping from two severed arteries in his left arm. From Steep Holm, Reed was also at the fort for training.

Sergeant-Major Withers started to organise the fort and when he called the roll, four soldiers were initially recorded missing until a further search found all except Haines. Withers tried to telephone Captain William Beardsley, the District Officer HQ Bristol Channel Fortifications at Bleadon, but the explosion had wrecked the line so he detailed a soldier to cycle the eight miles to Brean and then to report the incident.

By 8am Surgeon-Colonel Phelps, the senior Royal Army Medical Corps medical officer in the area, had been informed of the explosion, at his house, Beach House, in Knightstone Road. He hurried to the fort, and stabilised Reed before having him evacuated by rowing boat to Knightstone and then moved to Weston-super-Mare hospital.

A search of the wreckage then uncovered a naked body without its head, legs and left arm but a signet ring on the right hand identified the remains as those of Haines. Gunner William Keboe then reported that his Martini-Henry rifle

Pre-First World War postcard showing damage to the wall from the 1900 explosion. (Author's collection)

was missing from the arms rack at the head of his bed. During a search, Gunner Frederick Gibbs found the twisted barrel some six feet from Haines's body inside the wrecked magazine. Two police officers, Police Sergeant Kellaway and Police Constable Doble, then turned up and arranged for the remains of the body to be taken to the hospital mortuary.

The following morning Weston-super-Mare was abuzz with the rumour and reporters made every effort to find out what had happened, some venturing to the high ground overlooking the fort, while others were prevented from entering by the garrison. Visited in hospital by a *Weston Mercury* representative, Reed graphically described what had happened. He was sleeping soundly when he became aware of

> a terrible rumbling report, accompanied by a shock, and at the same time the room was filled with flying glass from the window and general rubbish. I was sleeping next to the window and felt something sting my arm. For a few seconds we were so dazed

with the shock that we could not form the slightest idea as to what had happened, and on opening the door everything was in confusion – a great cloud of heavy smoke and dust hung over us, and in all directions there was such disorder as I can't describe, rocks, girders lying on every hand. I had hardly got two steps beyond the door when I felt something warm and wet running down me, and then I found that a big stream of blood was pouring from my arm – in fact I was so badly hurt that I could not go further, and in a short time some of my comrades rendered First Aid and did their best to stop the flow of blood.

Later in the day, Captain Beardsley visited the fort but refused to give the reporters any information. An Army inquiry ordered by Lieutenant-General Sir William Butler KCB, GOC Western District, was assembled at No. 3 Cartridge Store by Major A.W.R. Gordon RFA, but its findings are not known and were not presented to the Coroner's inquiry.

Several days later, the inquest into the death of Haines was held at the Wellington Hotel (now the

Berrow Inn) before the Coroner, Dr Craddock, and a jury of twelve men. Before the proceedings began there was a debate about visiting the fort when a juryman, Mr J.A. Dare, felt so strongly about the need that he departed without his colleagues. Dr Craddock then suggested a visit would be worthwhile and everybody trooped out of the hotel and began to walk to Brean Down. After about two miles, they met a military vehicle with Mr Dare and a Royal Garrison Artillery officer, who explained that since a governmental Committee of Investigation had been ordered by General Butler, there was no need for a visit. This was eventfully agreed and the Coroner's inquiry jury returned to the Wellington Hotel.

The first witness, Sergeant-Major Withers, first outlined how Haines had arrived at Brean Down Fort from Steep Holm the previous week for training and then described how Haines's body had been found in the centre of the cartridge room floor with Keboe's carbine nearby. He said access to No. 3 Magazine was controlled and was approached by two sets of stairs. For ventilation in hot weather, the store was left open from 9am until 2pm Gunner Unsted had locked the door and returned the keys to Withers. The cross-examination continued:

"Was the body found inside?" from a juror.
"The body was found in the pit caused by explosion, just where the floor of the magazine would have been", replied Withers.
"Was the rifle inside?"
"It was found two or three yards from the body."
"Were the duplicate keys intact?"
"Yes", replied Withers.
"Then how did he get in?"
"I can't say."
"Would it be possible to shoot from the outside into the store and explode the contents?"
"It would if it struck any of the cartridges."
"Was the door opposite any of the ventilators?"
"No."
"Could he fire through any of the ventilators?"
"I cannot say – there is one at the top and one or two at the side."
The Coroner intervened: "Of course, if he fired from the outside, he could not get inside after the explosion?"
"If the man had got inside, in my opinion his remains would have never been found after the explosion", replied Withers.
"Where were the keys?"
"Over a fireplace in the barracks."
"Could anyone reach them?"

"Yes, if they got through the window."
"Was there a sentry on duty?"
"No", said Withers concluding his evidence.

Other witnesses called before the court included Johnson, Shillabeer and Keboe. Master-Gunner Sergeant Jonathan Brett, who was on temporary detachment to Brean Down for the training, could not offer further evidence about the incident but did confirm the magazine had held three tons of powder. Later Withers was recalled and testified that 100 rounds of ball ammunition were always kept in the book box. This was a secure container in which classified documents and other important items were kept. He had checked the box and all rounds were still accountable. At the request of the jury, he forced open the breech of the wrecked rifle and inside found a cartridge case. Sergeant-Major Withers confirmed it would be possible for someone to fire down into the magazine but since none of the zinc cylinders containing the powder was underneath the shaft, the bullet would have had to ricochet. He also described how Haines had left all his clothes neatly piled at the head of his bed.

Summing up, the Coroner concluded there could be no doubt that Haines had been killed by the explosion and he asked the jury to decide how the explosion occurred. He continued that, although Haines had drunk three beers at Burnham-on-Sea, he had also taken four hours to reach the fort and therefore there was the probability he might have had some more elsewhere. It was known that he stopped at the cottage of the Miller family near Squire's Gate, at the bottom of the Down, for a short time. They also must take into account the possibility that, since Haines was a violent-tempered man, he might have become "excited and deranged through knowing that he would be put under arrest for being late at the fort". There was no doubt that when he left his bed he was deranged, suggested Dr Craddock.

The jury was also asked to consider how the magazine exploded. If they came to the conclusion that Haines had nothing to do with it, they must record an open verdict. If the deceased detonated it, it must remain a mystery. The jury returned with the verdict that Haines had been:

Killed by No. 3 magazine on Brean Down exploding, with the explosion caused by the deceased firing a carbine loaded with ball cartridge down the shaft of the ventilator to the magazine whilst in a state of temporary insanity.

Photograph taken between 1900 and 1914, showing the damage to the wall from the 1900 explosion.
(Author's collection)

Nevertheless the entire incident remains shrouded in mystery. If Haines was responsible, why did he fire a shot into the magazine? Why did he leave his clothes piled at the end of the bed? Where did he acquire a bullet? (The day before his death was possibly a range day). How were his remains found to be in the wreckage of the magazine? To fire down its ventilation shaft, Haines would have had to stand on top of the magazine. It seems likely his body was blasted upwards and dismembered by the explosion and must have fallen into the gaping hole left by the explosion. Almost certainly the force of the explosion dismembered his body. It is likely that he died immediately.

Little is known about Haines because, since he died during military service, his records were probably destroyed. He had served in the Army for thirteen years and his wife lived at 236 Bristol Road, Bridgwater, but no evidence was presented in court to suggest any domestic trouble.

Known for his quick temper, he nevertheless was not drunk that night; indeed the walk from the Wellington Hotel, up the hill onto Brean Down, and on to the fort would probably have sobered him. There is no evidence that any action was going to be taken against him for being late. However, it had been noted that he was unusually quiet and morose a few days before he died, but the reason is not known.

The explosion effectively caused Brean Down Fort to become non-operational and by June the following year the guns were dismounted, loaded onto trailers and towed by traction-engine to Burnham-on-Sea railway station to be returned to Woolwich Arsenal. By 1903 the Severn Defences had been dismantled. Among those who served at Steep Holm and Brean Down was Corporal Joseph Walford, whose son would serve in the forts forty years later. By October 1909 the leases on all the forts were handed back to their original owners.

SEVEN

Brean Down in Peacetime

Brean Fort with a 'Malaya' class battleship passing by in the background, probably about 1930. Note the building in the moat. It is thought this was the generator house for the café. (Author's collection)

After the guns had been removed and equipment dismantled, following the 1900 explosion, the War Office vacated Brean Down Fort. It was handed over to the Wyndham Trust and remained unoccupied until 1910 when, for the first time, it was converted into a café, and then became known as the Old Fort Picnic Refreshment Room. The proprietor was a Mr R. Waterman from Brean. An advertisement in the *Weston Gazette* recommended visitors to come by taking a sailing or rowing ferry or motorboat from the small, sheltered inlet at Anchor Head, between Knightstone and Birnbeck, on the northern side of Weston-super-Mare.

Meanwhile, although the Bristol Channel forts had been dismantled, there was still some, more limited, provision for coastal defence. When the Territorial Army was formed in 1908, 1st Gloucestershire RGA was absorbed into 1st South Midland Royal Field Artillery, and responsibility for the south-west coastal defences was handed over to Royal Naval Volunteer Reserve. The battery at Portishead was taken over by one of the three Bristol companies and remained intact until the position was dismantled in early 1914. There is no evidence to suggest that any of the Bristol Channel forts was taken over by the military authorities during the First World War except for Steep

Lady on swing, c.1900. In the background are the soldiers' barracks. (Somerset Archaeological and Natural History Society)

Holm, which became an Admiralty signalling station.

On the outbreak of war on 4 August 1914, responsibility for the defence of the West Country remained with Southern Command. To defend Avonmouth docks, No. 2 Heavy Battery (Devon) RGA manned two 4.7-inch (120mm) guns on the lawn of the Royal Hotel in Portishead and camped there until barracks were built in a wood above the hotel. No. 1 Company 6th Devonshire Regiment RGA manned two 12-pounders, and then a 4.7-inch at Avonmouth. Since the barracks at Battery Point were too far from the guns, a large house called 'Eastwood' was used to accommodate the soldiers.

The South Wales coast was included in the North-Western Coast Defences sector, which stretched as far as Liverpool and Barrow-in-Furness. At Milford Haven, 591 (Pembrokeshire) Regiment RGA (TF) manned four 9.2-inch (234mm), six 6-inch (152mm) and eight 12-pounders while 531 (Glamorgan) Regiment RGA (TF) manned four 6-inch at Cardiff and two 6-inch and two 4.7-inch QFs at Barry Dock.

The Café between the Wars

In the early 1920s the fort was leased from the Wyndham family by Mr Joseph Chamberlain, who owned the Weston-super-Mare coal-merchants, W.H. Hillman Ltd. Renovating the Master-Gunner's accommodation to make at least six bedrooms and converting the soldiers' block into a café, in 1925 Chamberlain engaged the fifty-year-old Alfred Meredith and his wife to manage the café and gave them the Master-Gunner's block in which to live. A daughter, Gwen, used to visit during the holidays. Mr Meredith, who was from the Isle of Wight, was a trustee of the new Wesleyan Chapel on Church Street, Brean and one of the committee who voted to keep Brean a 'dry' village (with no public house). He grew vegetables in a garden where the Second World War-vintage hardstanding now is.

In a letter post-1945 supporting a proposal to convert the fort again to a café, a Mr H.E. Hodder of Clifton Road, Weston-super-Mare, in a letter to the *Weston Mercury*, recalled that as an apprentice plumber he was sent by his employers, Messrs H.C.

Sometime before the First World War, three ladies pose on top of a building, probably the soldiers' barracks. Note the chimney behind them. (North Somerset Museum)

Sleep & Son, to the fort to extend the water supply in galvanised pipes to the toilets by pumping water from a well inside the fort. Evidently Hodder needed to bring back some heavy equipment and pipes and asked Meredith if he could use his donkey and cart. Meredith agreed provided Hodder did not beat the animal. However the donkey would frequently stop to nibble at the lush grass, and Hodder and his colleagues would have to pull the wheels of the cart to get it going again.

To help them, the Merediths hired the twenty-two-year-old Irene Sampson and paid her ten shillings a week plus tips. She and her family had recently moved from Dartmoor to a cottage next door to the Methodist church in Brean. Her father, Arthur, first found employment with Mr Roland Frost, who was farming Brean Down Farm after its previous occupant, Mr Hawking, had been killed in 1918 by a bull. Frost was a keen gardener and created a beautiful walled garden below the down where he grew asparagus. In 1929 Arthur Sampson went to work for the Hicks family, who had owned Southfield Farm for several decades (and still do), where he remained until he retired. In 1950 the farm was taken over by Mr Vowles. The walled garden has since fallen into disrepair. Roland Frost's youngest daughter, Ruth, eventually became a nanny to the Conservative MP and former Paymaster-General, David Heathcoat-Amory.

Irene Sampson cycled to work every day, collecting – at the bottom of Brean Down – two cans of milk from a cowman at Dibble's Farm, which in

1995 was known as Tucker's Farm. She would also collect the mail for the Merediths and for a former Indian Army captain, Harry Cox, who, for 40 years until he died in 1949, was the warden on behalf of the Wyndham family. A stocky man, he lived in a tin shack, which came to be known as 'Old House', near a small copse south of Fiddlers Point. Miss Sampson would then push her heavily-laden bicycle up the hill, which was lined with railway sleepers, along Military Road and then cycle to the fort. She recalls wild strawberries grew along the sides of the road. Going down was easier and Irene let her bicycle freewheel from the top all the way to Brean Cottages (where the Bird Garden and its café now are). Squire's Gate, at the foot of the down on Military Road, was erected after the First World War. There is now a small stile there.

Cox was also warden for Steep Holm and would often take Irene and other youngsters across in a Watts Co. motorboat, which was in such a state that a treacle tin was used to bail it. Later the Wyndhams built him a stone house near the hill fort, known locally as 'New House'. Cox did not own a bicycle and usually walked everywhere including on his weekly Saturday shopping trips to Weston-super-Mare, when he used the Uphill ferry and then took a bus. The journey took about thirty minutes. If he went into Burnham-on-Sea, he would catch a Hardings Bus Co. coach, which used to go the base of Brean Down twice a day during the summer season.

A keen naturalist, Cox insisted that all dogs be on a leash while on the down. A mine of knowledge about Brean Down, he was a great favourite with the children of Brean and would lend them his binoculars to view the badger sett in some rocks. He was also a knowledgeable ornithologist and looked after a pair of ravens that nested every year in rocks in South Bottom. According to Donald House, who lived for four years with his uncle Roland Frost at Brean Down Farm, these birds were merciless and would often attack sheep that had fallen on their backs and could not get up, first pecking at their eyes and then feeding on their exposed stomachs. He once saw a ewe, which had survived being blinded in an attack, being looked after by her two lambs, who would gently nudge their mother to grass, water and shelter. Two peregrine falcons also regularly nested in the quarry near the ferry landing point opposite Uphill.

Miss Sampson recalls that Cox was reliant for drinking water upon rain collecting in a barrel from his gutters. On one occasion, after a long dry spell, she found him filling his kettle from the algae-covered water and said, "You can't drink that". To which he replied, "That won't kill me. Anyway I am going to boil it."

Two children play on a makeshift seesaw from a carpenter's trestle and a plank, also c.1910. (North Somerset Museum)

Harry Cox the Brean Down warden. Here he is pictured in about 1943 as a member of the Coastwatch Service, overlooking Berrow Sands with anti-aircraft and anti-landing craft obstacles. (Mac Hawkins collection)

By the mid-1930s, some of the many foxes that used to live on the down began to raid the thousands of chickens that used to range at will in large coops on the farms around Brean. About twice a year Stuart Hicks, whose family farmed at Southfield Farm, arranged shoots on Brean Down to control their spread. Harry Cox had no objection to this provided the shooters, usually armed with a 12-bore shotgun, did not disturb the badger sett. Generally the older farmers would wait on the high ground for the foxes to break while the younger and fitter ones scrambled through the bracken with their dogs. Later Stuart became a founder member of the Highbridge Young Farmers' Club and a Brean Parish Councillor for many years. In 1988 he attended a garden tea party at Buckingham Palace. Most of the foxes have since migrated to the farmland.

The café was open only during the summer months and a favourite place to visit. In March one of Hillman's lorries would bring a consignment of non-perishable food, fuel and other items needed by the Merediths, but otherwise the family relied upon Miss Sampson's daily deliveries, including paraffin for lighting and heating, deposited at the Brean Down cottages by traders. Thorn's Bakery of Berrow, for instance, delivered bread while Joseph Churchill delivered groceries in his horse and wagon. Otherwise it meant either a shopping trip to Weston-super-Mare by taking the ferry to Uphill or Mr Meredith cycling to the shops in Brean. According to Miss Sampson, the postman, Mr Washer, collected post from the Burnham-on-Sea General Post Office and delivered three times a week to the fort. He always hoped there would be no letters because it was a stiff climb and a long cycle to the fort. Every day Meredith pumped water, using a generator, from a well inside the fort. It was then boiled in Valor oil stoves behind the counter. Spring water was also collected from a rock near the vegetable garden. Oil-fired lamps were used for lighting throughout the fort.

On a summer's day 200 people could be expected to use the ferry and, on a Bank Holiday, at least 700

A family is enjoying a picnic on Brean Down, Good Friday 1933. (David Lock)

Foxhunting on Brean Down. Left to right are Stuart Hicks, Phillip Frost, Frank Champion, John Perret and Philip Champion.
(Stuart Hicks)

About 1925, Mr Bert Gillings and a Sunday school outing on the parade ground. In the background is the entrance to the café. (Stuart Hicks)

could be guaranteed. Meredith charged visitors one penny to enter the fort and employed boys to collect the money. At the end of the week, he usually had a heavy bag of money, which then had to be taken to the bank. Campbell Co. and Watts Co. boats ferried visitors in sailing cutters or rowing boats from Knightstone harbour or Anchor Head, in Weston, to the sheltered stony beach below the single 7-inch RML position. Still evident there are the steps cut into the rocks. An advertisement for the café suggests that another way was to take a bus to Uphill and then cross by the Uphill ferry. Coach parties from Bristol usually made a booking. The Bristol Channel is renowned for sudden changes in the weather and Miss Sampson recalls passengers from one of Campbell's boats being stranded by a storm and staying overnight in the café.

The café could seat 100 people on benches at five long trestle tables, which were covered in spotless white tablecloths boiled and cleaned in a copper tub heated by a fire in the washroom. Tea and food was served using gold-rimmed white cups, saucers and plates. There was no menu and nothing was cooked. A pot of 'Carwardine's of Bristol' tea and bread-and-butter cost one shilling. With cake, tea cost one shilling and three pence and with jam one and six-pence. Cups of tea taken onto the lawn, which is

now the stony parade ground, cost fourpence per cup. As Irene Sampson recalled, the tea was tested in Bristol and "Everyone said it was a beautiful cup of tea". Lemonade was sold by the glass. Cigarettes and chocolate sweets were also sold over the counter. At the end of the café were cloakrooms.

Three years after starting with the Merediths, Irene Sampson left. She trained as a children's nurse and for the next forty-seven years was employed by the Holt family, who lived at The Croft, Brent Knoll and were proprietors of Holts Bros., the brewery in Burnham-on-Sea (on the road to Highbridge).

Donald House was born one of six children at Chestnut House, in the village of Mark. Educated at Sexey's School, Blackford, for nine years from 1918, in termtime he cycled the seven miles to and from the school, invariably with the Fears, but they were always late. Leaving school he then found employment with Roland Frost at Brean Down Farm. In 1936 the Merediths closed down the café and contracted with Mr Frost to remove the furniture. Donald House made several trips with his carthorse mare 'Madam', removing furniture from the Master-Gunner's quarters and the café to a shed at the farm. It was gradually sold off, although his Aunt Phyllis kept a chair. House eventually owned Woolston Farm, near Stogursey, which he sold in 1962 and then moved to a large sea-front house in Burnham-on-Sea. During the war he was a special constable and in the latter stages had a German and an Italian prisoner-of-war allocated to him, to help run the farm.

During the late winter, while the wind was still blowing from the north, Brean residents were allowed to pick potatoes which grew on the damp southern flanks of Brean Down, and carry a sackful home. One of the residents of Brean Down cottages at this time was a Mr Widrick, a fishmonger from Weston-super-Mare, who used to exercise his greyhounds on the upper slopes.

The Uphill Ferry

Many of those who visited the café used the Uphill Ferry. Its origins are lost in time but the Romans and local Britons must have established a crossing point to the island of Brean to take materials and worshippers to the Romano-British temple. According to Major Heneage Wheeler, the river crossing can be walked when the tide is at its lowest, and air photography suggests evidence of a causeway. While the banks of the Axe are muddy, in midstream the riverbed is stony and relatively firm. The first mention of the ferry is in Collinson's *History of Somerset*, the chapter on Brean manor stating that in 1637 "Thomas Bond had already conveyed to Henry, Lord Danvers and others a newly built house, part of the manor ... also the down or warren called Brean Down and the passage or ferry belonging to the said manor".

There is no further reference to the ferry until the nineteenth century and it is probable that later crossings of the River Axe took place upstream at Hobb's Boat ferry, Lympsham, which was owned by the Andrews family of Axbridge for a time. In 1808 a bridge was built over the Axe near Lympsham but, as part of land reclamation, floodgates were installed and the river diverted. The owners of the ferry, Pophams and Petheram, two well-known local names, claimed compensation from the Commissioners of Sewage for the enforced closure of Hobb's Ferry. In the same year Weston-super-Mare built its first hotel and since Brean Down soon became a place to visit, the need for the Uphill ferry re-emerged. Interestingly, there is no mention of the ferry in connection with the fort, presumably

The Uphill ferry in about 1910, with Brean Down in the background. (North Somerset Museum)

A Flatlander on the beach at Anchor Head, about 1910. Such boats frequently took visitors to the fort. (North Somerset Museum)

because most of the supplies came from the south, along the road past Brean.

At the turn of the century the ferry was bought by William Pople but its infrequent use is reflected in Dutton's *Brean Down*, in which the author writes that the ferryman is on the river from 9.30am to 5pm, March to October, but so few people used it that a booking had to be made with Mr A.E. Pople (William's younger brother), at 4 Church Road, Uphill. The ferryman held a Board of Trade monopoly and had built safe landing places for use at low tides. A regular user was a local preacher who took services in Brean. In 1926 William's widow sold the ferry rights, ancillary equipment and property to Leonard Smart of Uphill for £30. 'Cap'n' Smart, as he became known, was granted crown lease on 11 March 1927. He used a 15ft rowing boat named *Mary*, after his wife.

'Cap'n' Smart was a seadog, who had spent most of his adult life either at sea, some of it before the mast, or on dusty ranches in Australia and New Zealand. He was blessed with a volume of stories, many of which were disbelieved by the astonished listeners, but were probably true. When he gave up foreign wanderings, he bought a

ketch, the *Jane*, which had been built in 1800 and was the oldest merchant vessel afloat, and led a relatively sheltered life transporting material for the Menai railway bridge and carrying goods on the Mersey.

Clearly a local character, 'Cap'n' Smart always wore a navy blue seaman's jersey, naval officer's cap and heavy gold earrings. He soon clashed with local fishermen, who regularly used his landing stages, which he used to keep clean when the tide dropped. At a meeting with Board of Trade officials, Smart said that he had no objection to anyone using his steps, provided they did not interfere with his business. Uphill Parish Council was asked to report annually on Smart's use of the ferry and the state of the landing stages. When 'Cap'n' Smart died in 1936, his widow took over the lease and employed men to row *Mary*. In due course A.E. Pople and Len 'Patchy' Patch managed the ferry on her behalf until the outbreak of war, when Brean Down became a restricted area.

At the end of the Second World War, the Bird Preservation Society actively discouraged visitors to Brean Down and this affected the ferry. Still owned by Mrs Smart, it was managed by Jim Brueford,

Dick Gross and Dicky Dykes between 1951 and 1957 on her behalf. They were forced to move the landing site 150yd downstream when the River Axe widened, causing the banks to collapse. When Dykes retired in 1957, Mrs Smart surrendered the lease, which was, in any case, due for renewal on 11 January.

At an auction presided over by Messrs Hartnell and Taylor on 17 July 1957, at the Dolphin Hotel, Uphill, it emerged that the tenancy was subject to a payment of £1 to the Board of Trade and also £20 to the owner of Brean Down Farm for the right of ferry passengers to cross his land. Mr Hayden, who ran small boats with the Weston Marine Co., suggested the purchaser should not be given sole right to ferry passengers across the Axe. The proceedings were further enlivened when Hartnell claimed that the ferry was a public service and therefore there was an obligation that it should be operated.

The meeting broke up but it later emerged that the tenant was not under such an obligation but had exclusive rights to operate the ferry whenever he felt

opportune. Eventually Mr Frank Watts, a member of the Weston-super-Mare lifeboat crew, purchased the lease for £6, which led Hartnell to comment, "I have sold a few things cheaply in my life, but I do not think I have ever sold anything quite as cheaply as this". The *Mary* was sold for £56.

When Mr Watts took the ferry over, he ran it economically, as he saw fit, but not being a permanent service, this drew several complaints. At a meeting at Weston-super-Mare Council Highways and Works Committee in June 1962, Mr Watts explained that it was ridiculous to expect someone to be on hand all day in the winter months to collect a few shillings. In short, the ferry was uneconomical except in the summer, and his suggestion that the council should consider providing some attractions on Brean Down for visitors was rejected.

Watts let the ferry later that year to Frank and Jim Brueford, and then to Bill and Reg Brueford, but they found that only about 130 people were using the ferry daily at the height of the season. Jim

Bert Gillings and family enjoy a day out on the beach c.1925. Behind them are the remnants of the 1860s harbour jetty. (Stuart Hicks)

Birnbeck Island and pier, near Weston-super-Mare, in 1925. One of the White Funnel ferries is tied up at the steamer pier on the right.
(North Somerset Museum)

Brueford kept going until 1970 by which time the landing stages were in a very poor state and the cost of rebuilding them, in the face of competition from cars, prohibitive. He laid the ferry up.

Five years later Reg Brueford and Gordon Gillam renovated the landing stages, bought a boat with capacity for twelve people and powered by a 8-horsepower outboard, named it *Macboat* and resumed operations with a ferryman named Gordon Ferryman. Two other boats were also used, a fibre-glass dinghy, the *Skylark*, with capacity for ten passengers, and a punt for use in slack water at low tide.

The River Axe has a very fast flow and on one occasion, when a considerable amount of rainwater was spilling into the river from the Somerset Levels, Mr Ferryman was rowing some people across the river when a rowlock snapped. The ferry, which had made very little headway, suddenly careered downstream but the ferryman grabbed a buoy and held on until a yacht appeared and towed him out of trouble. Nevertheless, even with a powerful engine at full speed, she could only make 7 knots (8mph/13kph) back to the jetty, such was the strength of the ebb.

The ferry was closed for health and safety reasons in 1996.

The Bristol Channel Steamers

Many of those who visited the fort reached Weston-super-Mare by one of the many paddle steamers that plied the Bristol Channel, and then took a boat from Weston to Brean Down. In each case, it was likely to be the firm of P. & A. Campbell that ran the service. As their name might suggest, Peter and Alex Campbell transferred their excursion steamers from the Clyde, where three railway companies ran steamers as well, and started sailing from Bristol in 1887.

Although in the early days mechanical troubles often hit the ships, trippers were not deterred from using the 40-minute service from South Wales. Competition was very fierce and ripping down posters advertising competitors' sailing times was common, as were unofficial races between the steamers. This eventually led to a collision off Birnbeck Pier between the Welsh-based *Lorna Doone* and the Campbell's *Ravenswood*.

86

The 1890s were the heyday of the steamers with 15,000 people a day disembarking at Birnbeck Pier. A low-water jetty was proposed but lack of funds, engineering difficulties and a storm in 1903 flattened the works and held up progress. It was not until Whit-Monday 1909 that the new jetty was finished. Meanwhile, in 1904, the Grand Pier had opened in Weston to land passengers nearer the centre of town, but steamers could only use it at high tides and the scheduled services continued to use Birnbeck Pier. By the outbreak of the First World War, competition had driven everyone to the wall except the Campbell's White Funnel Line. Of those ships that went to war, two were sunk, three were damaged beyond repair and nine returned.

Campbells, however, worked their ships up to their usual efficiency throughout the 1920s and 1930s but began to suffer from coach excursions and cars. A plan to introduce a screw-driven steamer was met with horror by the public: one of the attractions of the paddle steamers was going below to watch the engines. War again interrupted services, with the ships being pressed into minesweeping and coastal escort duties. Campbell's *Brighton*

Queen was not the only paddle steamer sunk at Dunkirk in 1940.

Even though Campbells had built two new paddle steamers in 1946/7, the post-war years saw a decline in steamer excursions and all the paddle steamers were laid up and scrapped when motor vessels took over. For a short period in 1963 a hovercraft travelled between Penarth and Weston-super-Mare, which led to some concerns by Weston-super-Mare Borough Councillor Gerald Wadham that Brean Down Fort could be used a hovercraft base.

In September 1971, Campbells announced they were withdrawing from the upper Bristol Channel because Clevedon Pier had collapsed and Birnbeck Pier had never really recovered from its wartime experiences as an experimental centre. Excursions still took place in the lower reaches from Ilfracombe to Lundy Island. Campbell's last services, in 1980, were operated by MV *Balmoral*, now preserved along with the 1947 Clyde paddle steamer *Waverley*. Both vessels now run services in the Bristol Channel each spring and summer, calling at Weston (Knightstone) as well as Clevedon Pier, now restored.

Campbell's White Funnel paddle steamers at Weston-super-Mare in 1925. The service from Cardiff was more a ferry than an excursion; note how full it is. (North Somerset Museum)

EIGHT

The Second World War

A 6-inch coastal artillery gun fires. (Imperial War Museum)

The threat of war had receded but it was not to be ignored altogether. In 1927 the world's first military missile was tested down the Bristol Channel. Developed at the Royal Aircraft Establishment at Farnborough for the Air Ministry, the surface-to-surface Larynx missile was designed to carry a 200lb (90kg) warhead at 200mph (320kph). Fired from the destroyer HMS *Stronghold*, the missile was guided on its 100-mile (160km) test flight down-channel by shore-based radio navigational beacons and telemetry direction units. The experiment proved the feasibility of remotely delivered bombs but after several trials with RAF Iraq Command, the project was quietly dropped. Within a few years, German scientists would begin their own experiments with missiles.

In 1932 Great Britain reorganised its defences so that, when war broke out seven years later, Coast Defences, Welsh Ports consisted of 591 (Pembrokeshire) Heavy Regiment RA (TA) protecting Milford Haven with 9.2-inch (234mm) and four 6-inch (152mm) coastal guns while Cardiff was guarded by two 6-inch guns and Swansea by two 4.7-inch (120mm) QFs manned by 531 (Glamorgan) Heavy Regiment RA (TA). The southern shores of the Bristol Channel appear to have had no coast artillery, apart from a naval battery at Avonmouth.

Ex-naval 6-inch Mark VII Coast Defence gun, showing projectile and bag charges of the type installed at Brean Down. (Ian Hogg)

When war broke out, Brean Down slumbered on, visited by the occasional Air Raid Precaution patrol taken by car to remain overnight in the fort watching for any fires that might help German pilots pinpoint their position. But its tranquillity was about to be disturbed for the second time within a century.

Severn Defences

The outbreak of war saw the Bristol Channel virtually defenceless from attack from the sea. Defending Cardiff port was Cardiff Fixed Defences, commanded by Lieutenant-Colonel E.C.J. Barry RA. Assembled around the Glamorgan Heavy Regiment RA (TA), with batteries at Nells Point and Friar's Point, it was supported by 588 Army Troop RE, formerly the Glamorgan Fortress Company RE, who operated the generators. At Portishead, the independent 365 Coast Battery began training and at Avonmouth Royal Navy gunners with 15-pounders claimed an unlikely hit on an enemy aircraft on 3 September 1939.

By mid-May 1940 the situation in Europe was desperate. The German Army had swept past the Maginot Line, defeated the Dutch in four days of spectacular *coups d'état* and efficiently fought battles, and were hard on the heels of the British Expeditionary Force, dogged in retreat to the sandy beaches around Dunkirk. The Belgians to the north were wavering and the French, shocked by the rapidity of the Blitzkrieg, were near collapse.

The government, well aware that morale was not high and the country was vulnerable to invasion, although the reality of such a venture by a country whose troops had never undertaken such an operation was deliberately not mentioned, finalised the idea of a volunteer home defence force. After the 9pm news on Tuesday 14 May 1940, Secretary of State for War Mr Anthony Eden made his famous call to arms for volunteers to join the Local Defence Volunteers (LDV).

Farmers Stuart Hicks and Philip Champion, both in their late teens, were the first to join the LDV when a friend called at their homes that evening seeking their commitment. Hicks, as a farmer, was in an essential occupation and did not have to enlist; nevertheless, equipping himself with his 12-bore shotgun and some ammunition, he reported to the LDV Platoon HQ in a Nissen hut below Brean Down (it still exists). The platoon commander was First World War veteran Lieutenant William Tucker and sergeants Foster and Dill assisted him. Those without guns armed themselves with drain rods.

Dressed in civilian clothes and with an orange LDV armband on their right arm, Hicks and his colleagues patrolled Brean and Berrow twice a week, a routine that was continued until the Home Guard was disbanded in 1944. Brean Down was also patrolled until it was taken over by the military authorities in 1941. Sometimes the needs of the farm seemed far more important than the defence of the country and on one spring Sunday, when he should have been on parade, Hicks was lambing. This did not prevent a brisk admonishment from Lieutenant Tucker.

In July 1940, the LDV was christened the Home Guard by Prime Minister Winston Churchill, and the Brean and Berrow Platoon formed part of 13th Battalion Somerset Light Infantry (Home Guard).

The Home Guard parade outside the hut, which is now the clubhouse of the Brean Land Yacht Club, near the entrance to Brean beach. (Stuart Hicks)

Within a few weeks, they were issued with battle-dress, '37-pattern webbing, a sidehat sporting the Somerset Light Infantry Jellalabad cap badge, a steel helmet and a Canadian first-world-war vintage 0.303in (7.7mm) Ross rifle, which was described by one Home Guard soldier as "unsuitable for Service conditions as any earth or dirt might cause a jam", and its 18-inch (457mm) bayonet. Later in the war the platoon was given a Browning automatic rifle (actually, despite its name, a light machine-gun of US origin), which could fire forty single shots in a minute or 550 on automatic, and a 0.303 Vickers machine-gun, which the First World War veterans instantly recognised.

To prevent enemy gliders from unloading troops on Berrow Sands, Royal Engineer and labour units dug in 10ft (3m) posts and built pillboxes to cover the beaches and the flat Somerset Levels. After the war Stuart Hicks had great difficulty in dismantling a pillbox on his farm. His brother undermined the foundations of another, covering the beach, causing it to sink beneath the sand. Amongst the army units

was the 10th Battalion Somerset Light Infantry on coastal defence duties, which later became 7th Battalion, the Parachute Regiment and dropped on D-Day. Its soldiers were accommodated in requisitioned houses or billeted with families with some feeding done centrally. Nevertheless parts of Brean soon became a hive of vehicle parks, tented camps and pathways of duckboards.

German aircraft frequently flew at low level along Berrow Sands. On one occasion in 1943 Hicks and Champion were part of a three-man Vickers gun detachment covering the beaches from a small hut, which is now the Brean Land Yachting Club, near the entrance to Brean beach, when a German aircraft arrived from the direction of Burnham-on-Sea within easy range of their Browning automatic rifle light machine-gun. Hicks was the gunner and, clearly identifying the swastikas on the fuselage, asked Lieutenant Tucker if he could open fire. Tucker replied, "Drop his eggs on us? We can't have that!" and they watched as the aircraft banked over Brean Down Farm, aiming to drop a mine in the River

Heinkel He 111s were often employed minelaying in the Bristol Channel. (Ken Wakefield collection)

Axe, but it missed. Instead the mine hit the ground at the foot of the down, near the present Bird Garden, and exploded with a massive bang, its shockwave toppling the watching Home Guardsmen and blowing a large crater in a field. Parachute silk and the lines were prized items and Hicks recovered about twenty lengths of silk line. Home Guard Private Roland Frost recovered sufficient material to make his four daughters a pair of gloves each.

By New Year the air battles and bombing over Britain were almost over and the Germans tended to send aircraft as single raiders or in small packs. Flying across the mainland from France, the Luftwaffe was sometimes diverted on to dummy targets. On 4 January 1941, over 500 incendiary bombs were dropped on open ground near Brean when oil-filled drums were set alight at the 'Shadow Factory', a ruse designed to lure German aircraft away from Weston-super-Mare and its important aircraft production factories near Locking. By this time Brean had several hundred evacuees and the Hicks family had built a robust large shelter capable of taking forty people, underneath a hayrick near their farmhouse.

The Defence of the Bristol Channel

With London and south-east under attack, the Bristol Channel became increasingly important as the anchorage for the Welsh ports and Bristol. However, its tidal range (the difference between high tide and low tide) is one of the greatest in the world, which meant that ships often had to wait before entering its ports, especially the River Avon, and were therefore at risk from marauding E-Boats, as well as mines and aircraft. This was compounded by two further factors. First, damaged ships and those with vital cargoes obviously received priority unloading. Second, because of the need to protect other convoys, escorts needed to refuel and re-arm in naval ports, such as Plymouth, and therefore would be unable to provide air and surface defence for the anchored merchantmen.

To defend Bristol, the light anti-aircraft guns of the ships, which collectively could put up a heavy barrage, were augmented on 24 August 1939 by the deployment of 76 Heavy Anti-Aircraft Regiment, with its 236 Battery first establishing a position near Pill before relocating to Gordano, on 18 December, and 237 Battery manning the Portbury site. Each site was purpose-built with gunpits for four mobile 3.7-inch (95mm) guns, semi-underground magazines and hutted accommodation. In September 1941, 411 Battery, 104 Heavy Anti-Aircraft Regiment took over from 236 Battery, which went to the Middle East.

Until early 1941, 205 Mobile Heavy Anti-Aircraft Regiment manned sites at Sims Hill, Stoke Gifford, Baileys Court Farm, Portbury, Rockingham, Cribbs Causeway, Brickfields and Easton-in-Gordano. In May the defences were increased to twenty positions with static anti-aircraft guns defending the docks at Avonmouth, railways and power station, the aircraft manufacturing factories at Filton, the city centre and the approaches from the north-west. In December 1942 the city was further strengthened when Lodge Farm, Pilning and Rockingham were defended by four 4.5-inch (114mm) guns manned by 2nd Anti-Aircraft Group. When 205 Heavy Anti-Aircraft Regiment departed for overseas duty, the Home Guard took over the air defence of Bristol.

In South Wales, there were air defence sites J5 at Sully and J6 at Bulwark. Site J4 near the old fort at Lavernock Point was equipped with 4.5-inch dual-role anti-aircraft/coastal guns, and all three batteries were assigned an anti-shipping role in addition to air defence.

Severn Fixed Defences

On 26 June 1940, the independent 365 Coast Battery at Portishead, commanded by Captain J.S. Lee, was reinforced by eight men from 2nd Super Heavy Regiment and forty-seven men from 52 Heavy Battery to man two 6-inch Mark VII beach battery positions, two mobile searchlights and a single Coast Artillery Searchlight (CASL). On 5 September 1940 the Glamorgan Heavy Regiment (TA) was reorganised into 531 Coast Regiment (TA), with A Battery at Nell's Point and B Battery at Cardiff.

Responding to a Home Forces instruction dated 23 September, Admiral Sir Frederick Dreyer CB, KCB, GCB, who had been recalled to the active list after retiring in 1939, was tasked with surveying the coastal defences of the country and identifying beaches across which troops could be landed. Based at the Admiralty's Office for Miscellaneous Services at HMS *President* in Chatham, he tasked Captain D.T. Graham-Brown RN, MVO, also mobilised from retirement to active service at the shore establishment at HMS *Lucifer* in Swansea, to reconnoitre

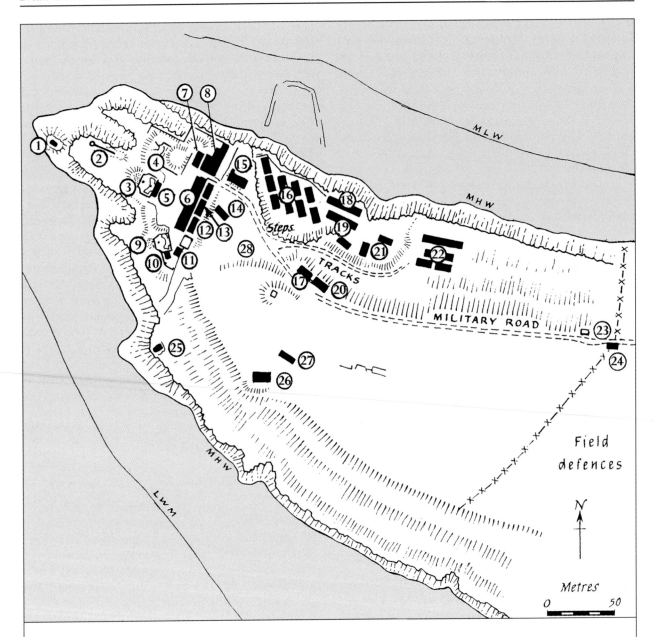

1. No. 1 Searchlight
2. DMWD rail
3. No. 1 6in gun emplacement
4. Coal heap
5. No. 1 Detachment shelter
6. Cookhouse/NAAFI
7. CO's office
8. Officers' mess
9. No. 2 6in gun emplacement
10. No. 2 Detachment shelter

11. Ablutions
12. Generator store
14. Pay office
15. Fort HQ
16. Accommodation blocks
17. MT Section with inspection pit
18. Ablutions
19. Training wing
20. Master Gunner's office
21. Medical and RAOC Sections

22. Sergeants' mess
23. Bren gun trench
24. Guardroom
25. No. 2 Searchlight
26. Fire Command
27. Fire Command offices
28. Fuel, oil and lubricant dump

the feasibility of siting "batteries and three Defence Electric Lights for the defence of the Bristol Channel from Lavernock Point to Flat Holm to Steep Holm to Brean Down". Both men were expert in naval gunnery.

Graham-Brown appointed Lieutenant-Colonel Barry (from HQ Coast Artillery, Western Command) to his reconnaissance team of naval and Western Command army officers. By November he had completed his report, finding that while there were limited defences in South Wales, the English coast had been abandoned virtually since the turn of the century. In discussing the threat, he concluded that this would come from three directions:

- Sea – raids and mine-laying submarines
- Land – Amphibious and parachute raids
- Air – High- and low-level bombing, parachute drops and minelaying

Much of the report centred on Steep Holm and Flat Holm, and the logistics of equipping them and then supplying them. This included the need for a medical officer and three RAMC orderlies on Steep Holm, with a boat to allow them to go to Flat Holm. Water was also seen to be a major issue and No. 3 Water Transport Company RASC was warned to supply the islands. As far as Brean Down was concerned, the report concluded:

Brean Down – one battery approved in existing obsolete work on Somerset mainland

Access – road said to be passable by lorry and car

Accommodation – required for 120 men

There is a suggestion in this assessment that the reconnaissance team did not visit Brean Down.

Graham-Brown acknowledged that the Bristol Channel was vital to the nation's security and although the Victorian forts were in a poor state of repair, they nevertheless provided suitable gun positions. The report suggested that there should be two regimental-sized Fire Commands covering the Bristol Channel, one in Cardiff and the other in Swansea. The problem of Brean Down and Portishead being in 8 Corps, Southern Command's area was resolved by placing the defence of the Bristol Channel with Western Command.

There were two types of coast artillery positions during the Second World War: first, the permanent fixed defences, such as the huge offensive railway guns in Dover; and second, defensive emergency batteries equipped mainly with 6-inch guns, fitted for the duration of the war. Generally, its organisa-

tion was units of two guns, each manned by a 30-strong Gun Troop, and a Headquarters Troop, which included command and control and also support elements. Total strength was about 120 all ranks.

The victory of the Battle of Britain and the approach of winter decreased the likelihood of invsion but nevertheless Western Command moved quickly to defend the Bristol Channel ready for the spring by creating two Fire Commands.

On 15 October, to cover the Western Approaches, the 21st Coast Artillery Group, which was retitled 559 Coast Regiment, was formed in the Port Talbot and Swansea area from 401 and 402 Coast Batteries and B Battery 531 Coast Regiment. On New Year's Eve, 365 Coast Battery at Portishead and 366 Coast Battery, which was commanded by Captain R.G. Hickson at Cardiff, were incorporated into 531 (Glamorgan) Coast Regiment, commanded by Major D.P. Horsley.

Joe Walford – whose father, also called Joe, had served at Steep Holm and Brean Down during the Victorian era – was called up on 18 May 1940 and was sent to the Royal Artillery training unit at Topsham in Exeter. He recalled:

After six weeks' training, the intake was posted to different regiments. I and many other Bristolians were posted to Barry Island to start our coast defence training and then on to Queens Dock, Cardiff to man two 6-inch guns of 366 Battery, Captain Hickson being our commander. The battery was just being formed and the site quite basic. We were told to form ourselves into groups of six to seven and were each given a bell tent. My early days as a scout and with my knowledge of knots, splices and rigging, we had our tent up in no time. Rats soon infected the tents and coal dust from the coal trains going to Queens Dock was also a problem. Nevertheless we were never short of coal.

Of the five in his tent, Gunners Haywood, Woolley, Stone and Fry survived the war but Gunner Chenowith was killed in action. On 3 March 1941, 366 Battery's position was bombed causing some minor damage.

On 9 March, HQ Southern Command issued orders to implement the scheme to defend the Bristol Channel:

As a step towards implementation of the Bristol Channel Scheme (12 x 6" guns), it is recommended that sites be prepared for 2 x 6" gun batteries (4 guns) on Flat Holm. Anti-Aircraft Command should be consulted when selecting these sites.

German Schnellboote (E-Boats) tie up at Haslar Creek, Gosport, after the German surrender. It was this type of vessel that was a threat to the Bristol Channel. (National Maritime Museum)

The same day, air defence at Portishead was strengthened by the arrival of eight Lewis guns manned by a troop of 145 (Z) Anti-Aircraft Battery, commanded by Captain R.D. Smith RA, and eight Coast Artillery gunners. They were soon in action on the night of 11 April during the last large raid on Bristol. Other reorganisations quickly took place with the newly formed 192 Battery joining 531 Coast Regiment, who were then joined, on 1 July by 145 (Z) Anti-Aircraft Battery, who moved to man the 4.5-inch guns at Lavernock Point. In due course, they were joined, for a short time, by 351 Heavy Anti-Aircraft Battery.

On 3 July 1941, 930 Port Construction and Repair Company RE (Major David Bertlin RE), arrived at Nells Point from Woolmer in Hampshire, with orders to fortify the Bristol Channel defences against enemy forces. Consisting of a high propor-

tion of Territorial Army and Reservists, most of them formerly employed in marine and civil construction, the company was formed specifically to build fortifications and support facilities for the Bristol Channel forts and the Drake's Island defences in Plymouth.

Bertlin set up his headquarters at 42, Redbrink Crescent, Barry Island, with the Stores Dump at Ping-Pong Sidings in Barry Dock. In support was a section of 29 (Railway Survey) Company RE, commanded by Lieutenant I.T. Goodchild RE, to examine the feasibility of building narrow-gauge railway tracks at Steep Holm and Flat Holm. Labour was provided by 116 Company, Auxiliary Military Pioneer Corps (AMPC) and 690 General Construction Company. Royal Signallers from Western Command (Severn) Signals laid 3in (76mm) submarine cables, each with 25 telephone lines, to connect HQ Severn Fixed Defences with the two islands and Brean Down. Royal Indian Army Service Corps (RIASC) muleteers and their mules, almost all of who had been evacuated from Dunkirk, were at Steep Holm. Civil contractors provided support.

All work to build the forts and supply them during construction was done from Barry. To add to the small flotilla of requisitioned and Royal Navy vessels, such as the launches *Wanderer*, *Haslar* – which frequently towed targets for the guns – and *Corrigoyle*, one of Major Bertlin's first acts was to requisition from Everards of Greenhithe, on the Thames, the coaster MV *Assurity*, which was often beached to unload stores. The *Peter Piper*, a motorised Thames barge with a derrick, and the barge *Yumbi*, which sank off Steep Holm in rough seas with a full load of cement on 2 October 1941, were also much in evidence.

It took the Royal Engineers a year to complete their task and on 7 July 1942, 690 General Construction Company took over the work when 930 Port Construction and Repair Company RE

were posted overseas. They were sent to repair captured docks in Italy and Normandy so that supplies could be landed in greater bulk than was possible across beaches.

With the forts all but operational on 19 December 1942, Cardiff Fire Command, commanded by Lieutenant-Colonel C.J. Ferard RA, MC, was reorganised into Fire Commands at Brean Down, Flat Holm and Cardiff Docks under HQ Severn Fixed Defences. It was commanded by Lieutenant-Colonel E.M. Bolt at HQ Western Command, with his headquarters at 12 James Street, Cardiff. Now Cardiff Fire Command consisted of HQ 531 Coast Regiment. Its 192 Battery was disbanded.

To defend the Bristol Channel northern approaches and the channel between the mainland and Flat Holm, 570 Coast Regiment (Major C.W. Galloway RA) was formed with headquarters at 'Craiglands', Redbrink Close, Barry Island and administrative offices at Barry Pier railway station. Under command were 188 and 189 Coast and 145 Anti-Aircraft Batteries. At Portishead, 366 Battery, from the disbanded 531 Coast Regiment, joined 365

A group of coast gunners pose outside a Cardiff gun emplacement in August 1941. Note the camouflage net. Rear, alone: *Gnr Brown.* Rear row: *Gnrs Downton, Britton and unknown, Corporal Stone, Gnrs Mosedale and Gorman.* Front: *Gnrs Platt, Walford and Underhay.* (Joe Walford)

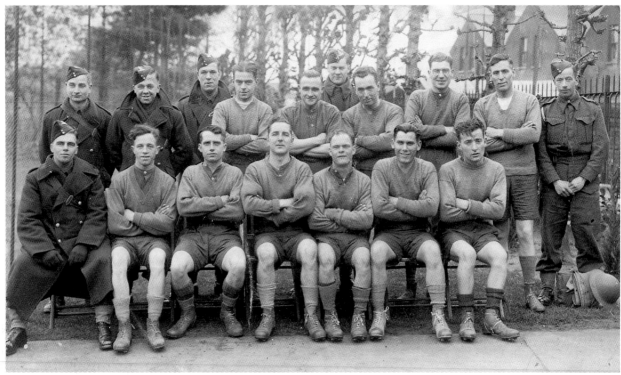

December 1940: 351 Coast Regiment football team pose in Cardiff. Back row: *Young, Sheppard, Butler, Stone, Chanowitch, Fisher, Walford, Davies, Pooley.* Front row: *Capt Davies, Frost, Beard, Taylor.* (Joe Walford)

Battery to form 571 Coast Regiment, commanded by Major Hickson, since promoted, to defend the southern approaches to Bristol. Headquarters were temporarily at Portishead.

By 1942 the likelihood of German invasion or surface raids was low and, throughout Home Forces, units were examined to see where military personnel could be replaced by the Home Guard. Since volunteers fell short, in June Southern Command ordered that eight coast artillery batteries be disbanded or handed over to the Home Guard, with eighty volunteers to each battery. One of those selected by Western Command was 365 Battery at Portishead and 7th Somerset (Long Ashton) Home Guard began converting to the 6-inch guns in May. By September they had taken over Portishead on the basis of twenty Permanent Staff, sixteen Coast Artillery School instructors and seventy-five Home Guard. Also, 365 Battery became an independent unit and joined 511 Coast Regiment at Hartlepool.

Still under command of Commander Severn Defences in Western Command, on 20 June 1942 Severn Fixed Defences was redesignated Coast Artillery South Wales and included 559 Coast Regiment from Swansea and Port Talbot. Flat Holm and Brean Down were still Fire Commands. On 26 April the headquarters were moved to Swanbridge and Lieutenant-Colonel Ferard was placed in command.

Brean Down

With the Royal Engineers constructing jetties and derricks on the two islands, the 930 Port Construction and Repair Company diary recorded:

Sunday 13 July 1941. Weather very heavy storms. Sea rough. The MV Assurity has been loaded for Breendown.

14 July 1941. Weather stormy, high winds. Sea rough. 30 men of the AMPC have been sent to Breendown for duty. The MV Assurity carried personnel and stores to Breendown.

26 July 1941. Construction work at Flatholm, Steepholm and Breendown continues.

5 August 1941. Orders have been received from TN5 at the War Office to cease work on the pier construction at Breandown. Arrangements have been made to withdraw the section employed and transfer them to Steepholm.

Brean Down did not have a jetty and most of the equipment and construction material was brought by Tank Landing Craft 24, which was supporting

930 Port Construction and Repair Company; it and the MV *Assurity* were usually beached to be unloaded.

By 29 July communications were established from Brean Down to Headquarters Severn Fixed Defences. On 11 August, 188 Battery was incorporated into 531 Coast Regiment and earmarked for Brean Down.

11 August 1941. Col. Bruce White, AD TN (D), the War Office arrived at Breandown. The (pioneer) section withdrawn from Breandown has arrived at HQ Barry and is preparing to sail for Steepholm on the 12th inst.

9 November 1941. Assistance was given to land telephone cables from Breandown.

Coast Artillery Units.
A muzzle-loading gun and a stack of cannon balls in black on a circular background divided in red and blue was the badge of the Coastal Artillery Fire Commands, Regiments and Batteries. This badge was used as a vehicle marking.

The Coast Artillery School.
The Coast Artillery School formerly at Shoeburyness was re-established in the war years at Llandudno, moving later to the Citadel, Plymouth. Its badge was a 'Hong Kong' target in black and white on blue wavy lines (for the sea) set in a circle.

Coast artillery insignia. (Author's collection)

On 5 September, an advance guard of thirty men of 116 Pioneer Company under the command of Lieutenant R. Forbes moved to Brean Down. Setting themselves up in a tented camp in the old quarry, they cleared the Victorian gun sites, removed all but one of the George III cannons used for the Dwarf Traversing Platforms, unloaded stores and equipment from vessels, laid tarmac over the stones of Military Road and carved several lay-bys into the grassy banks. The lawn was covered with stone shingle and in the moat a robust building housed the Lister diesel 5kW generators, which supplied power for the fort.

Two emplacements were built. No. 1 Emplacement faced almost exactly north-west. The parapet was low and the barbette was raised on a semi-circular concrete platform with ready-ammunition recesses at ground level protected by steel doors. Overhead protection to the ammunition from air attack was given by a reinforced concrete roof supported on steel stanchions. The detachment shelter consisted of two small rooms left and right of the entry to the position. These were equipped with a stove, some chairs, small table, dartboard, books, cards and sometimes a wireless. To prevent an explosion in the emplacement affecting the remainder of the fort, and to reduce the impact of a bomb or a mine affecting the gun action by exploding outside, the entire position was surrounded on three sides by a reinforced concrete blast wall fixed to metal stanchions.

For the local air defence of the battery, a Lewis gun on an AA (anti-aircraft) tripod was mounted on this emplacement. Lewis machine guns in Severn Defences were expected to engage all enemy aircraft and ships except for parachute mines, whose mid-air explosion could be extremely dangerous.

No. 2 Emplacement was placed over the wreckage of the 1900 explosion and faced slightly south of west, towards the open sea, and was also protected by a blast wall. Its detachment shelter was in a purpose-built room to the left of the emplacement. Opposite this emplacement was the ablution and latrine block for those working inside the fort.

The fort was equipped with two naval 6-inch Mark VII breech-loading guns both mounted on P.IX mountings. They were two of a large number of guns that had fortuitously been removed from decommissioned warships by the Royal Navy and placed in storage. The guns for the Severn Fixed Defences, serial numbers 2742 and 2749, were issued from Naval Armament Supply Office in Cardiff.

Lewis gun in air defence. (Imperial War Museum)

One gun had been manufactured by Armstrongs, and in August 1902 had been fitted to the cruiser HMS *Drake* until it was fitted on RMS *Mauretania* in January 1918. At the end of the war it was placed in storage until deployed to Brean Down. The second gun had been made at Woolwich Arsenal and fitted to the cruiser HMS *Euryalus* in December 1902, transferred to Hong Kong coastal defence in 1918 and then moved around from depot to depot until June 1940.

Since they were designed to be fitted to the deck of a ship and had different mountings to the land 6-inch coastal guns, a concrete base was built for them. In 1942, Royal Army Ordnance Corps gunfitters slotted a 3.7-inch anti-aircraft gun sleeve inside a gun and tested its capability, without much success, to use lower-calibre ammunition, which was more plentiful than 6-inch.

Dug into the hillside above the fort was a split-level bunker which, during the war, was draped with camouflage nets. The upper level was the battle headquarters of 571 Coast Regiment, controlling the operations of the Brean Down Fort and Steep Holm (South) batteries with sub-surface telephone cables and radios to HQ Severn Fixed Defences at Lavernock House, Swanbridge and Fire Command Flat Holm.

The lower level was the Battery Command Post for Brean Down Battery, and its local defence, and housed the duty command post watch, which consisted of the Fire Commander, usually the Troop Commander of the duty troop, his Troop Sergeant, and several JNCOs and gunners, one of whom operated the Barr and Stroud rangefinder, while others manned the telephone exchange and radios.

The Fire Commands, the batteries and then the guns each had their arcs of fire and ranges that they covered. The arcs for Brean Down, for instance, were 36-degrees to 180-degrees out to a range of 6,000yd (5,486m). The fort also provided the fullback position to deal with any ships that managed to break through the island barrier by firing behind Steep Holm and Flat Holm.

Two Coast Artillery Search Lights (CASL) posts were a vital element of the defences and connected by telephone to Fire Command and the guns. The gunners manned them. Searchlights had been developed, as a weapon from the 1870s, although there is no evidence that they were deployed at Brean Down during the Victorian period.

Both CASL positions were of a similar design. Two roomed and semi-circular, No. 1 CASL was perched on Howe Rocks in front of No. 1 Emplacement and was originally approached over a concrete bridge, into which were built two metal pipes through which electrical cables were fed for the searchlight and telephones. A back room housed a small stand-by generator to power the light, which was mounted on small rails in the front room. Its windows were protected by overlapping armoured plates on rails. No. 2 CASL was positioned near the cliff edge to the south of the fort to support No. 2 Emplacement.

Primary power for the CASLs came from a 22kW generator in a concrete building in the moat. Also in the moat was another building that housed the 5kW generator which provided power for the Nissen hut lighting. However, the gunners considered the 40–60kW light bulbs insufficient for this and very frequently exchanged them for 100–150kW bulbs in the pubs in Burnham-on-Sea. This frequently overloaded the system so that orders were eventually given for the hut lighting to be connected to the searchlight generator.

Protecting the landward approaches were barbed wire entanglements and sandbagged defensive positions across Brean Down. A guardhouse, which is still evident, was erected on Military Road and was covered by a Bren gun position about twenty yards inside the perimeter. A 75mm mountain gun for local landward and inshore defence against E-Boats was issued to Brean Down in 1942 and was trialled by the officers and SNCOs firing it out to sea. In the same year a 2in (50mm) Unrotated Projectile, a rocket-propelled anti-aircraft system, was set up near the quarry but no one knew how to use it. The pyrotechnics and ammunition for it were kept in a magazine inside the fort. It could be fired at anything in the air except flares. This was in fact a Parachute and Cable (PAC) anti-aircraft device. The system fired a cable by rocket into the path of an oncoming aircraft, the idea being either to persuade the pilot to bank into a killing zone of anti-aircraft guns or to snag the cable onto the aircraft.

Steep Holm

On 6 July 1941, an advanced party of an NCO and twelve men was taken by the *Assurity* from Flat Holm to set up a camp on Steep Holm. After a con-

siderable amount of work, frequently broken by poor weather, gantries, trackways and paths were built from the landing beach. On 30 September, the four 6-inch guns, generators and equipment were landed and the following day two guns were hoisted into position. Some difficulty was experienced in landing the guns and there is a contemporary account they were dumped over the side with marker buoys and then dragged ashore.

Steep Holm was divided into two sectors. The Summit Battery emplacement, designated as Steep Holm (North), reported to Fire Command Flat Holm while Garden Battery, as Steep Holm (South), reported to Fire Command Brean Down. Both bat-

Barr and Stroud rangefinder. (Imperial War Museum)

A battery of 2-inch Unrotated Projectiles (UP) being fired at enemy aircraft. (Imperial War Museum)

teries had observation posts and supporting low-level CASLs on Calf Rock, South Landing, Rudder Rock and on the northern cliffs. It was sometime between 7 and 13 February 1942 that 188 Coast Battery was posted to Steep Holm (North) and came under command of 571 Coast Regiment.

By now Sergeant Walford had been appointed as the Training Sergeant for small arms for all the coast defence batteries. When he rejoined 366 Coast Battery after a course in Liverpool, it had moved to Steep Holm and with his expertise as a steel erector, he was placed in charge of the 44ft (13.4m) gantry that dropped into the sea at the end of the pier. At the end of the pier was a crane. Despite frequent warnings not to do so, soldiers going on leave frequently crowded on to the jetty and one occasion the hook caught in the webbing cross-straps of one soldier and swung him over the hold of the ship. Fortunately the straps held.

The Victorian barracks were taken over as the other ranks' dining area while an organised sprawl of Nissen huts adjacent to the barracks and near Tombstone Battery housed a total of 120 men.

Generators provided power and a narrow-gauge railway was built around the island to transport shells and stores to the guns. Water was pumped by diesel generators to tanks on the island, but it was often short and a soldier from Royal Indian Army Service Corps died of typhus. When it was found that the water was infected, it then had to be brought in 'flimsy' jerrycans and consequently was even scarcer, with twelve men using the same water to wash. Seagulls' eggs provided a welcome relief to the compo rations.

Poor water frequently meant that shore leave had to be cancelled. Life was tedious, broken only the air raids on Cardiff. Entertainment was rare, although on one memorable night, 31 October 1942, a troupe from the Entertainment National Service Association (ENSA) was stranded by a storm. Although it is thought that only two photographs were taken of Steep Holm during the war, the artist Ray Howard-Jones completed a couple of paintings of activity there at the time.

Howard-Jones lived in Penarth and when war broke out she pleaded to be appointed a war artist, but it was not until July 1943 that she given permission by the War Office War Artists Advisory Committee to paint activities on the fortified islands in the Bristol Channel for a fee of 20 guineas. All work was to be property of the Crown and subject to censorship. By October she had completed most of the work, but in a letter to E.C. Gregory of the Committee she admitted to being a little battered after "the boisterous crossings". She also commented:

> The weather, even for a Welsh summer, has been wild – much time spent on storm routine ... easels blowing away, tearing seas ... biscuits and beans.

Two of Ray Howard-Jones's works, in gouache and oil, are now in the Imperial War Museum and show *Fortified Islands in the Bristol Channel: 2" Naval UP projector* in 1942 on Steep Holm. She died in July 1996.

R. Howard-Jones' painting 'Fortified Islands in the Bristol Channel: 2" Naval UP projector in 1942'. (Imperial War Museum)

Flat Holm

Flat Holm is exceptionally well placed to defend the approaches to Cardiff and its port and, as a consequence, the decision was made that its main priority would be an air defence platform. As with Steep Holm, Flat Holm was divided into two areas, with the batteries at Well Battery and the Lighthouse designated as Flat Holm (South), and Farmhouse and Castle Rock batteries as Flat Holm (North). Each position was fitted with 4.5-inch Anti-Aircraft/Coastal Defence dual-role guns, all brand new, supported by a Mark 1 Anti-Aircraft Predictor, which could spot aircraft up to 45,500ft (13,870m).

On 4 July 1941, most of 930 Port Construction and Repair Company were landed on Flat Holm, where a tented camp was built and the Old Cholera Hospital turned into a mess hall, kitchen and recreation room. An old laundry at the base of the lighthouse was Fire Command. With the urgency to complete the work, Major Bertlin was quick to start; however, poor weather hampered operations. On 15 July, a stormy day with rough seas, the bad weather led to tragedy.

When HMS *New Roseland* set off to deliver supplies to Flat Holm and Steep Holm, Major Bertlin asked that three newly-posted Royal Engineers, Sergeant John Harwood, Corporal Cyril Bull and Sapper Morse, be taken ashore to join Lieutenant Hopper on Flat Holm. However, all were drowned when their small rowing boat capsized shortly after shoving off. It seems the soldiers were wearing their full webbing but not life preservers. Their Royal Navy coxswain survived. For the next five days, shipping operations ceased until the weather improved.

Extracts from the Company diary give a flavour of German activity in the Bristol Channel:

> <u>6 October 1941</u> At 20.50hrs enemy aircraft dropped sea mines in the Channel between Steepholm and Brean Down.

> <u>7 October 1941</u> Further mines were dropped during the evening and one struck Flatholm and exploded at approx. 20.55hrs injuring one Sapper of this unit.

Both attacks were carried by the highly versatile Junkers 88 from III Gruppe, Kampfgeschwader 30 (III/KG30), flying from Melun in France. In addition to the sapper, there were twenty-nine other casualties, including four pioneers. A 4.5-inch position and several buildings were damaged. Poor weather closed Barry Docks and precluded vessels from recovering the casualties. On the 8th and 9th, medical stores were successfully dropped by an aircraft to the RAMC orderly dealing with them. The Admiralty also issued orders that all ships going to Flat Holm must now be armed. In fact it was not until 10 October that the naval launch *Corrigoyle* managed to reach Flat Holm, by now very short of rations and water, and evacuate the five seriously wounded soldiers. The skipper of the *Assurity* could not be found!

On 17 September, TLC 24 had beached on West Beach and a working party of pioneers from Brean Down and the Stores Dump at Barry had unloaded the first 4.5-inch and its predictors. The second gun followed three days later and was mounted at Lighthouse Battery. Although their emplacements were not constructed for another year, the guns were

On 17 September 1941, a 4.5-inch gun is being unloaded from Tank Landing Craft 24 onto Flat Holm. (Public Record Office)

desperately needed to defend Cardiff. On Christmas Eve 1941 gunners from 351 Heavy Anti-Aircraft Regiment from Lavernock were sent to Flat Holm to man the guns and on Boxing Day were joined by a detachment from 440 Battery, 127 Light Anti-Aircraft Regiment to man the two 40mm Bofors guns.

The guns first engaged the Germans on 26 April 1942, when 351 Heavy Anti-Aircraft Battery fired, with 4.5-inch guns, at aircraft flying between 8,000 and 12,000ft (2,440–3,660m). No hits were registered. This was the first of fourteen times that the Flat Holm batteries opened fire on German aircraft. By 18 May, Flat Holm had become a formidable 'stone AA position' with four 4.5-inch guns and Gun Laying Mark 2 Radars manned by 351 Heavy Anti-Aircraft Battery, two 40mm Bofors light guns and two air-defence Lewis guns manned by rotating sections of 465 Battery, 72 Light Anti-Aircraft Regiment, with a Defence Electric Light site controlled by 450 Battery, 67 Searchlight Regiment. When raids on Welsh targets took place, Flat Holm found that when the anti-aircraft batteries at Cardiff fired rockets, their lethal motors regularly fell on to the island.

On 3 July 1942, the men of 184 Coast Battery, from East Blockhouse, Cardiff joined 570 Coast Regiment to man the two 4.5-inch guns on Flat Holm (North) in the coast artillery role; but they stayed only until 18 August when they replaced 365 Coast Battery at Portishead, who in turn moved to Hartlepool. In their place, 205 Independent Coast Battery was posted to Flat Holm, having been transferred from the Faeroe Islands to form part of 532 Coast Regiment at Pembroke Dock.

After 45th (South Wales) Anti-Aircraft Brigade (who controlled air defence in South Wales from their HQ at Penylan Court, Tygwyn Road, Cardiff) and Coast Artillery South Wales had agreed that, to save men, the four 4.5-inch guns on Flat Holm would be converted to a dual role, 351 Heavy Anti-Aircraft Battery began to train the coast gunners on the guns but, within a fortnight, found that it was being hampered by coast artillerymen doing fatigues.

Nevertheless, by 1 January 1943, sufficient numbers had been trained that HQ 45th (South Wales) Anti-Aircraft Brigade handed over the two 4.5-inch guns and their equipment in the North Battery on Flat Holm to 570 Coast Regiment, 205 Coast Battery at 9am on the 3rd, leaving a troop of C Section, 306 Battery, 98 Light Anti-Aircraft Regiment to man the four light anti-aircraft sites, while the 4.5-inch guns of Flat Holm (South) were manned and maintained by 351 Heavy Anti-Aircraft Battery section, based at Lavernock.

During this period in 1943, there were frequent changeovers in the gunners manning the four Lewis anti-aircraft sites. On New Year's Day, 306 Battery, 98 Light Anti-Aircraft Regiment was listed at Flat Holm but, by 11 January, B Section, 440 Battery, 127 Heavy Anti-Aircraft Regiment were listed as having taken over. Seven days later C Section, 306 Light Anti-Aircraft Battery had returned. The reason for 306 Battery's seven-day absence is not known but it may have been to give the men a week's unit block leave.

Within days, 205 Coast Battery's range predictor failed and some cables had to be replaced. On 1 February, 146 Coast Battery took over the air defence commitment from 351 Heavy Anti-Aircraft Battery at Flat Holm (South) so that 570 Coast Regiment now had total control of the defence of Flat Holm. While 351 Heavy Anti-Aircraft Battery still provided technical support for the 4.5-inch guns, the three sections based on Flat Holm were redeployed to Newport, Cardiff and Caerwent on anti-aircraft duties. The new coast gunners soon had their first engagement, on 16 February 1943, when both batteries fired on two German aircraft with eight rounds loosed but no hits observed. By June, 98 Light Anti-Aircraft Regiment had left Flat Holm and was replaced by 282 Battery, 82 Light Anti-Aircraft Regiment, whose headquarters was at Nore Park House, Portishead.

Lavernock

On 25 August 1941, a 6-inch Mark VII gun, three Mark V Anti-Aircraft Searchlight Projectors and a diesel generator were delivered to 145 Battery/531 Coast Regiment, and the gun was mounted by 2 September. A second gun was mounted eight days later.

The guns of the Severn Fixed Defences were never brought into action against enemy ships, because none appeared, but were no doubt a welcome sight to the seamen of battered convoys at the end of their gruelling voyage across the Atlantic Ocean. There is only one recorded incident of any of the Bristol coast

A 4.5-inch dual-role coastal/air defence gun. (Imperial War Museum)

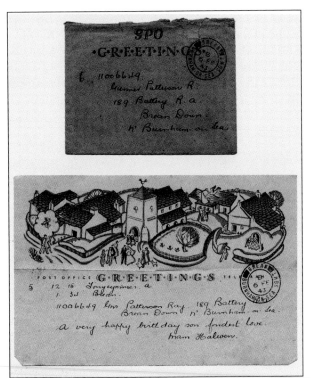

The 21st Birthday greetings' telegram (and its envelope) sent to Gunner Patterson at Brean Down from his mother. (Ray Patterson)

batteries opening fire on a ship. At 7am on 13 June 1941, Severn Fixed Defences had its only maritime challenge when 130 Coast Battery opened fire on an unidentified tanker about a mile offshore. One round was fired but the ship, later identified as the SS *Overton, en route* to Burnham-on-Sea, disappeared into the mist.

For those based on Brean Down, the most southerly of the Severn Fixed Defences, getting to headquarters was difficult. Unlike the two holms, Brean Down did not a have a jetty or reliable beach, apart from the stony beach on the north side, used by local boatmen. Since the Uphill ferry was closed throughout the war, the only route was by vehicle or bicycle to Weston-super-Mare and then by train to Barry Docks. The requisitioned motorised Thames barge *Peter Piper*, manned by the Royal Army Service Corps, supplied Steep Holm while the *Snowflake* serviced Flat Holm. One of the few times when a boat did arrive on the beach below the fort at Brean Down was to land the body of a soldier who had died on Steep Holm, to be collected by Red Cross volunteer driver Miss Hams. Based at Wadham Street in Weston-super-Mare, she drove a Chevrolet ambulance.

By the time, in 1942, when two 20-year old gunners, Reg Stevens and Ray Patterson, joined 570 Coast Regiment, Severn Fixed Defences was nearly operational. By 11.30am on 31 March, Brean Down's first 6-inch gun was connected to No. 2 CASL and became operational. The incumbent 430 Coast Battery exchanged with 366 Coast Battery, from 571 Coast Regiment, and, passing under command of 531 Coast Regiment, set up in Alexandra Docks, Cardiff operating 75mm guns on anti-motor torpedo boat duties. Over the next fortnight the second gun was installed at Brean Down, and Headquarters 571 Coast Regiment moved from Portishead before moving to Brean Down on 4 April. Two flights were made over Brean Down to check its camouflage.

Both Reg Stevens and Ray Patterson had been drafted into the Army under the 1939 National Service (Armed Forces) Act, which made all men aged between 18 and 41 'liable for service for the duration'. After completing the six-week basic training course at the Royal Artillery depot at Paignton, they joined the Coast Regiment Training Centre and Depot at the Citadel, Plymouth where Stevens attended the six-week rangefinding course. Patterson trained to be a gunlayer. They both found the Coast Regiment strange. Many of the men were in their late twenties and early thirties. Younger men were being posted to field and anti-tank regiments where youth was seen to be an advantage. Most were volunteers and this, combined with their above-average age, meant that discipline was relaxed and adult.

Stevens' intake was originally earmarked for the Far East but when the drafting authorities arrived at the letter S, they found there was no further requirement in that theatre where, in 1942, the war was not going well for the Allies. Returning after fourteen days embarkation leave, he found that he was go to 570 Coast Regiment at Portishead not far, to his delight, from his home at Clevedon. About a month later he was posted to Brean Down and was employed as a rangefinder in Fire Command. After two months, Stevens was posted to 188 Coast Battery on Steep Holm and was taken by a motorboat, which picked him up from the rocky beach below the quarry.

On Steep Holm, Stevens was employed in the Quartermaster Stores but after a month was offered promotion to sergeant if he stayed. Deciding he had had enough of isolation at the 'stone frigate', he returned to Brean Down, where he was employed as the clerk to the Master-Gunner in addition to his role at Fire Command. Although Stevens had no clerical or typing skills, he found this a useful slot to avoiding the routines of a Coast Artillery garrison and took every opportunity, when he was not on duty, to acquire a leave pass and cycle the twenty-two miles to his parent's house on his three-geared bicycle. He found cycling to the top of Brean Down exhausting and just once managed to make the summit in one.

Patterson also joined 188 Coast Battery on Steep Holm for several weeks and was glad to leave. He also found life there dull and would volunteer to do almost anything to keep himself occupied – sorting the mail, clerical work and general duties. He also worked in the Pay Office. By 1944 daily pay for a Private was 4/-. Married men received a Family Allowance of £1/8/6 for the wife and 12/6 for each child, paid direct to the wife.

Inevitably, life at Brean Down centred on the two 6-inch guns. At its maximum, each gun was manned by twenty-seven soldiers (broken down into three detachments of a duty watch), a recess party and a magazine supply party. Casualties were replaced by the corresponding gun numbers of the support watches. If these were unavailable, the duty watch was expected to continue the action with reduced ammunition numbers. For longer actions, detachments could be relieved on the gun but would be expected to support the watch. At Brean Down, because of the shortage of men, between six to eight gunners were assigned daily as the Alert Detachment. These were the Number One, who was a sergeant, the elevation and traverse gunlayers, loaders, rammer and ammunition handers.

On 11 May 1942, 366 Coast Battery carried out its first live practice at towed sea targets, the first of just nine live firing shoots from Brean Down throughout the war. For target practice, a Hong Kong target was towed, usually by the Royal Navy-manned target launch *Haslar*, although on one occasion in 1942 a gunner laid on to the launch. On another occasion, a shell whistled straight through the target, ricocheted off the water and exploded on Steep Holm, which resulted in several furious signals of complaint.

Instruction in firing the guns was given in the 1932 edition of *Coast Artillery Training: Volume One*, which was issued to every Coast Regiment officer, SNCO and JNCO. A definitive book on coast artillery operations, it contained a mass of information ranging from the organisation of fixed defences

in peace and war, fighting a counter-bombardment action and organising close and local defence, to the science of coast artillery, taking in ballistics, rangefinders, and countering the effects of the tide and currents. Many found the mass of information suitable only for impressing examination and promotion boards, but nevertheless it was the bible for coast artillery operations.

Assembling all the information available to him, the Battery Commander made his own plan for the use and deployment of his unit in the Fort Fighting Book, which was kept in Sector Fire Command. With the aim being to engage the enemy in a co-ordinated fashion, coast artillery rules did not allow for independent fire except under strict conditions authorised by the sector Fire Commander, for instance to engage unidentified submarines or an obvious enemy ship that had managed to sneak into the upper reaches of the Bristol Channel or, at night or in very poor visibility, to challenge an unidentified vessel or any vessels attempting landings. Allied warships countering enemy activity always took precedence over coast artillery operations. Nevertheless in spite of the standing orders, it was always up to the local Battery Commander to use his initiative and make decisions, provided he could justify them later on.

Every battery under command of Severn Fixed Defences had a copy of *Fire Commanders Standing Orders for Severn Fixed Defences*, which was a highly classified accountable document and was formally signed between Fire Commanders, and contained, for example, the following information:

- the threat, detailing likely forms of attack and probable enemy objectives
- detailed plans of the 570 and 571 Coast Regiments Fire Scheme covering the Bristol Channel and including the topography and layout of battery positions
- local Royal Navy responsibilities in the sector
- communications
- rules of engagement for opening fire and the use and choice of projectiles
- states of readiness, ground defence plan, landward firing and passive and active air defence plan
- synchronisation and organisation of watches and duty detachments
- deployment and operation of the searchlights
- all CASL detachments were to be trained in chemical decontamination and if the engine

Rare photograph taken inside Fire Command. Note the silhouettes of aircraft and ships on wall charts behind the gunners. (Imperial War Museum)

failed, then the searchlights' traverse was to be cranked manually
- tide-tables
- alarms
- document security

Since no warships had been allocated for the defence of the Bristol Channel, the identification of friendly ships was critical and therefore gun detachments and observers were expected to know the description and pennant numbers of Allied ships. The means of communication varied from the submarine telephone cable across the Channel, the No. 17 radios operated by Royal Signals, visual communications using Aldis lamps and semaphore flags, pyrotechnic alarms and carrier pigeons. Generally, by day enemy ships were to be engaged as soon as they were spotted and at maximum range. At night, the leading or most dangerous ship was to be fired at. Batteries were not expected to fire barrages.

Aerial photograph of Brean Down Fort taken from a helicopter in August 1996. (Author's collection)

All gun emplacements and CASL engines were to be manned from one hour before Official Night until one hour after Official Dawn. The composition of fighting patrols, stretcher-bearers and fire picquets was listed, as was local bomb disposal measures. HQ Severn Fixed Defences issued orders that the CASLs were expected to be kept in action: "Neither gas attack, dive-bombing nor shellfire must cause a light to be dowsed or stopped voluntarily. Arms and battle order are to be kept at the duty post."

All Command alarms were to be tested twice a day at Stand-to. Several types of alarm were standard issues throughout the Coast Regiment:

- coastal artillery by bells
- anti-aircraft by siren
- landward threat by bugle
- gas by rattle
- chemical spray by word of mouth
- fire by gong

To maintain security, there were instructions on the disposal of codes, cyphers and classified documents in the event that the battery was overrun. This was generally to rip up documentation and then burn it. The Fort Fighting Book was regularly inspected to ensure amendments had been correctly inserted and grave were the consequences if it could not be produced immediately.

By the Second World War, rangefinding in the Coast Regiment was carried out by the Barr and Stroud rangefinder. The auto-sight method was applied only when the target was at a very short range. Both systems laid the graticule pointer of their telescopes on the bow waterline of the ship, and Fire Command then calculated the necessary adjustments for wind, tide, direction of travel, estimated speed and point of impact. The gun was then directed on to the target.

Once the range had been calculated, the next step was to hit the target. One method was to bracket the target before and beyond the target with the third round to hit. The next method was the 'ladder' when the rounds were fired above, or short of, the target and adjusted to hit by steps without bracketing. The third method was by battery salvoes during which the guns were fired and the corrections given according to which gun's shells landed closest to the target. The other guns then adjusted to the first gun.

August 1941: Sergeant Stone poses beside the breech of a 6-inch gun. (Joe Walford)

Two methods of fire control were generally practised. 'Gun fire' was when the guns were fired independently of each other at ordered intervals. 'Salvo fire' was controlled by Fire Command and all guns fired together. The order for salvo fire was delivered by telephone to the Gun Position Officer and it was up to him to ensure that the guns were ready by making sure the Number 1s, usually sergeants, could communicate with him. At Brean Down, the No. 1s stood outside their emplacements and placed themselves so they could see the Gun Position Officer at Fire Command and their detachments could see them. When their detachments were ready, they raised their right hands. If both guns did not fire simultaneously it was considered poor gun drill.

Soldiers operating the CASLs were expected to know the science of light and its application, most of which was contained in the 1939 War Office publication *The Elementary Electrical and Optical Principles of Searchlights*, which covered magnetism, electricity and elementary principles of electrical machinery, such as a searchlight, cables, batteries and the most effective use of searchlight. The pamphlet states that "in order to produce a powerful concentrated beam of light, it is essential to have a source that is very small and at the same time be very bright" and then goes on to describe the properties of the electrical arc that gives light.

The CASLs were manned – only at night – by two or three men, although in foul weather this was often reduced to just one. The lights could be operated manually or automatically from Fire Command, and in spite of the blackout frequently swept the channel to Steep Holm and south across Berrow Sands. The searchlight detachment also provided all the electricity for the garrison's accommodation. While on Steep Holm, Sergeant Walford did a CASL course at the School of Coast Artillery in Llandudno. At Brean Down, he served in Sergeant-Major Levers' searchlight detachment. In Stan and Joan Rendell's *Steep Holm: The Story of a Small Island*, he describes life in a CASL emplacement as remote:

The emplacements were very uncomfortable, especially in rough weather, when they were manned by just one person, his sole companion to help him pass the time and keep awake were books, a home-made crystal-set radio, and bits and pieces for model making. When the searchlight was switched on it was not easy to pick up the ships; and you also had to be careful not to keep the beam away from the guns' line of sight.

Squad 8 passing out at the Royal Artillery basic training camp, Topsham, August 1940. (Joe Walford)

Life in a Brean Down emplacement can have been no different.

Training was an important aspect of life at Brean Down. Fire Command staff dry training took place in a Nissen hut adjacent to their bunker. A large raised board containing numerous small holes and representing an area of sea was placed at one end of the hut, and a curtain prevented observation onto the board. The Fire Commander and his team would place themselves at the other end of the hut in an area representing Fire Command. On the command, 'Take Post! Prepare for action stations!', the curtain was drawn and, peering through binoculars, the Fire Commander would first locate the target. He would then issue a stream of orders such as 'Alarm! CASE II! Take Post! Target E-Boat moving left, bearing 130 degrees, add 300! Fire!' and then wait. An instructor concealed below the board would wait for a suitable time to simulate the flight of the shell and then push a match to represent shell splashes. The Fire Commander would then give corrections using of the three principal ranging methods until the target had been hit.

A detailed debrief highlighted errors. As Reg Stevens recalled, "The gunnery instructor would explain, very forcibly, everything that had gone wrong and the reasons why it had gone wrong. In fact there seldom to be anything right!" Dry gun drills were usually held on a dummy 6-inch gun platform in the Training Wing.

Although there was a need for vigilance, the men were not permanently at action stations. The routine at Brean Down was common throughout Coast Artillery, with the Duty Troop on alert for twenty-four hours in the shelters: their duty incorporated manning the searchlight at nights, guns drills and maintaining the guns. The Reserve Troop slept fully clothed and carried out some fatigues and other duties to administer the garrison. The third troop was on 24-hours Stand Down but this included military training, off-camp fatigues and leave days. According to Sergeant Walford, small-arms training and grenade throwing took place on Berrow Sands out to sea, at targets erected in the mud so that the fall of shot could be observed.

On the handover, the Gun Position Officer ensured his Troop and its equipment were ready for action. From Fire Command, which was continually manned, the Gun Position Officer checked that the telephones and the Watkins Dial, which was used to pass electrically ranges to the guns, were working. Once satisfied, he waited until the Number 1s had

taken over their guns. There was usually competition to finish first. The Gun Position Officer then paraded the gunners to ensure his men were properly dressed and equipped with their personal weapons, respirator and clothing appropriate to the weather. He then checked the guns by firing an electrical tube to ensure the circuits were functioning. He also tested a percussion tube for when the gun had to be operated manually. When the Gun Position was happy, he would report to Fire Command, 'Battery ready for action!'

Invariably there were formal visits by senior officers with 1 June 1942 being a particularly gruelling day when Colonel Ferard visited in the morning and Lieutenant-Colonel D.S. Holt, GSO1 Coast Artillery Western Command in the afternoon.

At night, to avoid betraying the position, noise and light were kept to an absolute minimum. The sentry also needed to listen and watch for raiding parties. Duty detachments were expected to remain fully dressed with rifles neatly stacked in the racks. To fall asleep was an extremely serious offence and was usually rewarded with a severe punishment. When it was cold, a tot of rum was removed from the Battery Commander's safe and issued, but it had to be consumed in front of the Battery Commander, either neat or in a mug of tea (a combination known as 'Gunfire'), the idea being to ensure that the old sweats didn't get a double ration by 'persuading' the new members of the Battery to pass on their ration. The Coast Artillery tradition of the soldier who could throw a dart nearest the bull being given an extra tot was continued. Since rum was still accountable, the Battery Sergeant Major accompanied the Battery Commander and recorded the tot and to whom it had been given.

The only people to be accommodated in the fort were the officers, who used nine rooms in the Victorian Master-Gunner's quarters. Its large sash windows and doors were narrowed with concrete to accommodate 3ft (0.9m) square windows to reduce collateral blast damage. A small Nissen hut placed outside the Officers' Mess was the Battery Commander's office.

The rest of the garrison were housed in and administered from twelve Nissen huts on concrete plinths inside the quarry. Each troop occupied two huts, each consisting of a large open space and a single room for the Troop corporals. The huts were spartan, with each soldier being allocated a wire-sprung metal bed with mattress, sheets, blankets and a pillow, which had to be made into a bed block during the mornings. Clothing was kept in a 6ft high and 2ft wide (1.8 x 0.6m) wooden locker, with helmet and webbing stored on top. A single stove heated the room, with coal fatigue parties collecting coal in a bucket from the fort. The huts were inspected daily for cleanliness by the hut corporal, who had the privacy of the only single room.

Other accommodation was for HQ 570 Coast Regiment staff. Their three Nissen huts were set on a higher level: one was the Sergeants' Mess for the warrant officers and SNCOs. A large hut served as an ablution block and another was the Training Wing. A Royal Army Medical Corps section ran a medical centre and, although there was a Medical Officer on Steep Holm, most of those reporting sick were sent to Burnham-on-Sea Memorial Hospital by lorry.

The Royal Army Service Corps Motor Transport Troop looked after the 3-tonners, jeeps and 15cwt (760kg) trucks. A small unit of the Royal Electrical and Mechanical Engineers (which was formed in 1942) had a workshop with a vehicle inspection pit, where they maintained and repaired the guns, generators and vehicles, and an inspection bay. The Royal Army Ordnance Corps helped the Battery Quartermaster run the stores and provided technicians for the guns.

Another hut near the fort entrance was the Royal Army Pay Corps Pay Office. Pay parade, a formal event, was held every week in the canteen, at which the soldiers would march to the Paymaster, who sat behind a table, check their money, 'Pay and paybook correct, sir!' in the time-honoured fashion, salute and about-turn to his duties.

A track suitable for light vehicles led into the quarry and a set of concrete steps led to the fort. Nissen huts could be cold and every day the coal pile in the fort, near Victorian Gun Position No. 3, was painted white to ensure no-one illicitly collected more than their fair share.

The soldiers ate in the soldiers' block inside the fort, which was divided into a kitchen, pantry area and serving hatch behind a roller-shutter, a large eating area with a fireplace at each end and a small extension added for the Sergeants Mess dining room. Army Catering Corps cooks prepared the three meals per day of fresh and tinned food. The Orderly Officer, generally accompanied by the Orderly Sergeant and Cookhouse Sergeant, would regularly visit and ask each table, as he was required to do, 'Any complaints?' Few did. During the evenings, the block became the main social centre with a NAAFI bar.

Reveille for Brean Down was 7am, which was normally sounded when the Orderly Duty Sergeant woke up the huts. Sometimes this was done gently, but on other occasions, there was lots of shouting and banging of dustbin lids. By this time Sergeant Walford's family had been bombed out of Avonmouth and moved to a house in Cross Street, Weston-super-Mare and on his leave day he cycled the twelve miles from Brean Down to see them. However, he had to get up early and recalls tearing through dark, frosty lanes and arriving at Brean Down in a bath of sweat ready for his first parade. But, as he admits, "We were very happy and very fit."

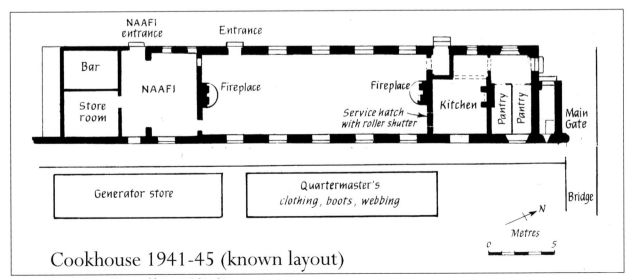

Cookhouse 1941-45 (known layout)

Map 9: *Brean Down Fort cookhouse, 1941–45.*

1943: A group of coastal gunners pose on the beach beneath the quarry area. Gunner Patterson in extreme left at the rear. To preserve the security of the location, the photo is marked 'Burnham-on-Sea'. (Ray Patterson)

Early-morning physical training of a run, regimented exercises and short competitive games, was taken by a physical training instructor and followed by a shower and shave and then breakfast. Dress was a woollen vest, long blue shorts, woollen khaki or grey socks and black plimsolls. Manning parade was at 8.30am when the roll was called and each man

might be inspected. Weekly inspections by Troop or Duty sergeants ensured that the soldiers themselves kept their huts and ablutions clean, as all armies have practised throughout the ages.

Soldiers nominated on the daily orders provided fatigue parties to collect rations, help cooks prepare the food by peeling potatoes and cleaning pots and

111

A 75mm mountain gun of the type used by coastal defences against enemy landing craft. (Imperial War Museum)

pans, ensuring the dining area was clean, collecting and disposing of waste and rubbish, providing men to clean the Officers' and Sergeants' Messes, indeed undertaking any other task needed to keep Brean Down fort self-sufficient, operational and effective. Others collected rations in a 3-tonner from a supply depot, near Lower Langford on the A38, the main road to Bristol.

At about 10.30, the fort almost came to a complete stop when everyone took advantage of NAAFI break, a half-an-hour stop for a cup of tea and a sticky bun. Training and normal duties then continued until lunch. Sports in the afternoon included basketball on the parade ground inside the fort and running over the down. The 1942 Regimental Sports Day was held on Brean Sands where a sergeant bet on Stevens, as favourite, to win a running race. However Stevens collided with another front runner, picked himself up, apologised, dusted him down and promptly lost the race, much to the fury of the sergeant. Sergeant Walford recalls watching this race.

Throughout the day guards based at the guardhouse provided security checks and patrolled the perimeter. Guard mounting, at 6pm, was a formal event with the Troops providing about eight men, each of whom was dressed in pressed battledress, with highly polished and shiny boots, and carrying their personal weapons, usually a 0.303 rifle. The Duty Officer inspected them. Patrols, often armed with Sten guns, scouted the down throughout the night. At dusk, the fort went into a night routine of strict blackout and patrols.

In the evening a liberty truck took some off-duty soldiers to a canteen run by Mr and Mrs Bert Gilling, assisted by their niece Eileen Hicks and other ladies, in the schoolroom of the Wesleyan Chapel in Brean. Other soldiers met with the Land Army girls working on farms. On Fridays and Saturdays, the liberty truck took off-duty soldiers to Burnham-on-Sea where the favourite pastime was the dances at the Pavilion.

For those who remained in camp, they would either gather in the NAAFI to chat, play games, such as Ukkers (a board game where you try to remove all your opponent's pieces), or remain in their huts reading, cleaning kit or perhaps dozing. The summer months allowed a little more flexibility with some fishing off the rocks or perhaps an evening walk. In the winter months, a member of each hut would collect coal from a small barbed-wire compound inside the fort.

Inevitably a close relationship developed between the regular gunners and the Home Guard. One of Sergeant Walford's tasks was to train them in small arms. Sometimes the Brean and Berrow Home Guard Platoon attacked the fort to exercise the garrison. On 6 September 1942, Brigadier R.J.P. Wyatt MC, Commander Somerset and Bristol Area (Southern Command) watched such an exercise. The Master-Gunner told Stevens he was in charge of the enemy and spreading his men across the down, they found the Home Guardsmen creeping along the cliffs on the leeward side of the fort. Hurling several thunderflashes and firing blanks, he had the satisfaction of seeing the Home Guard retire in some disorder whence they came. The security of the fort was once again assured although it was commonly said that two Germans armed with rifles could have captured the fort.

Inevitably the boredom of the routine invited some soldiers to mischief. On one occasion Stevens was stalking some nesting birds and was about grab a sheldrake when it flew off. He ran into the Master-Gunner's hut, grabbed a 0.22in (5.6mm) rifle and fired at the returning flock, winging one which then plunged into the sea, much to Stevens' frustration. Grabbing his bicycle, he pedalled hard along Military Road, past Harry Cox's house and sped down the hill. As he arrived on the beach, the dead bird was being gently pushed ashore. Stevens thrust the soaking corpse into his battledress jacket, cycled up the hill, crept past Cox's house and secreted the bird until his next pass and took it home. On another occasion he and a colleague stunned rabbits by shining a torch at them until an alert officer in Fire Command ordered them to "Put the bloody light out! And what the hell are you doing, anyway!"

Brean Down was also used by the RAF to train navigators and bomb-aimers, which was achieved by dropping bags of white chalk, and from 1943 by Airspeed Oxfords of 116 Squadron helping the air defence to calibrate their guns. The detachment set up in a range-control bunker of the cliff overlooking the Bird Farm. To help the pilots, a large area arrow was set in concrete pointing in the direction of the range. It was probably just as well the calibrators were protected for Reg Stevens remembers that the area around the arrow was covered in large white splodges from the sacks bursting on impact with the ground. Plans to establish a radar site on the down were rejected.

Above the northern cliffs near the hillfort, a battery of six Lewis guns, in a dual anti-motor torpedo boat and anti-aircraft role, mounted in circular chest-level emplacements, covered the low-level seaward approaches to Weston-super-Mare but it seems likely they were never manned. Nearby is Harry Cox's 'new house'. John Tucker can recall these guns being fired at targets towed by aircraft, which confirms Hazel Riley's interim report on Brean Down that the area was used for training.

The Americans had begun to arrive, with the Pontins holiday camp being converted into a US Army camp for 507 Ordnance Company. It also proved a valuable source of timber in exchange for local produce for farmer Hicks and his family. Italian prisoners-of-war, captured in the Western Desert and spread in prison camps throughout Somerset, were often seen in Brean cleaning out the rhynes (drainage ditches) using long handled shovels. Bill Tucker had a very sweet tooth and he frequently bargained geese in exchange for sugar so that by the end of the war, he had accumulated hundreds of bags.

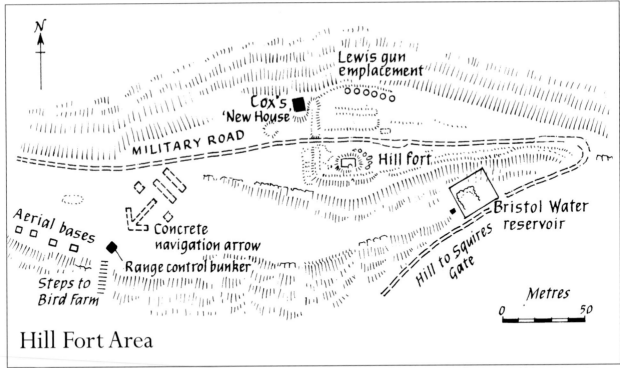

Map 10: *The hillfort area and range control. Note the concrete navigation arrow and Lewis gun emplacements, which survive today.*

Evidently some access to Brean Down was permitted and there is evidence that a Special Constable proposed to his future wife while overlooking Berrow Sands. John Tucker, son of Captain Bill Tucker, also visited with his father and can recall the guns being fired.

It was at the beginning of 1943 that 571 Coast Regiment ordered several battery exchanges to reduce the boredom of serving on Brean Down. On 20 January, 366 Coast Battery at Brean Down changed places with 189 Coast Battery on Steep Holm (North), a move that took just four hours, so the weather must have been good. Then 188 Coast Battery at Steep Holm (South) changed with 189 Coast Battery on Brean Down on 12 March but within five days the unit in charge of the two guns at Steep Holm (South) was reduced to a Care and Maintenance party of twelve men. Then 188 Coast Battery exchanged places with 366 Coast Battery, who returned to Brean Down on 27 May. A fortnight later, over two days seaward shoots with a 6-pounder anti-tank gun entertained the gunners brought by the Royal Ulster Rifles. The gunners showed the infantry a 6-inch shoot. One can only imagine the NAAFI that night must have been noisy!

By mid-October the war in Europe was beginning to turn against Germany although in the Far East the Allies were finding the Japanese a tough opponent. The threat of invasion was remote. One of the consequences of the fighting was to post regiments for front-line duties, in particular in the Mediterranean theatre where the Coast Regiment was tasked to defend the coasts against marauding E-boats and aircraft. This meant that batteries were reduced in strength. According to Sergeant Walford, there were a lot of postings to and from the Bristol Channel forts as the Allies' fortunes waned and then improved. He remembers a very short officer, who had seen active service, turning up, who regularly took his Troop for runs, during which they had to collect in their packs six house-bricks each, one by one, deposited at various points along the route, presumably to toughen them up.

Gunners Patterson and Stevens were posted to 120 Anti-Aircraft Regiment, which was equipped with 40mm Bofors mounted on Crusader tanks. Earmarked to support 4th Special Service Brigade for the D-Day landings, the regiment joined the Royal Marine Armoured Support Group. Stevens' landing craft was severely damaged by the weather and began to sink, but a destroyer about to take them in tow was diverted to deal with an E-Boat threat. Eventually they were towed to

Portsmouth and within 24 hours Stevens was on the Normandy beaches. Patterson's tank managed to leave its LCT but then bogged down on a sandbank. Patterson and Gunner Roy Clegg were left to man the guns while the remainder of the detachment landed. For the next six hours, as the tide flooded, Patterson and Clegg watched for German aircraft and kept themselves warm with cans of heated soup.

Subsequently, 120 Anti-Aircraft Regiment advanced in Germany and is credited with sinking a midget U-Boat near Flushing. They finished up in Dortmund and after a six-months' extension, Sergeant Stevens was demobbed and returned to his civilian occupation as fruit grower. Patterson was employed in a furniture factory until he took early retirement in the early 1980s.

Sergeant Walford transferred to the Royal Army Service Corps in 1943. Six days after D-Day he led a detachment towing 5.5-inch guns ashore on Gold Beach and eventually ended up in Bremen hauling spares for the *Prinz Eugen*, which was being prepared

for the atom-bomb test off Bikini Atoll. Discharged in May 1946, he returned to the Port of Bristol Authority and worked in various capacities until he retired, living in the same prefab that he and his wife had moved into after the war.

On 20 October 1943, Commander Royal Artillery Western Command initiated Operation Flood Tide to reduce the number of Coast Artillery units under the command, by reducing the batteries at Brean Down, Steep Holm (North) and Lavernock to Care and Maintenance basis. A senior gunnery instructor, Sergeant Reg Stone, from Weston-super-Mare, had served his entire war with Severn Fixed Defences and was posted from Brean Down as NCO-in-charge of thirty men to Steep Holm to close down both batteries. The one officer and eight other ranks of 184 Coast Battery at Portishead were placed with the Home Guard battery.

At Brean Down, within weeks equipment began to be removed. On 16 November the 22kW search-light generator was replaced by a 5kW generator capable of providing lighting and was handed to

A 6-pounder anti-tank gun. (Imperial War Museum)

115

A poor quality but very rare photograph taken in 1944 shows Captain Bill Tucker (nearest the shield) and other members of the Brean and Berrow Home Guard sitting on a 6-inch gun. (Stuart Hicks)

Commander Royal Engineers, Wells, three days later. The reduction of the 366 Coast Battery to Care and Maintenance clearly caused a few difficulties, as outlined in a memorandum to the War Office on 18 November from Headquarters Severn Fixed Defences. It seems likely that the original idea was to have a small caretaker unit to look after the fort:

Item 4: BREAN DOWN

The difficulties relative to this Battery are principally administrative. The caretaker will have to be:

(a) capable of working the diesel water pump(such an NCO is already earmarked)

(b) supplied with rations (it is 9 miles {14km} to the nearest shops)

(c) issued with one GS bicycle

(d) authorised with a generous scale of oil for light and fuel for heating, as the site is very exposed. Tentative enquiries are being made with Somerset sub-District relative to the foregoing. It is anticipated that these matters, with the exception of item (c) one GS bicycle, will be solved locally.

Item 5: Early disposal instructions for the service ammunition at Brean Down and the two Steep Holm batteries would be greatly appreciated.

Regrettably, the War Office reply is not known but it does seem that Brean Down was very soon downgraded. Its last recorded live firing was on 29 October 1943.

The Brean and Berrow Home Guard Platoon undertook some interesting training on the 6-inch guns at the fort, but it seems that the big guns were no longer fired. Instead, they used the 1-inch (25mm) aimable rifle on top of the gun-barrel to simulate live firing, but without the recoil, dust and noise. Hicks recalls that training took place on Sunday mornings under the instruction of Royal Artillery gunners. After parade at Platoon HQ, the Brean and Berrow Home Guard's Nissen hut, which was situated near the present-day Bird Garden, they boarded the Bristol Bus Company's No. 91 double-decker service bus for the journey by Squire's Gate and along Military Road on top of the down to the fort. Some of the Home Guard seem to have felt they were more at risk from this journey than they were from enemy action, and not without reason. As Hicks recounts:

> We young fellows sat on the bus and all the older people, 60 to 66, thought they would be killed going up and over so they wouldn't ride in the bus. So they walked it. We then had to sit at the top and call out 'Come on!' and they would be struggling up the hill. And then when we went down, they would walk down, the soldiers would march.

The soldiers were trained to handle a 100lb (45kg) projectile by laying the nose into the crook of the left arm. It was then passed from hand to hand between four soldiers, from the ready lockers to the gun where it was loaded. The cordite bag charge was then loaded and the breech closed. Hicks was detailed as layer and was strapped into a seat alongside the barrel. He recalls

> pedalling like mad to bring the gun around to the target, which was usually a buoy, out to sea

and when we lined it, we would say "Whoa, whoa! OK, fire!" I will always remember the power of the explosion and I was sitting in the chair and the barrel went back like this and then back again.

On 1 April 1944, HQ Severn Fixed Defences and 571 Coast Regiment were both disbanded under a total reorganisation of Coastal Artillery. At the same time 570 Coast Regiment, with its headquarters at Nells Point, Barry Island, took under its command all the operational and care and maintenance batteries. By 19 July, five weeks after D-Day and with most of the ports in occupied France recaptured, Severn Fixed Defences was reduced to Z – Flat Holm (North), Y – Flat Holm (South), both with two 4.5-inch guns, X – Cardiff) with two 75mm guns, and V – Works (Portishead) with two 6-inch guns. Non-operational batteries under care and maintenance, including Brean Down, were each placed in the hands of two RAOC armourer/storekeepers.

Members of 13th Bn Somerset Light Infantry (HG) before the stand-down dinner. The front rank was the battalion's officers. Behind them are members of the Brean and Berrow Home Guard. (Stuart Hicks)

On Sunday 3 December 1944, the Brean and Berrow Platoon paraded for the last time. The Stand Down of the Home Guard was sounded on 31 December and a year later, with the German surrender seven months old, the formation disappeared into legend and history. With the other organisations that had sprouted up throughout the country, it had provided a focal point for community spirit and patriotic outlet during the dark days of 1940 and although it was ignored as a threat in German intelligence and operational orders for Operation Sea Lion, it nevertheless filled a useful gap in the country's defences by expanding into transport, medical support, bomb disposal, air defence, coastal artillery and the nucleus of armed resistance. Altogether 1,206 Home Guard were killed and 557 wounded or injured by enemy action or accidents. Brean and Berrow Platoon lost no-one. Two George Crosses and thirteen George Medals were awarded to Home Guard soldiers.

After the war ended on 8 May 1945, and 570 Coast Regiment was finally disbanded on 1 June, the coastal strip gradually emptied of the troops and returned to its tranquillity to await the return of holidaymakers. The concrete posts on the beaches were dug up by the army or covered in sand but the fort remained largely forgotten.

Cartoons from the rear of the stand-down dinner menu. (Stuart Hicks)

NINE

Admiralty Department of Miscellaneous Weapons Development

During the shambles of Dunkirk in May 1940, a former naval Commander attempted to prevent low-level air attacks by flying kites. From these inauspicious beginnings the Admiralty formed, from civilian and military scientists and inventors, the Department of Miscellaneous Weapons Development (DMWD), who, over the next four years, researched and developed rocket-propelled weapons and systems. Most were pitchforked into uniform at a moment's notice and were unfamiliar with Service tradition, jargon and customs. One naval officer drafted to DMWD was the author Nevil Shute.

Early experiments were instigated in universities and laboratories throughout Great Britain, most aimed at creating havoc for invading German forces, such as spilling burning fuel onto the sea. The problem was that much of the smoke blew inshore onto the defenders. Other projects, such as 'Dazzle Gun', which was intended to blind enemy pilots, never reached production.

The rocket-propelled Parachute and Cable (PAC), developed by the Schermuly brothers, was, in effect an emergency balloon barrage, designed to foil low-level aircraft by firing a rocket carrying 500ft (152m) of steel cable, which then gently floated to the ground by parachute. At the height of the Battle of Britain, a PAC crippled a Dornier 17 attacking RAF Kenley and there are several recorded instances of 'kills' by ships carrying the system. As aircraft flew higher to avoid the PAC, the need arose for a more powerful system, which emerged as the Type-J. This could propel a cable rated at 5 tons 600ft (183m) aloft.

In 1941 Sub-Lieutenant John Francis arrived in Weston-super-Mare looking for a place where he could test his spigot mortar and came across the deserted 75-year-old Birnbeck Pier. The sandy beaches provided an excellent test area and the high rise and fall of the tide was ideal for testing underwater weapons. Francis persuaded its owners to give him a small room for his experiments and some RAF airmen volunteered to provide security. Other inventors then arrived.

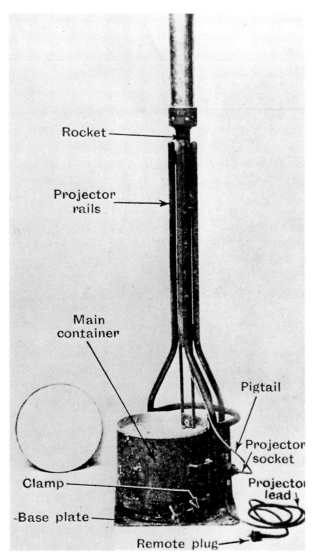

Rocket-propelled J-Type Parachute and Cable anti-aircraft device. (Mac Hawkins collection)

When the Admiralty learnt about the unauthorised use of Birnbeck Pier, they formally requisitioned it for DMWD and named it His Majesty's naval shore establishment HMS *Birnbeck*. It was initially commanded by Naval Officer, Watchet, Vice-Admiral John Casement, who later moved his

Brean Down Fort today: the ramp for projecting rocket-propelled experiments is still extant. To its left are the remains of No. 1 searchlight emplacement. (Author's collection)

headquarters to Weston-super-Mare. Bombs, mines, other weapons and odd-looking shapes were soon being sent to Weston-super-Mare by couriers travelling by train, and the pier was soon playing a memorable role in Admiralty research.

The slot machine hall was converted into a sleeping quarters for visitors and the damp chill was warmed by an efficient Tortoise stove. The permanent staff used the Tea Room. Messing was a little erratic, with a combination of local purchase, scrounging and formal issue. Informality between ranks was not discouraged. Several PAC Type-J posts were placed on the pier in the hope that enemy bombers bound for Bristol would pass close to Weston-super-Mare; none did, much to the frustration of the scientists.

In 1942 at the height of the Battle of the Atlantic, an early weapon to be tested was the 'Expendable Noise Maker'. Fired from shipborne mortars, it emitted a series of rhythmic detonations below the surface to attract enemy acoustic torpedoes. For some reason, the army was entrusted with

testing the prototype. With the launch tube on a wing of the pier about 40ft (12m) above sea level and aimed across Weston Bay, the first round sailed clean over the water and exploded in mid-air near a café. Puzzled by the trajectory, the soldiers adjusted the elevation, fired and watched in horror as the second round landed outside the office of Vice-Admiral Casement, showering the staff inside with debris, glass and stones.

After this episode, Expendable Noise Maker trials were moved to Brean Down Fort where a launch-pad, in the form of an 80ft (24m) rail with a five-degree slope, was laid between No. 1 Emplacement and its searchlight. Strict orders were issued to the garrison that no-one was to mention what they had seen, and indeed security was so tight on Brean Down that there are few wartime photographs of the fort. Some tests failed with spectacular results, much to the amusement of the watching gunners. In one instance the first round behaved as expected but the next projectile behaved quite differently. All went well initially and then it careered inland, eventually exploding inside a chicken coop at Brean Down Farm, covering the farmer working inside with dirt, chicken feathers and smashed eggs. His reported reaction was "Not another cock-up!", according to Gunner Reg Stevens. The scientists returned to the drawing board and designed a rocket-propelled container, which ejected several small acoustic devices across the sea to confuse the torpedoes.

Another anti-submarine device apparently tested, according to Rodney Legg, at Brean Down Fort was 'Amuck'. This consisted of twelve 2-inch (52mm) rockets fixed to a Mark II Depth Charge, which boosted the range to at least 500yd (455m) on calm day, considerably further than conventional dischargers. If there was a need to reduce the range, corresponding pairs of the rockets were removed. Initially, Amuck entered service on a ramp mounted on the bows of destroyers and corvettes but this was replaced by a turntable, also on the bows, to give nearly 300-degree angle of coverage and therefore greater flexibility. 'Rocket Spear' was the simplest of devices. Literally a rocket-propelled spear with a cast iron flute, it was designed to rip a hole in the pressurised hull of a U-Boat. Within eight weeks of being invented, it had entered service and accounted for a U-Boat.

In early 1943 DMWD were instructed by the Admiralty to carry out an "investigation of the effects, size, density, moment of inertia, speed and height of launching of Baseball". Although no work was done at HMS *Birnbeck* on Barnes Wallis's bouncing bomb, 'Baseball' was a naval version of the dambusting skipping bomb, designed to be fired from motor torpedo boats. One of the country's greatest fears was that if a German battleship, such as the *Tirpitz*, breached the Allied blockade, it could wreak havoc in the Atlantic convoys. The raid by No. 2 Army Commando in March 1942 on the large dry docks at St Nazaire was designed to keep German capital ships away from the English Channel but had led to high casualties.

The idea was to fit rails along the deck of the MTBs from which rocket-propelled trolleys would launch the 70lb (31.8kg) steel circular canisters, which would bounce along the surface of the sea to the target, sink and explode. Hydraulic cylinders at the end of rails were designed to act as buffers to bring the trolley to a complete stop. Initial trials were encouraging although the speed of the missile at about 200mph (320kph) threatened to take the pier with it. However, setbacks were experienced in launching a bomb successfully. Even the combined

speed given the projectile by a fast boat and the rocket-propelled ejection from its launch rail was insufficient to make the device spin far enough.

On 15 February 1943, the rocket-propelled trolley hurtled down the rail and was stopped by the ram but the force of the rockets was not controlled and their concentrated blast ripped apart sandbags. The first timed trial took place on 27 February, using four 5-inch (127mm) rockets to drive the carriage. The trolley was stopped at 172ft per second (117mph/187kph) but the launching mechanism failed. The same day, another trial using six rockets saw the speed raised to 230ft per second (158mph/245kph) but this time the ram struck the cylinder, severing twelve bolts retaining the assembly unit and, out of control, the entire contraption smashed into the sea some 80ft (24m) offshore, a mass of crumpled metal and flying hawsers.

On the day, Cyril Lemon, who was employed by the builders' merchants Leslie Dyer of Weston-super-Mare, was visiting Brean Down Fort to see how his men were getting on building a large concrete base sunk into the ground and fitted with all sorts of restraining chains and bolts for some sort of device. Lemon, who was in the Home Guard, was stopped by a sentry at the guardhouse and told he could go no further. He said he never had any problems before but nevertheless he was told he could not enter the fort. There was then a huge explosion. Lemon later learnt that several of his workmen had been bowled over and that the force of the blast had ripped up the concrete. The track had to be re-levelled and a 7ft 6in (2.25m) bunker dug into the bund protecting the deep Victorian central magazine.

Trials of Baseball continued, so that it could be fired at 400ft per second (272mph/436kph). The new catapult was located at Middle Hope Cove, to the north of Weston-super-Mare, where the catapult could be stopped in sand dunes and the secrecy of the developments secured. In spite of the hard work, many trials and relative success of the Dambuster raid on 16 May 1943, Baseball never quite worked satisfactorily.

As the Allies adopted a more offensive strategy in 1942 and could think about attacking the Axis, so the work of DMWD turned to projects to help assaulting units disembarking from landing craft. One of the greatest difficulties was clearing obstacles on beaches, in particular mines, without decreasing the momentum of the assault. Dr Guggenheim had developed the shipborne anti-submarine weapon 'Hedgehog', which could fire up to 24 depth charges 200yd (180m) ahead of the ship. Sinking fast in a circular pattern of 130ft (40m) diameter at a prescribed depth, the canisters exploded, which either damaged and forced an enemy submarine to the surface or sank it. Although Hedgehog was a lethal weapon, the conservatively-minded Royal Navy took time to accept it; nevertheless, by 1945 it was credited by them, together with Commonwealth and other Allied navies, with at least fifty submarines as 'kills'.

The circular pattern of Hedgehog anti-submarine depth charges: on the extreme right two projectiles can be seen about to hit the surface. By the time Hedgehog entered service with the Royal Navy, well-developed tactics with depth charges had evolved. The weapon was more readily embraced by the US Navy in its operations against Japanese submarines in the Pacific theatre. (Mac Hawkins collection)

Using the same principles, Guggenheim developed 'Hedgerow', a predecessor of the modern 'Giant Viper' mine-clearing device, and it was first tested on Berrow Flats. Using several hundred captured German Teller mines, lifted from the Western Desert and relaid on Berrow Flats, the beaches were cleared by Hedgerow mortar bombs fired from batteries of spigots in specially designed Landing Craft Assault (LCA). The spigots were mounted at different angles and could achieve a range from 315yd (96m) to 475yd (145m), blasting a path 120yd (36m) long and 8yd (2.5m) wide. The system was first used at the Salerno landings in Italy and although used by quickly trained crews, one barrage cleared a path through a minefield in scrub. On

D-Day, 45 Hedgerows accompanied the first waves of the invasion force and helped breached German defences.

Not all the work was for the Royal Navy. The War Office asked if the PAC Type J could stop tanks. The Guards Armoured Division drove a Valentine tank to the beach below Brean Down but not before it suffered a steering failure and had crashed into a pub, much to the embarrassment of its commander. The trial was a success and the Valentine was brought to a shuddering halt. It took two days to untangle and cut the cable from the tracks.

In 1943 Airborne Forces asked DMWD to develop a method to drop vehicles, guns and heavy stores by parachute accurately and without damage. The scientists installed a nest of rockets underneath the loaded platform, which when ignited slowed the rate of descent. The project was known as 'Elijah'. The time came to photograph the descent of the device and the sea around Birnbeck Pier was selected. After dropping the first loaded platform too far out to sea, the Lancaster pilot was asked to drop it nearer the pier. Bomb doors open, the aircraft thundered in at 2,000ft (600m) and out tumbled the platform. Unfortunately the rockets failed to ignite and with deadly accuracy, the platform smashed into the engineering shop on HMS *Birnbeck*, sheared a steel joist, and demolished a covered way leading to a jetty and narrowly missed a group of Wrens preparing lunch.

One of the more spectacular systems was the firing of rocket-propelled grapnels for Combined Operations Headquarters. The system was tested on 3 June 1943 and showed that a rope ladder could be fired 200ft (60m) up a cliff and a 2½-inch (65mm) rope at least 300ft (90m). However, the system was too noisy for raiding, but it achieved fame a year later when D, E and F Companies, 2nd (US) Rangers successfully climbed cliffs at Pointe du Hoc to assault a German battery, in spite of losing fifty of the two hundred of their number.

One of the first hazards faced by the assaulting troops was 'cross-decking' from transport ships to landing-craft, with heavily-laden soldiers stepping over the side and climbing down nets into landing-craft, which were being tossed about by the sea. It was dangerous and time consuming. Falls into the sea between the two vessels were not uncommon. Shortly before D-Day the Army requested a method to speed up this 'cross-decking'. DMWD developed

A bank of Hedgerow rocket-propelled landmine-clearing device spigots on board a landing craft. (Mac Hawkins collection)

'Helter Skelter', which consisted of a long, ribbed rigid-rubber tube down which soldiers could slide into landing-craft standing off from the transport. Using US troops from camps in Berrow, the trials were carried from the end of HMS *Birnbeck*. After initial trepidation, the soldiers found the experiment such fun that DMWD had difficulty in persuading them to return to their units. Helter Skelter was introduced into service and fitted to several Castle-line troopships for D-Day.

A problem faced by D-Day planners was the construction of a safe harbour to supply the beachhead. An observation by an American scientist noted that bubbles of air tended to calm waves. The initial sea trials of 'Bubble Breakwater' proved inconclusive, although, to be fair, the tests were carried out in poor weather and driving rain, but the finding that it needed to be anchored to the seabed was important. In the event Bubble Breakwater proved impractical but from it emerged floating 'Lilo' breakwaters, which were just one of the measures used to protect the Mulberry Harbour off the Arromanches beaches from up to Force 6 winds. HMS *Birnbeck* also carried out trials to test the unwinding of the Pipe Line Under The Ocean (PLUTO) and made special buoys to mark its route. PLUTO was an ingenious method to ensure the rapid transfer of petrol from the United Kingdom to Normandy and avoided the need for fleets of tankers.

All inventors and scientists, even those in uniform, are often thought to be slightly odd. However, without their eccentricities and strange ideas, many events of the Second World War would not have happened and things that we use today would never have been invented. The scientists at DMWD played their part in the development of rocket-propelled weapon systems and although not all worked, some such as Hedgehog and Hedgerow, were vital in winning the war. Those who worked at HMS *Birnbeck* were fondly known as 'The Wheezers and Dodgers'.

TEN

Brean Down Fort, 1945–2000

'THE KNOCKERS-DOWN AND DIGGERS-UP'

Aerial photograph taken on 13 January 1946, showing buildings and field defences. (English Heritage)

Early in 1945, the guns were removed and by June two military caretakers were the sole occupants of Brean Down Fort. While Steep Holm and Flat Holm remained relatively inaccessible to the public, and therefore their fortifications are relatively well preserved, the post-war story of Brean Down Fort – abandoned to the elements and again a venue for inquisitive Sunday afternoon walkers and summer visitors – is a sorry tale of bureaucratic disagreement, several reports and over the years a failure to conserve an important part of Great Britain's military history. In the meantime the buildings crumbled, largely ignored except minimal repairs to make them safe. In 1949 Captain Harry Cox died, after several decades as the respected guardian of Brean Down.

View from the air, taken 11 March 1948, showing hillfort area, RAF range control arrow and buildings. (English Heritage)

Back under civil control

Weston-super-Mare Borough Council considered buying Brean Down from the Wyndham Trust, to whom the fort had been returned by the War Office, but were beaten to the post by Axbridge Rural District Council, who paid £3,000 in 1954 with the proviso that there should be free and unrestricted

access to the down. Any part was prohibited from being used for business, trade and entertainment.

To commemorate the Festival of Britain, Axbridge then handed 155 acres (62.7ha), which was all of the down except the fort, to the National Trust, who then leased it back for 99 years at the rent of 10 shillings per annum. The police and Army Cadet Force regularly used the Brean Down cliffs to climb and practice rescue techniques.

So far as the fort was concerned, Weston-super-Mare Council purchased it from the Wyndham Trust for £1,500. However, much of the Second World War accommodation and defences was becoming derelict and dangerous. Somerset County Council accepted an offer by Mr Michael Dewar, whose father had pioneered the National Parks movement, to bring volunteers to help clear up Exmoor, the Quantocks and other open spaces, including Brean Down. With the threat to the nation now seen to be from the air, the Coast Regiment – formerly in charge at Brean Down – was disbanded in 1956.

In August 1958, Cambridge University undergraduate John North and five individuals interested in conservation, including a Dutchman and a Pakistani, cleared some of the buildings, electricity poles and corrugated iron left over from the dismantled Nissen huts. The field defences were particularly difficult to clear because they had become entangled with eleven years' worth of undergrowth. Reinforced gloves provided by Axbridge RDC wore out within two days. Two buildings too difficult for the students to tackle were later blown up by 205 Field Squadron RE (TA).

On the down were also a group of archaeologists from Bristol University Speleological Society under the direction of Mr Arthur Simpson, archaeological lecturer at Queen's University, Belfast, who between 1956 and 1958 excavated the site of the Romano-British temple. They had already found coins, parts of a skeleton and pottery, although it was thought that early Christians might have looted the site looking for pagan religious artefacts.

Both groups stayed in the fort and although their accommodation was basic, Somerset County Council, who paid their travelling expenses and food, provided a barrel of cider. Known by the local newspapers as 'The Knockers Down and Diggers Up', their meals were prepared by Ann Duckett and Marion Davies, both on a course at the Bath College of Domestic Science. Every two days the archaeologists and the 'Knockers Down' hauled a 180-gallon

Cambridge University 'Knockers and Diggers' students demolish a building in the quarry area, August 1958. (Author's collection)

(800l) bowser to Brean Down Farm to fill it with water and then back to the fort. An article in a local newspaper mistakenly suggested that the fort had been built by French prisoners-of-war during the Napoleonic wars.

The following summer 12 apprentices from London's East End and Mr Gordon Stead, of Holme Valley Grammar School, and 6 boys of Leysian Mission Boys' Club in Shoreditch, working under a Civic Trust work scheme formed by Home Office minister Duncan Sandys, spent a fortnight dismantling the defences. They were one of nearly thirty groups of young people who volunteered to give up part or all of their holidays to restore beauty spots throughout the country. Most were unpaid, but were given their rail or bus fares and food, which they cooked for themselves.

At a Weston-super-Mare Borough Council debate at the end of June 1961, Councillor Gerald Wadham, a National Trust member and lecturer, suggested that if the fort was to avoid being spoilt by a service establishment, a hovercraft base, a nuclear power station or a hotel being built on the site, it should be handed to the National Trust. If this was rejected, he suggested that it should be used for something useful and proposed a casino complete with a yachting marina to attract the wealthy. Wadham learned that the buildings were 'of some historic interest' but seems to have assumed they were of the early nineteenth-century Napoleonic Wars period, as opposed to the period of Napoleon III. Members, by a large majority, re-

affirmed the council's intention to retain the land on which the fort stood, but did not publicly declare why this decision had been reached. This was the first of many debates about its future.

In September, the borough council rejected Wadham's idea of a casino and confirmed its intention to keep Brean Down Fort, but nevertheless expressed a determination that it and the land should remain open space. As the debate gathered pace, an editorial in the *Weston Evening Post* reported that the fort was in a dilapidated state and asked what were the Council going to do about it. A month later Wadham continued his campaign to hand the fort to the National Trust but Alderman Holcombe, although not against the trust having the fort, was in favour of the council retaining some control over it. Councillor Salisbury suggested the fort should be used for youth activities.

An editorial in the *Evening Post* dated 13 October 1961 was highly critical of the borough council's decisions, declaring:

> It is woolly thinking on the part of Weston Councillors to suggest the Trust might change their mind over the future of Brean Down. The Trust are forbidden to exploit their possessions or develop them in the way that some councils have seen fit to deal with their beauty spots.
>
> Rather the council are acting like a small child grimly hanging onto its possession without having the least idea why it should do so.

At no stage during the debate about the disposal of Brean Down did Weston-super-Mare Borough Council or its successors ever state their intentions about the fort. No doubt mindful of the vested interests common in politics, Councillor Wadham was correct to challenge his fellow-councillors for their views but when, in July 1963, a Mr Andrew Gibson applied to open a café at the fort, it took two years for the council to turn down his application as uneconomic.

By January 1966 so many cars were being driven onto the down that Axbridge Rural District Council sought the help of Brean Parish Council to appoint wardens to keep Squire's Gate locked. However, the locks were either stolen or broken, and so recommendations were made to place a car park near Brean Down café. Although the people of Brean were still allowed to take their cars to the fort once a year, the banning of cars otherwise effectively meant that only the fit and healthy could visit the down. On 22 October 1971, a Mr D. Hutchins of Burnham-on-

Sea believed he had found the fort's main gate keys on the beach, and he handed them in to Burnham-on-Sea museum.

On 6 March 1973, Weston-super-Mare Borough Council finally offered the fort to the National Trust because councillors felt that with the imminent local government reorganisation, the fort would fall outside its jurisdiction and therefore its perceived close link with the town would be lost. On 11 September the Finance and General Purpose Committee were advised that the trust had rejected the offer on the ground that it was not prepared to pay for the fort's repair and maintenance. The members agreed to offer it to Axbridge Rural District Council, because they had originally administered Brean Down and had also entered into the deed of covenant relative to Brean Down with the National Trust. The *Western Daily Press*, which reported on the meeting, seemed to think the fort was a relic of the 1914–18 war.

In a debate a week later, Axbridge Councillor Frank Adams said the fort was not so much a white elephant as a white dinosaur, but nevertheless the council agreed to buy it at a nominal cost. Councillor Mrs Rosemary Unwin agreed that, while

the fort was a national asset, it was "an eyesore ... and should be demolished and the land allowed to go back to nature like Sand Point".

In 1974 the four acres (1.6ha) surrounding the fort were acquired from the National Trust, subject to protective covenants that the land would be as retained as 'open space' with no development permitted except with the permission of the trust. This provision that the trust must be included in any projects for the fort's future use was rigorously applied thereafter to the disadvantage of the fort.

In April the same year, a proposal to re-activate the wartime communications cable from Weston-super-Mare to Brean Down Fort and then underwater to Steep Holm, to provide a telephone link for Mr Peter Rees, of Dorchester, who had just taken over on the island as the Kenneth Allsop Trust warden, foundered when GPO and 10th Signal Regiment personnel, using geophone detectors, found that a considerable length had been removed, probably stolen, for scrap.

The new Sedgemoor District Council absorbed Axbridge Rural District Council and one of its first acts, on 16 February 1977, was to invite a twenty-

A hovercraft on Weston-super-Mare sands. There was a suggestion that Brean Down Fort should become a hovercraft port. (David Lock)

127

strong detachment from the Dover-based 54 Squadron Junior Leaders Regiment RE to demolish the 10-ton reinforced roofs of the two 6-inch gun emplacements, which had become corroded. Commanded by the commando-trained sapper Captain Russ Tolley from Clevedon, the sappers, whose average age was seventeen, had recently passed their combat engineer Level 3 course and this was their first practical experience at demolition. The troop camped on the hard-standing in the quarry.

Inviting the army to blow them up was much cheaper than engaging a commercial demolition company and indeed kept the army in the public eye. Major Len Wilson, Tolley's airborne-trained squadron commander, also visited the site as did a local BBC crew. The BBC were later pestered into giving Wilson's mother a private showing of their film because she had missed seeing it on television.

For two days members of the public were banned from Brean Down, the sea around Howe Rocks was closed to shipping and the airspace above the fort denied to aircraft. The original intention was to carry

Major Len Wilson and Captain Russ Tolley. Note the covered emplacements and the generator building in the moat. In the background the bridge to No. 1 CASL is still intact. (Lt-Col Len Wilson)

out the demolition on the Sunday but this was changed to Monday so as not to disturb people. The operation was in two stages. By placing plastic explosive around their base and then electrically firing the fuses, the outer steel supports were severed. The same exercise was repeated with the inner supports. More explosive than necessary was used: the explosions were heard over a wide area and windows rattled in Weston-super-Mare and Berrow. When council workmen moved in to remove the debris, the Area Works Manager, Mr John Houlker, later declared that he was very pleased with the army's work.

Sedgemoor District Council were now faced with a problem: what to do with Brean Down Fort? Records show several files of correspondence and reports from the council and several other elected and conservation bodies keen to do something sympathetic to the character, history and environment of Brean Down. However, in the background remained the National Trust with its direct responsibility for Brean Down and its restricting covenant over the fort.

During the late 1970s, several inquiries examined harnessing the tidal power of the Severn Estuary by building a dam from Brean Down across to Sully Island. The waters of the Bristol Channel are not deep and some fears were raised that, since the upper reaches would become a lake, industrial pollutants from both north and south banks would damage the environment. An alternative view was that without tidal flow, sediment would drop to the seabed, as opposed to being washed to and fro by the tide, and, since the sea bed is bedrock, the lake would become clear water and therefore an attraction, Mediterranean-style, for safe sailing and an expanding leisure industry that would benefit Weston-super-Mare. The greatest concern, however, was the environmental damage to the area during the building phase. The proposal to build a dam has haunted some people in Brean ever since and this fear surfaced more than once during proposals to restore the fort. By the end of the decade the proposals were shelved.

In October 1977, Sedgemoor Council and the National Trust produced their 'Brean Down, Somerset: Management Plan', which was the first comprehensive study of Brean Down and its relationship to local use and tourism. In paragraphs on the natural history, it emphasised that ecologically "the community is unique in Great Britain" and had that year been listed as a Grade 1 site in the White Conservation Review and was also a Site of Special Scientific Interest. In an interesting review of the management of Brean Down, the report listed two

February 1977: sappers blow up parts of the fort. Note the demolished overhead cover of No. 2 6-inch emplacement. No. 1 emplacement has already suffered the same fate. (Westair).

prime objectives, conservation management and recreation management.

So far as conservation management is concerned, the four principles proposed by the report to preserve the natural and historical features were

- protection from excessive pressure and development
- conservation of the important plant communities and bird life
- conservation of the archaeological features
- sympathetic maintenance of the remains of the nineteenth-century fort

In relation to recreation, just two principles were listed as necessary to present the property as an attractive and interesting place, namely

- control of vegetation to give unrestricted pedestrian access where possible

- presentation and interpretation of the important features for the general public

Although the National Trust appeared assiduous in protecting the ecological and botanical features of Brean Down, it remains the case that few members of the public know where the archaeological sites are, because they are unmarked, and pedestrians can go virtually anywhere, with consequent erosion of the terrain. The historical features have not been interpreted and as consequence, the Iron Age fort, the nineteenth-century fort and the RAF range-control post have largely been ignored and allowed to degrade. There is no doubt that, while the spirit was evident, the willingness to preserve the historical conservation was weak. Nevertheless, very many aspects of this joint report were included in the 1998 lottery bid to preserve the fort and its associated facilities.

Explosion as sappers demolish a building. (Bristol Evening Post)

In some circles Brean Down Fort was still seen to be a tourist attraction. In November 1977 a plan to build a narrow-gauge railway from Uphill to Brean Down was refused by the planning authorities on the grounds that, although an excellent facility for tourists, it was more important to "safeguard the natural amenities of Brean Down and National Trust property".

Sedgemoor Council then said they were "taking steps to schedule the fort as an ancient monument" and that they would be erecting signs to tell people what had happened at the fort. The National Trust erected the only signs, but these gave minimal information about the fort, its history and buildings.

In July 1980 a report, commissioned by the National Trust, on the structural survey of the fort by the surveyors Houghton, Greenless & Associates found the buildings to be in good condition although faults were beginning to emerge, namely, inherent weaknesses in the construction materials, and prob- ed by age, leaks, weathering and finally by and other unknown influences. It seems ational Trust began to carry out essential ng young people under the Youth es Programme but when there were two

accidents, the work was handed over to a contractor.

In November 1983 a group of eleven local men, supervised by Mr Paul Richards, were employed by the Manpower Services Commission to make the buildings safe. Sponsored by Sedgemoor District Council, who gave £10,000 to the project, and the National Trust to restore the fort; the local media made much of the fact that the men would be working in wet and windy conditions. Shortly afterwards Brean Down had its second fatality when one of the men, from the village of Mark, was found dead on the beach. With his wheelbarrow still on the cliff, it is not known what actually happened. The man left a widow and two small daughters.

In February 1989, Mr Victor Smith BA, Conservation Officer of the Fortress Study Group, carried out an extensive survey of the fort on behalf of the National Trust to examine the feasibility of restoring and interpreting the fort. His findings were printed in a report entitled 'Images of Brean Down Fort, 1870–1945'. Knowing that its disposal had been discussed for several years, Mr Smith hoped to bring

that consideration to a conclusion so that a programme for the positive development of the fort may result. With the rising tide of public interest in visiting post-mediaeval artillery fortifications, the time is right for this to happen.

For the first time a person with experience in presenting the fort to the public suggested that guides were a labour-intensive and inefficient means of visitor management whereas a self-guiding booklet would allow visitors complete freedom to explore the place at their own pace. Smith suggested that physical security measures, including closed circuit television cameras, were important to protect displays. It was largely on the strength of this report that eight years later Sedgemoor District Council led its failed bid to the Heritage Lottery Fund. The response by the National Trust to this forward-thinking report is not known but judging by the continued 'ruinisation' of the fort, the recommendations were largely rejected.

Two years later the engineering consultants Mann Williams examined the two Coastal Artillery Searchlight positions, on behalf of the National Trust, to determine the risk of their dilapidation. By this time, access to Number One position was achievable only by scrambling over the rocks. The bridge had been blown up the Royal Engineers and can still be seen between the rocks.

In 1992 Brean Parish Council complained to Sedgemoor District Council of the filthy state and untidiness of the fort and asked that something be done about it. A young man had fallen to his death when an eroded sheep track collapsed, pitching him over the cliffs. At about the same time a visitor found evidence of satanic rites being held in the large magazine, namely a five-pointed star with candles at the apexes and the centre. In February the next year English Heritage affirmed that the fort was of national importance.

In 1993 the first historical survey of Brean Down Fort and its relationship to the defence of the nation was written by Dr John Barrett, a member of the Fortress Study Group, and published as *A History of the Maritime Forts in the Bristol Channel, 1866–1900*. Reviewing the forts and paying tribute to the Coast Regiment, he suggested that a single 7-inch RML should be mounted at Brean Down because, unlike Steep Holm, where Rodney Legg had carried out conservation work, the fort was the only one of the

Severn Fixed Defences that survived and was also still accessible to the public.

The Manchester Metropolitan University Study

The same year, in October, Sedgemoor District Council, English Heritage and the National Trust commissioned the Centre for Environmental Interpretation of Manchester Metropolitan University to carry out an in-depth assessment of the feasibility of converting the fort into a visitor centre. One of those consulted was Mr Alan Wynn, a quantity surveyor from Burnham-on-Sea.

Manchester's report recommended several options, including restoring and developing the fort as a visitor centre, with a field study centre, and converting the Master-Gunner's quarters into holiday cottages. The report commented that the fort was already a significant destination for visitors, most of who had no idea about the history of the place. It was a fascinating place but the report continued:

> The fact that the site, a scheduled ancient monument, is unmanaged and has an air of dereliction and neglect, reflects badly on Sedgemoor District Council as owners of the Fort and, by association, the National Trust as managers of Brean Down.

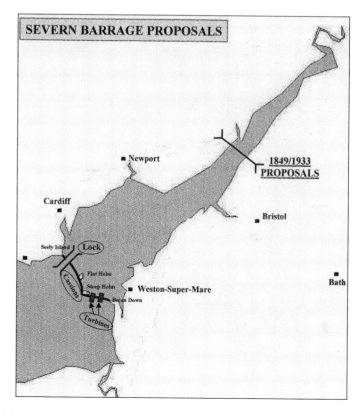

(Right) **Map 11:** *Severn Barrage proposals in the 1970s would have involved the linking of Brean Down, Steep Holm, Flat Holm and Lavernock Point. This was doomed to failure for environmental reasons, apart from the enormous costs involved.*

It was a damning indictment of the conservation record of the National Trust, as a national conservation body, in particular.

In 1994, Sedgemoor District Council commissioned the civil engineers Whybrow Associates to examine the fort. They found the buildings slowly deteriorating with weathering and age, and in need of refurbishment.

Meanwhile, four private individuals formed themselves into the Brean Down Fort Group and in 1994 began to negotiate with Sedgemoor District Council to instigate action to preserve and interpret the fort. Initially, Sedgemoor District Council offered the Group the chance to take the fort off their hands for £1 and to give a £40,000 endowment to enable the new owners to improve the "crumbling landmark" but, attractive though the option was, it was rejected for several reasons, not the least of which was liability in the event of an accident, as well as the National Trust's powers of veto lurking in the background.

The Sedgemoor Lottery Bid

Eventually common sense prevailed and Sedgemoor District Council brought together several heritage and environmental agencies to discuss what to do with the place. By October, an outline plan had emerged, the idea being to breathe life back into the fort by establishing a visitors' centre, an educational and cultural centre, and by refurbishing the gun positions and associated facilities.

In spite of the claims of opponents, from the very start the balance of retaining the tranquil nature of Brean Down with the commercial pressures of renovating the fort was deemed to be critical. In a proposal to Sedgemoor District Council, the Brean Down Fort Group proposal stated that

> the key issue in the proposals is to balance the commercial nature of the proposals against the ecological and environmental nature of the headland, bearing in mind that it is owned by the National Trust.

Air photograph of Brean Down Fort taken in August 1996. (Author's collection)

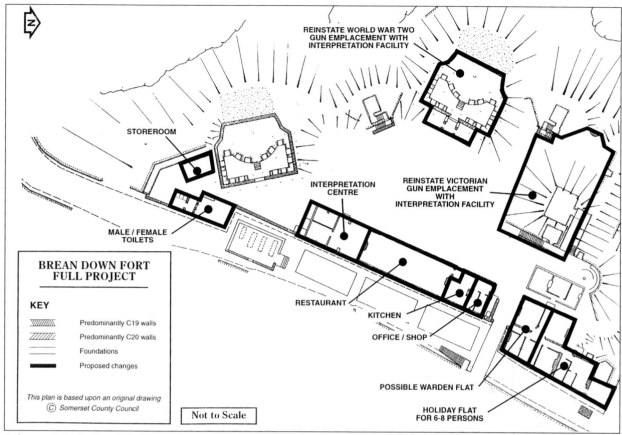

REINSTATE WORLD WAR TWO GUN EMPLACEMENT WITH INTERPRETATION FACILITY

STOREROOM

MALE / FEMALE TOILETS

INTERPRETATION CENTRE

REINSTATE VICTORIAN GUN EMPLACEMENT WITH INTERPRETATION FACILITY

BREAN DOWN FORT FULL PROJECT

KEY

⬛ (hatch)	Predominantly C19 walls
⬛ (hatch)	Predominantly C20 walls
—	Foundations
▬	Proposed changes

This plan is based upon an original drawing © *Somerset County Council*

Not to Scale

RESTAURANT

KITCHEN

OFFICE / SHOP

POSSIBLE WARDEN FLAT

HOLIDAY FLAT FOR 6-8 PERSONS

Sedgemoor District Council's plan for the restoration of the fort. (Sedgemoor District Council)

At a Leisure and Tourism committee meeting the same month, Sedgemoor District Council allocated £40,000 to the repair of the fort.

In the New Year the first major meeting took place at which everyone, including English Heritage, agreed that any proposals must also achieve a balance between conservation needs and financial viability. English Heritage also expressed a willingness to consider diverting funds towards the refurbishment. On 16 November the National Trust wrote that

> The National Trust would like to see the buildings put into good repair and suitable use made of them, which would particularly conserve their historical integrity.

The aim was to open the refurbished fort to the public on 5 July 2000, exactly 100 years after Gunner Haines had blown half of it up, apparently with a well-aimed shot into No. 3 Magazine.

Throughout 1995 the project gained momentum with management and architectural meetings. The fort was registered with the Royal Commission on the Historical Monuments of England and the Defence of Britain Project. Brean Parish Council, who evidently saw themselves as guardians of Brean Down, initially agreed with the plans. Meanwhile other forts, such as Fort Nelson near Portsmouth and Fort Nothe in Weymouth, were being restored and shown to the public, some by consortia of private individuals and others by councils.

Victor Smith's belief – that the public was interested in the history and functions of Palmerston's forts – was bearing fruit. It was hoped that Brean Down Fort would provide that interest in the northern part of the south-west region. Other parties expressed an interest in the project including English Nature, who not unnaturally wished to preserve the ecology of the down but were happy to see the fort provide interpretation facilities. Somerset County Council was also generally supportive and the heritage architects, Architectron of Bristol, were engaged to carry out the design work.

By the middle of 1995, Architectron had a developed a plan to interpret a Victorian 7-inch RML and Second World War 6-inch emplacement, create a museum, convert the Officers' Mess and Master-Gunner's accommodation into several small holiday flats, and refurbish the soldiers block as a refreshment area and shop, thereby bringing the fort back to life. The magazines were also going to be interpreted. A charitable trust would manage the fort and its activities. Lord Jeffrey Archer of Weston-super-Mare and Mark was one of several people invited to become a patron to the fort, although he declined.

To keep the military dimension of the fort and preserve the tranquillity of Brean Down, no vehicles, except something like a jeep, were going to be permitted. This would give the disabled and infirm a military-history experience and a company that could convert suitable military vehicles was identified. This also would have been suitable for parents with babies and toddlers. Otherwise, visitors would be encouraged to walk to the fort along Military Road and not all over Brean Down, something which the National Trust has done little or nothing to stop. Bearing in mind that, before the war, boatmen from Weston-super-Mare ferried visitors from the town, a plan emerged to build a jetty on the beach below the single 7-inch RML position.

The National Trust, wary as ever and as they would fatally remain throughout the project, said "the fort is very important historically and archaeological and the National Trust would be very interested to talk to the local authorities". At a meeting at the council offices, the first wavering of the National Trust was detected when their Brean Down warden said he did not wish to damage relations with local farmers. Nevertheless, in March 1995 the National Trust were supportive of the project.

When a decision was agreed to seek a grant from the Heritage Lottery Fund, Sedgemoor District Council began grinding through the bureaucratic complexities of a bid. Part of the process was to gauge public opinion and throughout the year briefings were given. At a private meeting, Brean District Council indicated general support in the village. Present at that meeting was Councillor Stuart Hicks, who had served at the fort as a Home Guardsman. Sedgemoor District Council also distributed several hundred questionnaires and thus it was with some confidence that Somerset County Council, Sedgemoor District Council, and the Brean Down Group faced a formal meeting on 8 November 1995 at Brean.

However the political framework of local parish councillors led to opposition. The Brean Residents Association were hostile, and one of their members, while claiming to be conservationist, suggested the fort should be "razed to the ground". A farmer then said he was apprehensive about the role of a member of the Brean Down Group because McAlpine's had been trying to get a foot in Brean for years, a reference to the dam project. McAlpine employed the individual member. Another delegate refused to believe that big business was not behind the proposal. At the end of the meeting, thirty-two delegates voted against the full scheme, seven were in favour and twenty-nine believed the fort should be maintained at public cost.

The meeting spawned interest from the local and national media. Unfortunately, many of the proposals had been badly misinterpreted by the Brean Residents Association, who by now had gained the support of Dr David Bellamy, the media personality. They seemed to think the fort would become something akin to Blackpool's illuminations, which had never been the intention. On the other hand, local leisure businesses in Brean declared their support, as did several Sedgemoor District Councillors after visiting a similar-sized fort managed by the National Trust on the Isle of Wight.

In June 1996 the Environment and Property Department, Architectural and Historic Heritage Group at Somerset County Council finished a lengthy initial archaeological survey of the fort. The survey was to:

> provide an accurate set of drawings that could be used for design work, a preliminary survey and description of the remains. In addition it was hoped to be able to reconstruct the plan of the Victorian battery, as no plans are known to exist.

Useful information about how the fort could be managed was gathered during comparative visits to the batteries at Steep Holm and Needles Battery. The report found new information on the architecture of the site but some interpretation was hampered by the lack of documentary evidence.

However, the opposition from local politicians continued when Somerset County Council and North Somerset County Council both accused Sedgemoor District County of keeping the proposals for the fort under wraps and were therefore not supportive. Presumably they had not read local newspaper reports about the disposal of the fort. A Somerset county councillor, noted for his pomposity, told a Mendip Hills Advisory Committee meeting that few county councillors were aware of the project and there was no way he could support this "cock-eyed idea". He felt the fort was too far for people to walk and the down would be damaged. A North Somerset county councillor, who had been appointed to the proposed charitable trust, drew up her own plan, but she did call for a partnership between business and Sedgemoor District County Council to preserve the down's heritage.

After three years' work, Sedgemoor District Council were nearly ready to submit the £1.5 million bid when the National Trust essentially undermined the proposal by withdrawing their support on the grounds that the fort was unlikely to be visited by 30,000 visitors per annum. Others involved in the project felt this claim was unsustainable, particularly when compared with the tourism in Somerset and the relative success of the less accessible Needles fort. The Trust's decision was a minority one and seems to have been based more on preserving the scientific status of Brean Down than on preserving a balance between this and enhancing its modern history. In spite of this serious setback, the remaining parties decided to submit the bid more in hope than anything else. The support of the National Trust throughout the project was seen as critical to its success.

It was therefore little surprise when, on 24 March 1998, Sedgemoor District Council received a fax that their bid for a grant had been turned down by the Trustees of the National Heritage Memorial Fund. In drawing up their reasons, the trustees concluded

there were significant concerns about the long-term viability and the detrimental impact of the scheme on the site and it was therefore not possible for the present application to be supported. The Trustees noted that the fort required a minimum of 30,000 paying visitors in order to make the project viable. They were not convinced that such numbers could be drawn from the current visitors to the Down but rather that greater numbers of people on to Brean Down as a whole would need to be encouraged. They expressed concern that any increase in visitors to the Down could have damaging impact on the archaeological and nature conservation interest of the site. Finally the Trustees also considered the divided management of the Fort and the Down as an added problem.

There was great disappointment amongst those who had worked hard over three years but it was also felt by some that the reasons offered by the trustees did not stand up to close scrutiny. It was also felt that perhaps there had been behind-the-scenes lobbying by interested parties.

In the media furore that followed the decision, a Sedgemoor District Council spokesman said:

Ours was the only proposal that appeared to give the fort a lifeline. The Trust agreed it was the way forward. But then the Trust moved from positive support to neutrality, with an element of undermining.

A National Trust manager was quoted as saying:

We own the adjoining land and have a covenant on the fort itself, meaning we can veto any plans for it. We felt the plan was flawed so we did not feel we could be partners in the Lottery bid.

The Trust also claimed it was never officially involved – which was news to many in the project team – and therefore could not lend its support.

Clearly, the spokeswoman was badly briefed because her predecessor had been involved from the beginning of the project, and had indicated his support for the project. As one of the Brean Down Fort Group was told by a National Trust manager, "There was nothing wrong with your bid. Everything was done correctly but we didn't like it". After the disappointment Sedgemoor District Council wrote to the Brean Down Group, again offering them the fort for £1 but this was again rejected on the grounds of the National Trust's claim that it could veto any plan. As a member of the group put it, "The National Trust are the neighbour from hell".

The National Trust Lottery Bid

Having successfully undermined the bid, literally within months, by December 1998 the National Trust had put together a bid for £350,000 to the Heritage Lottery Fund to fund the capital repair and consolidation to the fort. There were three elements to the National Trust offer.

Firstly, the Trust proposed to purchase the fort and the five acres (2ha) of land still owned by Sedgemoor for £1. This was the amount for which the council had originally offered the land to the Brean Down Fort Group in 1994 – and again in 1998 – but had been turned down as impractical. If this offer were accepted, the Trust would then own the land and would declare it 'inalienable', which meant it could never be bought or sold or mortgaged and would be kept for the benefit forever of everyone. The National Trust would nevertheless manage the fort. Secondly, the Trust promised to provide an endowment to finance the maintenance of the fort and thirdly, to project-manage the repair, maintenance and consolidation with other interested parties, on behalf of Sedgemoor District Council.

As opposed to a major interpretation of the fort, the National Trust proposed to stabilise the existing buildings and provide a lesser interpretation of the fort, relying on trained guides and boards to illustrate the purpose of the fort and the use of buildings. Noticeable when reading the names in the project-management team was that the Brean Down Fort Group, the four private individuals who had persuaded Sedgemoor District Council to take care of the fort, were excluded in favour of representatives of official conservation bodies.

After a short delay, during August 1999, the Heritage Lottery Fund announced its support for Brean Down Fort by granting £364,000 to repair the structures, make it safe and provide some interpretation for visitors. English Heritage donated £100,000 toward the project, which is expected to last two years. Once the project is complete, the National Trust will then own the site, and its management has undertaken to set up an endowment fund to cover future costs in running the site. With the Trust's policy of 'ruinisation', it remains to be seen if Brean Down Fort will remain as a focus for telling the story of the defence of the upper reaches of the Bristol Channel or whether it will be allowed to fall into disrepair and then demolished as a hazard. It is now up to the National Trust to show its colours.

A westerly-looking view of Brean Down shows part of the old causeway exposed by the low tide. Steep Holm is beyond and in the distance on the extreme left is North Hill near Minehead. (Author's collection)

Brean Down Fort today

(All photos taken by the Author on 15 March 2000)

Overall view of the fort as it is today.

A similar view of the fort showing the relationship of the Second World War fire command bunker, which is on the left.

Parade ground and buildings, with the steps down to the old main magazine on the left and No. 1 RML gun position beyond. Inset: *Latrines and ablutions building. The rear of No. 2 6-inch gun emplacement is on the extreme left.*

Inside view of the soldiers' barracks, taken from the site of the Second World War kitchen area. The overhead beam is in fact the housing for the roller shutter blind to the cookhouse.

The moat and the remains of the generator house in the centre, beyond which are the redbrick abutments supporting the bridge.

No. 1 6-inch gun emplacement and shelter; the steps to No. 2 Magazine are on the extreme left. In the background is No. 2 7-inch RML gun position. Inset: Nos. 1 and 2 6-inch gun emplacements, with No. 1 searchlight position in the background on the extreme left. In the foreground is the concrete pillar for the Victorian Depression Range Finder.

The Second World War fire command bunker.

Second World War Nissen hut area with the fort beyond and Steep Holm in the distance.

The DMWD ramp.

Cox's 'new house', with the Lewis gun emplacements beyond.

The Lewis gun emplacements.

Concrete directional arrow, possibly for the RAF ranges south of here. Besides the one at Sand Bay, just to the north, the RAF had one for practice bombing on Pawlett Hams and another for gun firing on Steart Flats, which were located on opposite banks not far from the mouth of the River Parrett.

A view looking east towards Uphill and the Mendips, with Military Road threading across the down. The Lewis gun emplacements are in the left background beyond Cox's 'new house', whilst the RAF range control bunker can be seen opposite on the right, where Brean Down Farm nestles close to the banks of the River Axe.

A hazy view of Brean village and sands, with the bird garden in the foreground. It is interesting to compare this scene with the picture postcard in chapter one.

Census Statistics at Brean Down

Brean Down Fortifications, 1871 census

Name and age	Occupation	Place of birth
George Goodwin, 48	foreman of works/stonemason	Hinckley, Leics.
Rebecca Goodwin, 47	wife of George	Warwick
John Lumsden, 54	asphalt maker	Tavistock
William Blake, 41	labourer	Wensley
Edward Duckett, 20	labourer	Monmouth
George Gimlett, 27	labourer	Michaelsay, Somerset
William Manley, 49	labourer	Taunton
Anne Manley, 54	wife of William	Taunton
James Parker, 27	labourer	Devon
John Paul, 22	labourer	Somerset
Edward Smith, 37	labourer	Hereford
Charles Wiffen, 44	labourer	Worcester
Frederick Harris, 28	boatman	Weston-super-Mare

Brean Down Fortifications, 1881 census

Master-Gunner's quarters

Master-Gunner John Bond, 40	Scotland
Sarah Bond, 31	Kingston, Canada
William Bond, 11	Quebec
Elizabeth Bond, 9	Bermuda
Anne Bond, 7	Woolwich
Walter Bond, 5	Dover
Charles Bond, 3	Cornwall
Agnes Bond, 1	Woolwich

Brean Battery

Gunner James Cable, 36	Surrey
Gunner James Dunn, 45	Lancaster
Gunner Charles Jones, 48	Surrey
Gunner James Robinson, 41	Leigh, Worcestershire
Elizabeth Robinson, 26	Dublin

Gunner Henry Giffard, 40	Plymouth
Elizabeth Giffard, 39	Plymouth
Alfred Giffard, 4	Somerset
Anne Giffard, 7	Highbridge, Somerset
Gunner Luke Ruff, 33	Devon
Gunner William Scott, 27	Wiltshire

Brean Down Fort, 1900: Royal Garrison Artillery District Establishment

Sergeant-Major James Withers
Bombardier John Shillabeer
Gunner Frederick Gibbs
Gunner George Johnstone
Gunner Keynes
Gunner William Keyboe
Gunner Reed
Gunner John Shillabeer
Gunner Unstad

Brean Down Fortifications, 1891 census

Master-Gunner William Stretton, 38	Scotland
Mary Stretton,	Rutland
Arthur Stretton, 6 months	Northampton
Bombardier John Reed, 35	Warwick

Source: Local History Department, Weston-super-Mare Library, except for 1900, which is taken from information collated during the inquest into the explosion (1901 census data not yet available)

Specifications and Gun Drill

7-INCH RIFLED MUZZLE-LOADED GUN

Specifications of the 7-inch Mark III Rifled Muzzle-Loader were:

Weight	7 tons (7112kg)
Overall length	12ft 4in (3.76m) of toughened steel
Barrel bore length	10ft 6in (3.20m)
External width of breech	2ft 7in (787mm)
Muzzle width	7in (178mm)
Muzzle velocity	1,561ft per sec. (1,064mph/1,712kph)
Range	(see contemporary range tables)
	3,960yd (2?ml/3.62km) at an elevation of 8°
Ammunition	Shrapnel and Case anti-personnel, 69lb (31.3kg) Drill, 112lb (50.8kg) Palliser Shells, 115lb (52.2kg) Common, 159lb (72.1kg) Double Palliser Shot and Segment Shells
Penetration	With a 30lb (13.6kg) charge and Palliser Shell the Mark III was capable of penetrating 8in (203mm) armour at a range of 1000yd (914m)

Identification

On the top of the breech was the Royal cipher and the left trunnion was stamped with identification markings. As an example, a gun on Steep Holm is marked as 'RGF No. 86, III, 1868' meaning, Royal Gun Factory, Serial Number 86, Mark III, manufactured in 1868.

Equipment

Before describing the gun drill, some components needed to be explained, as outlined by John Barrett in his book *A History of the Maritime Forts in the Bristol Channel, 1866–1900*.

Cartridges ignited the gunpowder, which then produced the energy to propel the projectile from its tube. Four types of cartridges were used for RML guns, namely a battering charge weighing 22lb (9.98kg); service cartridges weighing 14lb (6.35kg) for normal operations; 10lb (4.54kg) saluting cartridges; and drill cartridges made from raw hide. Manufactured at the Gun Powder Factory, Waltham Abbey, Essex, these were made of slow-burning black gunpowder and were usually stored in a flannel tube and placed inside lined metal cases, although by 1891 a contemporary source states that at Brean Down they were placed in zinc tubes. In the same year, cordite replaced gunpowder as the propellant.

Friction tubes were made from copper tubing, 0.200in (5mm) diameter and about 3in (76mm) long, and were the device that ignited the cartridge. Filled with fine gunpowder dampened with methylated spirit, the friction tube was placed in the vent. A copper friction bar with a roughened surface was placed in a small side-tube, called a nib piece, attached to the friction tube. A small patch of composition was then placed on both sides of the friction bar. The small side-tube was then carefully compressed with a pair of pincers. Both ends of the principal tube were then sealed: at the top with shellac putty, at the bottom by shellacked paper. When the time came to fire, the explosive mixture in the main tube was ignited by the friction generated by the roughened copper bar in the nib piece when the lanyard was pulled. A large bubble of inflammable gas then passed through a small channel to the pricked cartridge charge, leaking a trickle of gunpowder.

The quill friction tube was made on the same principle as mentioned previously. It was not used for naval service, as it could cause injury to personnel in confined areas between decks. The tube was supported by a metal crutch attached near the vent, whose purpose was to support the slender tube heads, as they were liable to bend when the friction bar was pulled by the lanyard. A guide-plate was fixed to the breech, which allowed the lanyard to be reached always from the same direction by the gun detachment's No. 1.

Wads were placed between the projectile and the cartridge, and reduced scoring in the barrel as well as forming a gas check. They also prevented erosion in the bore when the powerful battering charge was used. A common wad was the Bolton wad, which was a pulp prepared from 75 percent old rags and 25 percent of tarred rope coated with waterproof varnish. An earlier type was a *papier mâché* wad. By 1878, soft copper bandings had replaced the wads and these bands later became an integral part of the shell.

Gun Drills

The aim of gun drills is to ensure automatic obedience to orders in any conditions, including under fire, with maximum safety and minimum time lost in engaging the target. Strict discipline is exercised, each man being given a number and a specified task. Gun numbers are frequently changed, to give all members of the detachment experience in different positions.

In action the Gun Position Officer or the Master-Gunner relayed the range of the target and elevation to the Gun Sergeant, who was the Number 1. The order 'Load!' was then given, specifying the type of projectile. This order was repeated by the Number 1s to their detachments. Each gun number then proceeded with his allotted task, as follows:

- Number 2 moved into position at the muzzle, received the sponge from Number 6 and, assisted by Number 3, carried out the sponging operation, returning the sponge to Number 6 on completion
- Number 4 cleaned the vent of debris
- Number 8 fetched the cartridge cylinder from the magazine and handed it to Number 7, who was stationed at the muzzle
- Number 7 placed the cartridge cylinder upright on the ground, gripped the bottom between his feet and lifted the cartridge out by the choke, then handed the cartridge to Number 3, returned the empty cylinder to the rear of the gun platform and took cover
- Number 8 returned the empty cylinder to the store
- Numbers 2 and 3 rammed the cartridge fully down the bore, together with the wad provided by Number 5, and Number 2 retained the rammer

- Number 4 pricked the cartridge through the vent, making an opening in the canvas or flannel, thus permitting the friction tube to be inserted through the vent into the gunpowder
- Numbers 9 and 11 carried the projectile in a bearer from the magazine to the front, with Number 9 on the left and Number 11 on the right, and positioned it at the muzzle
- Numbers 2 and 3 rammed the projectile down the bore, after which Number 2 handed the rammer to Number 6 who returned it to a position clear of the platform
- Number 11 returned the bearer to the magazine after ramming was completed
- Number 9 took cover

The sponging procedure ensured that no hot particles remained in the bore from the previous round. With the 7-inch RML, difficulty was experienced with sponging because the rammer was 9ft (2.75m) long. Using the two-man bearer not only made for easier handling but the bearer also enabled the studs on the projectile to be correctly positioned for ramming.

Immediately the gun was served, the Number 1 reported to the Gun Position Officer (GPO) the number of his gun and that it was ready for firing, 'Number Two gun ready, Sir!', and raised his arm in the air. There was always competition to be the first gun ready. On receipt of gun reports, the GPO ordered 'Fire!' or perhaps 'One Round, Fire!'. The Number 1 repeated this order to his detachment, whereupon all stood clear of the platform while the Number 1 lowered the tangent scale, checked the elevation or depression for the range, inserted a friction tube in the vent, stood clear and fired the gun by pulling on a lanyard. After firing, the detachment immediately proceeded with the task of serving the gun, ready for the next fire orders.

The Victorian Coast Gunner

The publication *Clothing Regulations for the Army, 1887* listed the following items to be issued to enlisted gunners on home service:

- Helmet with large regimental insignia
- Pill-box sidehat
- Grey collarless shirt
- White long johns (*underclothes*)
- Dark blue, single-breasted worsted tunic, with a scarlet collar lined with yellow piping – the unit title was usually worn on the epaulettes, and badges of rank on the upper right arm
- Blue trousers with 2-inch red stripe
- White canvas trousers
- Braces

- Grey woollen socks
- Two pair of black leather, hob-nailed ankle boots
- Black leather gaiters
- White webbing, to include cross-straps, bayonet and bayonet frog, and water bottle
- Valise
- Cloth washing-satchel for razor and soap
- Towel
- Enamel mug and plate
- Knife, fork and spoon
- Boot brushes

Specifications and Gun Drill

6-INCH MARK VII COASTAL BREECH LOADER GUN

The Mark VIIs were introduced into service on 25 February 1898 to counter foreign navies producing bigger and better armed ironclads. Originally two variants were developed with the land version barrel rifling straight to 198.8in and increasing the twist while the naval versions were rifled straight from the breech to 211.06in from the muzzle, thereafter increasing to one turn in 30 calibre. In 1902 continuity prevailed and all guns were rifled to the naval design but with 36 grooves as opposed to 24. The performances of both were similar:

Weight: 7.3 tons
Bore length: 22ft
Muzzle velocity: 2,573ft per second
Normal range: 12,000yd
Extended range: 14,600yd with propellant charges.

The 100lb projectile could pierce 15in or armour at 1000yd. The ammunition came in three sections of an armour-piercing shell, a 27lb bag charge and a vent tube fuse, which were worn in a bandoleer by the Number Two on the gun.

Firing mechanism. Most Emergency Battery guns were fired mechanically, i.e. a gunner pulling a lever, as opposed to electrically. Hand-cranked gear mechanisms governed traverse and elevation that ranged from plus 15 degrees to minus 7 degrees. Firing mechanism was electric or percussion using a lanyard.

Gun Drills. 6-inch coastal artillery gun drills were in *Coast Artillery Drills Part III Gun Drills Pamphlet No. 8, 1940* for a short action are as follows:

Numbers	Duty Watch	Recess Supply	Magazine Supply
1	Command/ramming	In command	In charge
2	At breech	Cartridge supply	Cartridge supply
3	Loading	Shell supply	Shell supply in emplacement
4	Ramming	Shell supply	Shell supply in shell store
5	Loading	Shell supply	Shell supply in emplacement
6	Cartridge supply	Cartridge supply	Cartridge supply in emplacement
ASL	Auto-sight (layer)	Cartridge supply	Cartridge supply in magazine
RBL	Rocking Bar Sight (layer)	Action lookout	Action lookout
SR	Setter for Range	Reserve No. 1	Shell supply in shell store and operates hoist

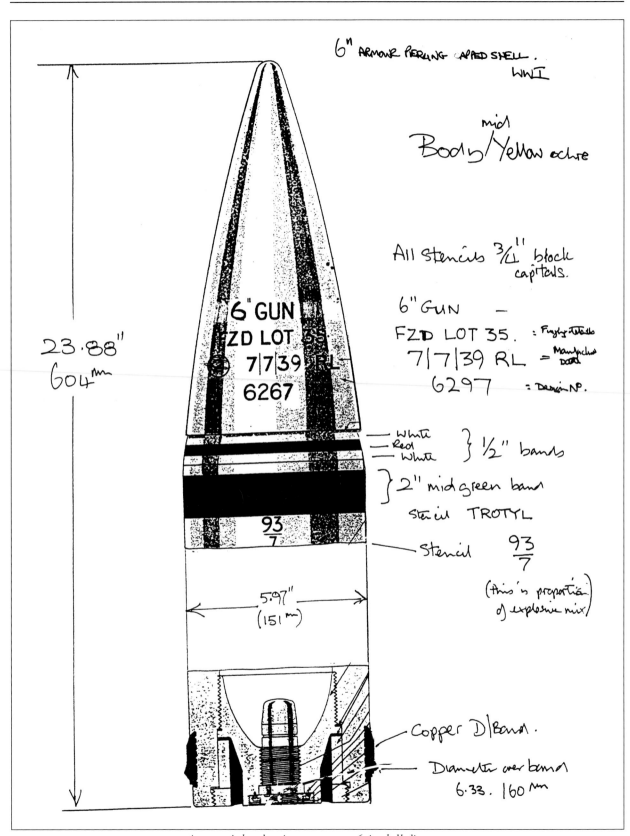

6" ARMOUR PIERCING CAPPED SHELL.
WWI

Body/Yellow ochre
(mid)

All stencils 3/4" block capitals.

6" GUN —
FZD LOT 35. = Factory details
7|7|39 RL = Manufacture Date
6297 = Design NP.

6" GUN
ZD LOT 35
7|7|39 RL
6267

White
Red   } 1/2" bands
White

} 2" mid green band

Stencil TROTYL

Stencil 93/7

93/7

(this is proportion of explosive mix)

23.88"
604mm

5.97"
(151mm)

Copper D/Band.

Diameter over band
6.33. 160mm

A gunner's hand-written notes on a 6-in shell diagram

The Second World War Coast Gunner

The Second World War coast gunner was issued with the following:

- Steel helmet
- Khaki sidehat with Royal Artillery badge *{Later dark blue berets were worn}*
- Cotton dark-khaki collarless shirt
- Thin khaki sweater
- Battledress blouse with rank insignia on both arms, Royal Artillery shoulder flash and Coast Regiment arm flash for parades and walking out
- White lanyard worn on right shoulder
- Battledress trousers
- Braces
- Greatcoat
- Black leather boots
- Webbing anklets
- Boot brushes
- 2 pair of grey woollen socks
- Pair of khaki woollen gloves
- Pair of denim one-piece overalls {to serve the guns}
- Two pair of denim battledress {for everyday use}
- Towel
- 2 pair drawers {underclothes}
- White and blue woollen pyjamas
- Pair of white or brown gym pumps
- PT vest, usually white
- Blue PT shorts
- '37 pattern belt
- '37 webbing, consisting of large park, small pack, two Bren-gun magazine pouches, metal water bottle in felt holder, braces, bayonet and bayonet frog
- Respirator
- Knife, fork and spoon
- Brown enamel mug
- Set of mess tins
- Brass button stick for polishing buttons {without getting the brass on clothing}
- 'Housewife' consisting of needle and cotton and darning wool
- Linen washing-roll including safety razor and shaving brush

Officers were expected to buy their Service dress, shirts and ties; but were issued with clothing and equipment for active service.

Rangefinding

Coast Artillery Sighting and Elevation (CASE) was the method used by the coast brigade/regiment to lay a gun on to the target at the desired point of aim, bearing in mind by the shell arrives on target, and the ship will have travelled a short distance. The point of aim was usually the bow. By the 1890s three service methods of gunlaying for coast defence had been developed:

- **CASE I:** The gun layer was responsible for line and elevation. Position Finders (PF) and Depression Range Finders (DRF) were used to calculate distance. Quick-firing (QF) guns were laid with this method. (CASE 1 was preferred when the range was not accurately known or instruments were not accurate due to mis-adjustment or breakdown).

- **CASE 2:** The gun was laid through the auto-telescope while a rangefinder, on a flank, computed the speed using a Watkins Depression Position Finder. This tracked the target on a gridded chart with bearings and ranges being calculated from the location of the gun to the target by a Watkins Dial electrical receiver, which then calculated angle and range to pass to the Gun Position Officer. He fed each calculation to the Number One who continually tracked the target until ordered to open fire. The gunlayer was responsible for laying the gun for line using straight edged sights whilst the Number One superintended elevation. PF and DRF were used to measure the distance of the target. This method was suitable when the target was obscured for night firing, salvoes and middle distant targets

- **CASE 3:** The sights were not used and the gun was laid by quadrant elevation and training arc, for what was called 'predicted firing'. The PF supplied the range and training. The information was sent electrically and displayed on dials. The gunlayer traversed the mounting and the gun was then fired electrically. This was used when the target was invisible to the gun detachment and indirect fire was applied using remotely by located rangefinders, for instance aircraft, radar or another battery.

APPENDIX VII

Severn Fixed Defence Shoots, 1940–44

Entries for Brean Down Fort are shown in *italics*. Engagements with enemy units are shown in **bold** type

Date	Gun	Direction	Unit	Location	Activity
1940					
07 July	6"	Seaward	365 Bty/531 Regt	Portishead	Practice
22 Aug.	6"	Seaward	365 Bty/531 Regt	Portishead	Calibration
11 Dec.		**AA**	**365 Bty/531 Regt**	**Portishead**	**Air raid**
1942					
23 April	6"	Seaward	365 Bty/531 Regt	Portishead	Practice
07 May	6"	Seaward	365 Bty/531 Regt	Portishead	Practice
	6"	Seaward	130 Bty/531 Regt	Nells Point	Practice
11 May	*6"*	*Seaward*	*366 Bty/571 Regt*	*Brean Down*	*Practice*
	3-pdr	Seaward	365 Bty/531 Regt	Portishead	Practice
14 May	6"	Seaward	365 Bty/531 Regt	Portishead	Practice
	6"	Seaward	430 Bty/531 Regt	Cardiff	Practice
17 May	6"	Seaward	365 Bty/531Regt	Portishead	Practice
13 June	6"	Seaward	130 Bty/531 Regt	Nells Point	Challenge SS *Overton* en-route to Burnham
05 July	6"	Seaward	430 Bty/531 Regt	Cardiff	Practice
	4.5"	**AA**	**351 HAA Bty**	**Flat Holm**	**German aircraft engaged – no hit claimed**
08 July	4.5"	**AA**	**351 HAA Bty**	**Flat Holm**	**German aircraft engaged – no hit claimed**
19 July	6"	Seaward	430 Bty/531 Regt	Cardiff	Practice
21 July	6"	Seaward	365 Bty/531 Regt	Portishead	Practice
22 July	6"	Seaward	365 Bty/531 Regt	Portishead	Practice
25 July	*6"*	*Seaward*	*366 Bty/571 Regt*	*Brean Down*	*Practice*
28 July	6"	Seaward	430 Bty/531 Regt	Cardiff	Practice
09 Aug.	4.5"	AA	351 HAA Bty	Flat Holm	Anti-tank landing craft practice
22 Aug.	3-pdr	Seaward	130 Bty/531 Regt	Nells Point	Sub-calibre practice
23 Aug.	6"	Seaward	130 Bty/531 Regt & Home Guard	Nells Point	Practice
25 Aug.	6"	Seaward	430 Bty/531 Regt	Cardiff	Practice
26 Aug.	*6"*	*Seaward*	*366 Bty/571 Regt*	*Brean Down*	*Night practice*
27 Aug.	6"	Seaward	184 Bty/571 Regt	Portishead	Practice
02 Sept.	4.5"	Seaward	All batteries	Flat Holm	Inspection
24 Sept.	75mm	Seaward	187 Bty/531 Regt	Newport	Anti-tank/landing craft practice
25 Sept.	75mm	Seaward	187Bty/531 Regt	Newport	Anti-tank/landing craft practice

Date	Gun	Direction	Unit	Location	Activity
	3-pdr	Seaward	130 Bty/531 Regt	Nells Point	Practice
27 Sept.	6"	Seaward	184 Bty/571 Regt	Portishead	Practice
06 Nov.	6"	Seaward	170 Bty/531 Regt	Nells Point	Practice
	6"	Seaward	430 Bty/531 Regt	Cardiff	Practice
	6"	*Seaward*	*366 Bty/571 Regt*	*Brean Down*	*Practice*
06 Dec.	6"	Seaward	7th Somerset Home Guard	Portishead	Practice
	75mm	*Seaward*	*366 Bty/571 Regt*	*Brean Down*	*Anti-tank/landing craft practice*
17 Dec.	*6"*	Seaward	*366 Bty/571 Regt*	*Brean Down*	*Practice*
	6"	Seaward	188 Bty/571 Regt	Steep Holm (S)	Night practice
	6"	Seaward	189 Bty/571 Regt	Steep Holm (S)	Night practice
1943					
21 Jan.	4.5"	Seaward	205 Bty/570 Regt	Flat Holm (N)	Practice
	3-pdr	Seaward	130 Bty/531 Regt	Nells Point	Practice
22 Jan.	6"	Seaward	170 Bty/531 Regt	Nells Point	Practice
	6"	Seaward	145 Bty/570 Regt	Lavernock	Practice
27 Jan.	75mm	Seaward	187 Bty/531 Regt	Newport	Practice
	6"	Seaward	170 Bty/570 Regt	Lavernock	Full charge practice
	6"	Seaward	145 Bty/570 Regt	Lavernock	Ranging salvoes
11 Feb.	6"	Seaward	170 Bty/570 Regt	Lavernock	Practice
	6"	Seaward	145 Bty/570 Regt	Lavernock	Practice
13 Feb.	4.5"	Seaward	205 Bty/570 Regt	Flat Holm (N)	Practice
15 Feb.	75mm	Seaward	187 Bty/531 Regt	Newport	Practice
	6"	Seaward	430 Bty/531 Regt	Cardiff	Practice
16 Feb.	**4.5"**	**AA**	**All batteries**	**Flat Holm**	**Two German aircraft engaged – no hit claimed**
22 Feb.	6"	Seaward	184 Bty/571 Regt	Portishead	Trials with Universal automatic sight
12 March	4.5"	Seaward	205 Bty/570 Regt	Flat Holm (N)	Practice
13 March	**4.5"**	**AA**	**All batteries**	**Flat Holm**	**FW 190 engaged – no hit claimed**
14 April	6"	Seaward	170 Bty/570 Regt & Home Guard	Lavernock	HG Training
16 April	3-pdr	Seaward	170 Bty/570 Regt	Lavernock	Practice
18 April	6"	Seaward	430 Bty/570 Regt & Home Guard	Cardiff	HG training shoot
19 April	6"	Seaward	187 Bty/570 Regt & Home Guard	Newport	HG training shoot
20 April	6"	Seaward	145 Bty/570 Regt	Lavernock	Practice
23 April	**4.5"**	**AA**	**205 Bty/570 Regt**	**Flat Holm (N)**	**German aircraft engaged – no hits claimed**
02 May	6"	Seaward	184 Bty/571 Regt & 7th Somerset HG	Portishead	HG training shoot
04 May	*6"*	*Seaward*	*366 Bty/571 Regt*	*Brean Down*	*Evening & night exercise*
	75mm	Seaward	188 Bty/571 Regt	Steep Holm (N)	Anti-tank/landing craft practice
	6"	Seaward	188 Bty/571 Regt	Steep Holm (N)	Practice
06 May	4.5"	Seaward	146 Bty/570 Regt	Flat Holm (S)	Practice
	4.5"	Seaward	205 Bty/570 Regt	Flat Holm (N)	Practice
	6"	Seaward	170 Bty/570 Regt	Nells Point	Practice

Date	Gun	Direction	Unit	Location	Activity
07 May	6"	Seaward	145 Bty/570 Regt	Lavernock	Night practice
	4.5"	AA	All batteries	Flat Holm	German aircraft engaged – no hits claimed
18 May	4.5"	AA	All batteries	Flat Holm	German aircraft engaged – no hits claimed
20 May	4.5"	AA	All batteries	Flat Holm	AA practice
06 June	6"	Seaward	187 Bty/570 Regt	Newport	Practice
08 June	6"	Seaward	170 Bty/570 Regt	Nells Point	Practice
10 June	6"	Seaward	184 Bty/571 Regt & 7th Somerset HG	Portishead	Practice
12 June	*6-pdr*	*Seaward*	*366 Bty/571 Regt*	*Brean Down*	*Anti-tank/landing craft practice*
13 June	6"	Seaward	184 Bty/571 Regt	Portishead	Practice
17 June	6"	Seaward	170 Bty/570 Regt & Home Guard	Nells Point	Mixed training
21 June	6"	Seaward	430 Bty/570 & Home Guard	Cardiff	Mixed training
22 June	6"	Seaward	145 Bty/570 Regt & Home Guard	Lavernock	Mixed training
24 June	6"	Seaward	All coast batteries	Flat Holm	Practice
08 July	6"	Seaward	170 Bty/570 Regt	Nells Point	Practice
	6"	Seaward	145 Bty/570 Regt	Lavernock	Practice
	CASL	Seaward	170 Bty/570 Regt	Nells Point	Searchlight practice
10 July	4.5"	Seaward	All coast batteries	Flat Holm	Practice
	CASL	Seaward	All batteries	Flat Holm	Searchlight practice
	CASL	Seaward	145 Bty/570 Regt	Lavernock	Searchlight practice
11 July	3-pdr	Seaward	145 Bty/570 Regt	Lavernock	Practice
14 July	*6"*	*Seaward*	*366 Bty/571 Regt*	*Brean Down*	*Practice*
22 July	CASL	Seaward	170 Bty/570 Regt	Nells Point	Searchlight practice
23 July	4.5"	AA	All batteries	Flat Holm	German aircraft engaged – no hits claimed
	6"	Seaward	145 Bty/570 Regt	Lavernock	Practice
24 July	6"	Seaward	170 Bty/570 Regt	Nells Point	Practice
	CASL	Seaward	145 Bty/570 Regt	Lavernock	Searchlight practice
26 July	4.5"	Seaward	146 Bty/570 Regt	Flat Holm (S)	Practice
28 July	4.5"	AA	205 Bty/570 Regt	Flat Holm (N)	Practice
31 July	4.5"	AA	All batteries	Flat Holm	German aircraft engaged – no hits claimed
10 Aug.	75mm	Seaward	184 Bty/571 Regt	Portishead	Anti-tank/landing craft practice
13 Aug.	*75mm*	*Seaward*	*366 Bty/571 Regt*	*Brean Down*	*Anti-tank/landing craft practice*
16 Aug.	6"	Seaward	187 Bty/570 Regt	Newport	Practice
17 Aug.	4.5"	Seaward	146 Bty/570 Regt	Flat Holm (S)	Practice
	6"	Seaward	430 Bty/570 Regt	Cardiff	Practice
18 Aug.	6"	Seaward	145 Bty/570 Regt	Lavernock	Practice
19 Aug.	6"	Seaward	170 Bty/570 Regt	Nells Point	Practice
10 Sept.	75mm	Seaward	145 Bty/570 Regt	Lavernock	Anti-tank/landing craft practice

Date	Gun	Direction	Unit	Location	Activity
13 Sept.	CASL	Seaward	Coast batteries	Flat Holm	Searchlight practice
	CASL	Seaward	145 Bty/570 Regt	Lavernock	Searchlight practice
15 Sept.	CASL	Seaward	170 Bty/570 Regt	Nells Point	Searchlight practice
17 Sept.	75mm	Seaward	187 Bty/570 Regt	Newport	Anti-tank/landing craft practice
	75mm	Seaward	430 Bty/570 Regt	Cardiff	Anti-tank/landing craft practice
18 Sept.	75mm	Seaward	170 Bty/570 Regt	Nells Point	Anti-tank/landing craft practice
19 Sept.	6"	Seaward	430 Bty/570 Regt	Cardiff	Practice
20 Sept.	6"	Seaward	187 Bty/570 Regt	Newport	Practice
	CASL	Seaward	145 Bty/570 Regt	Lavernock	Searchlight practice
	CASL	Seaward	All batteries	Flat Holm	Searchlight practice
22 Sept.	*75mm*	*Seaward*	*366 Bty/571 Regt*	*Brean Down*	*Anti-tank/landing craft practice*
	6"	*Seaward*	*366 Bty/571 Regt*	*Brean Down*	*Practice*
23 Sept.	4.5"	AA	205 Bty/570 Regt	Flat Holm (N)	Practice
26 Sept.	75mm	Seaward	184 Bty/571 Regt	Portishead	Anti-tank/landing craft practice
	6"	Seaward	184 Bty/571 Regt & 7th Somerset Home Guard	Portishead	Mixed practice
28 Sept.	2" UP	Seaward	170 Bty/570 Regt	Nells Point	Rocket training
	2" UP	Seaward	187 Bty/570	Newport	Rocket training
	6"	Seaward	184 Bty/571 Regt & 7th Somerset HG	Portishead	Mixed night training
29 Sept.	3-pdr	Seaward	188 Bty/571 Regt	Steep Holm (N)	Sub-calibre shoot
	6"	Seaward	188 Bty/571 Regt	Steep Holm (N)	Practice
14 Oct.	6"	Seaward	145 Bty/570 Regt	Lavernock	Practice
20 Oct.	6"	Seaward	145 Bty/570 Regt	Lavernock	6" guns placed in Care and Maintenance
	6"	Seaward	188 Bty/571 Regt	Steep Holm(N)	6" guns placed in Care and Maintenance
	6"	*Seaward*	*366 Bty/571 Regt*	*Brean Down*	*6" guns placed in Care and Maintenance*
21 Oct.	4.5"	AA	205 Bty/570 Regt	Flat Holm (N)	Practice
24 Oct.	2" UP	Seaward	170 Bty/570 Regt	Nells Point	Rocket training
	2" UP	Seaward	187 Bty/570 Regt	Cardiff	Rocket training
	2" UP	Seaward	430 Bty/570 Regt	Newport	Rocket training
25 Oct.	2" UP	Seaward	187 Bty/570 Regt	Cardiff	Rocket training
26 Oct.	4.5"	AA	205 Bty/570 Regt	Flat Holm (N)	Practice
	CASL	Seaward	184 Bty/571 Regt	Portishead	Searchlight practice
29 Oct.	*75mm*	*Seaward*	*366 Bty/571 Regt*	*Brean Down*	*Anti-tank/landing craft practice*
31 Oct.	2" UP	Seaward	184 Bty/571 Regt	Portishead	Rocket practice
	75mm	Seaward	184 Bty/571 Regt	Portishead	Anti-tank/landing craft practice
18 Nov.	4.5"	Seaward	205 Bty/570 Regt	Flat Holm (N)	Practice
	4.5"	Seaward	146 Bty/570 Regt	Flat Holm (N)	Practice
26 Nov.	4.5"	Seaward	205 Bty/570 Regt	Flat Holm (N)	Practice
	4.5"	Seaward	146 Bty/570 Regt	Flat Holm (N)	Practice
20 Dec.	4.5"	Seaward	205 Bty/570 Regt	Flat Holm (N)	Practice

Date	Gun	Direction	Unit	Location	Activity
1944					
10 Feb.	4.5"	Seaward	205 Bty/570 Regt	Flat Holm (N)	Practice
	4.5"	Seaward	146 Bty/570 Regt	Flat Holm (N)	Practice
11 Feb.	4.5"	Seaward	205 Bty/570 Regt	Flat Holm (N)	Practice
	4.5"	Seaward	146 Bty/570 Regt	Flat Holm (N)	Practice
14 Feb.	6"	Seaward	187 Bty/570 Regt	Newport	Practice
22 Feb.	4.5"	Seaward	205 Bty/570 Regt	Flat Holm (N)	Practice
23 Feb.	4.5"	Seaward	205 Bty/570 Regt	Flat Holm (N)	Practice
	4.5"	Seaward	146 Bty/570 Regt	Flat Holm (N)	Practice
27/28 Feb.	**4.5"**	**AA**	**All batteries**	**Flat Holm**	**Six German aircraft engaged – no hits claimed**
01 April	6"	Seaward	170 Bty/570 Regt	Nells Point	6" guns placed in Care and Maintenance
02 April	6"	Seaward	187 Bty/570 Regt	Newport	Practice
24 April	6"	Seaward	187 Bty/570 Regt	Newport	Practice
30 April	6"	Seaward	187 Bty/570 Regt	Newport	Practice
15 May	**4.5"**	**AA**	**All batteries**	**Flat Holm**	**Two German aircraft engaged – no hits claimed**
04–30 June	All guns	Seaward	570 Coast Regt		Home defence plan in support of Normandy landings
23 July	6"	Seaward	430 Bty/570 Regt	Cardiff	Practice
27 July	Radar	Seaward		Flat Holm	Gun laying AA Radar Mk III practice
30 July	6"	Seaward	184 Bty/571 Regt	Portishead	Practice
02–30 Aug.	**All guns**	**Seaward**	**570 Coast Regt**		**Severn Fixed Defences Command Shoot**
02–22 Oct.	4.5"	Seaward	205 Bty/570 Regt	Flat Holm (N)	Practice
	4.5"	Seaward	146 Bty/570 Regt	Flat Holm (N)	Practice
	6"	Seaward	184 Bty/571 Regt	Portishead	Practice
	6"	Seaward	430 Bty/570 Regt	Cardiff	Practice
23–30 Nov.	4.5"	Seaward	205 Bty/570 Regt	Flat Holm (N)	Practice
	4.5"	Seaward	146 Bty/570 Regt	Flat Holm (N)	Practice
	6"	Seaward	184 Bty/571 Regt	Portishead	Practice
03 Dec.	6"	Seaward	430 Bty/570 Regt	Cardiff	Practice
05 Dec.	4.5"	Seaward	205 Bty/570 Regt	Flat Holm (N)	Practice
	4.5"	Seaward	146 Bty/570 Regt	Flat Holm (N)	Practice
07 Dec.	4.5"	Seaward	205 Bty/570 Regt	Flat Holm (N)	Practice
	4.5"	Seaward	146 Bty/570 Regt	Flat Holm (N)	Practice
	All guns		570 Coast Regt		Non-operational
1945					
01 June			570 Coast Regt disbanded		All batteries placed in Care and Maintenance

Source: John Penny 'The War Diary of the Severn Estuary Coastal Defences, 1939–45'

Establishment of Severn Fixed Defences

Although an incomplete record, including formations, disbandments and subsequent battery incorporations, the following tabled extracts from war diaries give an indication of regimental strengths throughout the Second World War.

	570 Coast Regt		571 Coast Regt		530 Coast Regt		531 Coast Regt	
	Officers	*ORs*	*Officers*	*ORs*	*Officers*	*ORs*	*Officers*	*ORs*
1940								
05 September							Regiment formed	
1941								
12 December			Regiment formed					
19 December	Regiment formed							
1942								
31 January	11	348						
28 February	15	347	13	218				
01 April	16	360						
01 May	27	363	11	248				
28 May	18	365	10	218				
30 June	19	378	12	223				
31 July	16	389	12	217				
31 August	16	392	10	220				
30 September	16	402	9	237				
31 October			10	236	15	402		
30 November	17	403	10	236				
31 December	24	650	12	388				
1943								
31 January	26	605	17	398				
16 February	26	586						
28 February			18	365				
31 March	26	587						
30 April	23	584						
31 May	22	614	13	271				
30 June	23	622						
31 July	21	682	11	282				
31 August	25	611	11	257				
30 September	25	615	12	262				
31 October	25	585	13	245				
30 November					24	500	10	122
1944								
31 January	21	441						
29 February	20	434						
31 March	17	436						
01 April			Regiment disbanded					
30 April	23	603						
31 May	22	509						
30 June	23	492						
31 July	23	467						
31 August	25	487						
30 September	23	480						
31 October	24	479						
30 November	22	437						
31 December	21	434						
1945								
31 January	14	303						
28 February	12	261						
31 March	11	201						
30 April	11	204						
01 June	Regiment disbanded							

Source: John Penny 'The War Diary of the Severn Estuary Coastal Defences, 1939–45'

Appointments: Severn Fixed Defences

The date is that when the officer took command of the unit. *(Source: John Penny)*

Headquarters, Severn Fixed Defences
Lt-Col E.M. Bolt: 1 July 1940 from 570 Coast Regiment
Lt-Col C.J. Ferard: 9 Feb 1942
Lt-Col R.A. King: 16 Aug 1943 from 570 Coast Regiment
Disbanded 20 April 1944

570 Coast Regiment RA
Major C.W. Galloway: 19 Dec 1941
Lt-Col E.M. Bolt: 9 Feb 1942
Major C.W. Galloway: 8 May 1942
Lt-Col R.A. King: 20 June 1942
Disbanded 1 June 1945

571 Coast Regiment RA
Major R.G. Hickson: 12 December 1941
Major H.G. Mason MBE: 20 January 1942 to 561 Coast Regiment
Major M.W. McDonald: 8 August 1942
Captain R.E. Wilson: 30 May 1942
Disbanded 1 April 1944

Glamorgan Fortress Coy RE
Major G.W. Lunn: 28 August 1939

531 Coast Regiment RA
Major D.P. Horsley: 18 May 1941

29 (Railway Survey) Coy RE
Lt I.T. Goodchild: 30 May 1941
2Lt Whitehead: 13 June 1941

930 Port and Construction Repair Coy RE
Major D. Bertlin:
Captain McLeod: 13 July 1941

116 Pioneer Coy AMPC/RPC
Lt J.H. Forbes:
Lt R.F. Spoule: 14 August 1941

690 General Construction Coy RE
Lt F. Smith: 3 September 1941
Major M. Thompson RE: 1 January 1942

719 Artisan Works RE
Lt F. Milnes:
Lt J.D.H. Davidson: 11 Feb 1943

Maps: Defence of the Bristol Channel, 1941–44

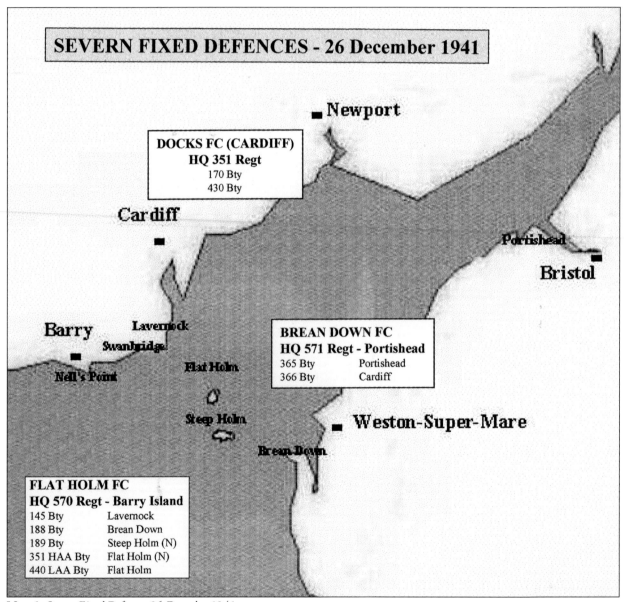

SEVERN FIXED DEFENCES - 26 December 1941

Newport

DOCKS FC (CARDIFF)
HQ 351 Regt
170 Bty
430 Bty

Cardiff

Portishead

Bristol

Barry   Lavernock
        Swanbridge

Nell's Point

Flat Holm

BREAN DOWN FC
HQ 571 Regt - Portishead
365 Bty   Portishead
366 Bty   Cardiff

Steep Holm

Weston-Super-Mare

Brean Down

FLAT HOLM FC
HQ 570 Regt - Barry Island
145 Bty   Lavernock
188 Bty   Brean Down
189 Bty   Steep Holm (N)
351 HAA Bty   Flat Holm (N)
440 LAA Bty   Flat Holm

Map 1: *Severn Fixed Defences, 26 December 1941.*

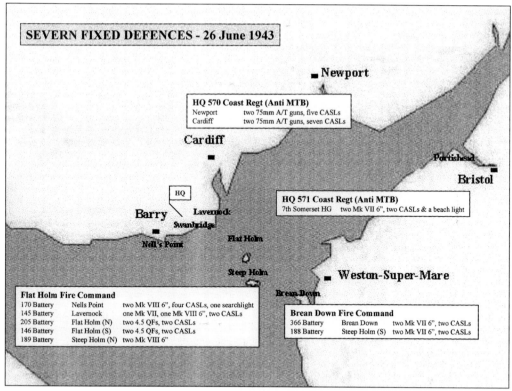

Map 2: *Severn Fixed Defences, 26 June 1943.*

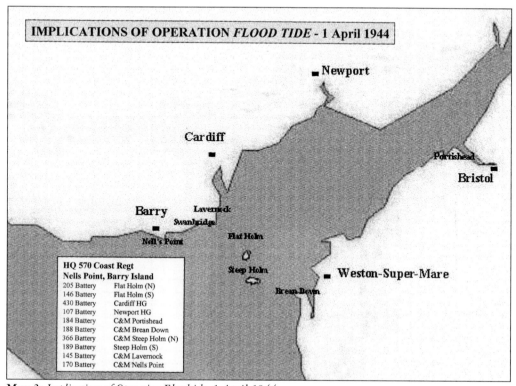

Map 3: *Implications of Operation Floodtide, 1 April 1944.*

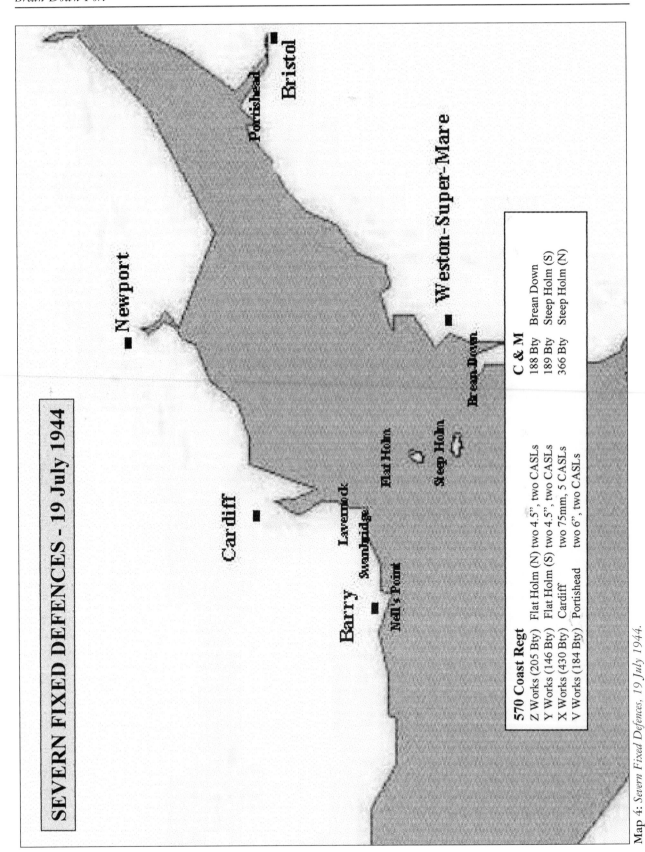

SEVERN FIXED DEFENCES - 19 July 1944

570 Coast Regt

Z Works (205 Bty)	Flat Holm (N)	two 4.5", two CASLs
Y Works (146 Bty)	Flat Holm (S)	two 4.5", two CASLs
X Works (430 Bty)	Cardiff	two 75mm, 5 CASLs
V Works (184 Bty)	Portishead	two 6", two CASLs

C & M

188 Bty	Brean Down
189 Bty	Steep Holm (S)
366 Bty	Steep Holm (N)

Map 4: *Severn Fixed Defences, 19 July 1944.*

Acknowledgements

Writing a history book is often collecting information from a variety of sources and then collating it under a single cover. This was the case with Brean Down Fort, about which remarkably little is known. I hope this book will help to fill the hole, but I have no doubt that more information about it will emerge, which can only be beneficial to local history.

While writing the story of Brean Down Fort, I have been fortunate enough to meet several people associated with its history. One of the most important is Alan Wynn, who sparked my interest when we were part of a group that contributed to the Sedgemoor District Council Heritage Lottery bid to restore this important part of Great Britain's and Somerset military and social history. He deserves credit for regenerating interest in its preservation, but it is sad that his commitment was cast aside. Let us hope that the National Trust will be as conscientious as Alan was about the fort's preservation.

Any writer on Brean Down owes a large debt to John Barrett, whose book *A History of the Maritime Forts in the Bristol Channel 1866–1900* was a result of long and detailed research. The same applies to John Penny for his unpublished work on the Severn Fixed Defences/Coast Artillery South Wales 1939–1945. I am grateful to them both for their permission to use and quote from their work.

In his book, Mr Barrett pays tribute to the soldiers of the Coast Brigade and Regiment; I concur.

During my research I was fortunate to track three members of a dwindling band of Coast Regiment gunners and a Home Guard soldier, who trained on the Brean Down guns during the Second World War. Fifty years after they were demobbed, I owe sergeants Reg Stevens and Joe Walford, Gunner Ray Patterson and Private Stuart Hicks a big debt of gratitude for their patience, photographs and momentos. This applies equally to Irene Sampson, who was a waitress in the café, and to Donald House for filling the gaps for the inter-war period. Mrs Betty Poole supplied with valuable her families' contribution to the building of the fort in the 1860s. Steve Dent helped me with the Admiralty's Department of Miscellaneous Weapons Development.

I made extensive use of museums and libraries and consequently must express my appreciation for their assistance – to Sharon Poole of North Somerset Museum for her information and photographs on the Bristol Channel steamers and Uphill Ferry; to Weston-Super-Mare Library for lending photos; to John Condor at Sedgemoor District Council for access to council records; to John Guy, Bernard Lowry and Major Tom Hitchins of the Fortress Study Group; Bristol City Council, Imperial War Museum, Royal Engineers' Museum, Royal Artillery Institute, National Maritime Museum, the Public Records Office, the National Monuments Records Office for giving me access to information. I am grateful to former Army colleague Martin Barratt and to Neil Hyslop for drawing the maps.

My editor and proofreader, Gerard Hill, was firm but very fair. Without his meticulous examination of the draft – all achieved by electronic messaging – this would be a lesser book.

I also owe a huge debt to Mac Hawkins for taking on this project. This was a difficult task, but as a keen local historian in his own right, he was a source of inspiration and also information.

Finally, thank you to my wife Penny and our daughter Imogen for your patience and understanding.

Nick van der Bijl
Mark, Somerset, April 2000

Bibliography
Books and ephemera

Books and ephemera

Architectron of Bristol: 'Brean Down Fort Project';
Sedgemoor District Council, November 1996

Barrett, John: *A History of the Maritime Forts in the Bristol Channel, 1866–1900;* privately published, 1993

Brown, Bryan, and Loosley, John: *The Book of Weston-super-Mare*; Barracuda Books; Buckingham, 1979

Dutton, Louie: *Brean Down;* [Weston-super-Mare], 1921

Hawkins, Mac: *Somerset At War, 1939–1945*; Hawk Editions, 1996

Hodder, E.H: 'Brean Down Café Memories'; *Weston Mercury*, 23 April 1965

Howell-Everson, Douglas: *Victorian Fortress Strategy in the United Kingdom;* Fortress Study Group, *Fort: The International Journal of Fortifications and Military Architecture*, Volume 15, 1987

Knight, Francis: *The Seaboard of Mendip*; Dent, London, 1902 [repr. Alis Press, 1988]

Manchester Metropolitan University: 'Brean Down Fort Feasibility Study'; unpublished report to Sedgemoor District Council and National Trust by Centre for Environmental Interpretation, October 1993

National Trust: *Brean Down, A Conservation Statement;* December 1998

National Trust: *Brean Down Fort: Project Proposals;* December 1998

National Trust and Sedgemoor District Council: 'Brean Down, Somerset Management Plan'; unpublished, October 1977

Pawle, Gerald: *The Secret War;* Harrap, London, 1956

Pinsent, Margaret: 'The defences of the Bristol Channel in the last two centuries'; *Fort: The International Journal of Fortifications and Military Architecture*, Volume 11, 1983

Rendell, Stan and Joan: *Steep Holm – The Story of a Small Island*; Alan Sutton, Stroud, 1993

Riley, Hazel: *Brean Down, Brean, Somerset: a new survey by the Royal Commision on the Historical Monuments of England;* June 1995

Rogers, H.C.B: *Artillery through the Ages*; Seeley Services, London, 1971

Smith, Victor: *Images of Brean Down Fort, 1870–1945*; A report to the National Trust, February 1989

Wall, Robert: *Bristol Channel Pleasure Steamers;* W.J. Holman, London, 1973

War Office: *Coast Artillery Drills – Part III – Pamphlet No. 8*; London, 1940

Webster, Chris: *Initial archaeological survey of Breandown Battery;* Environmental and Property Department, Architectural and Historic Heritage Group, Somerset County Council, June 1996[included in National Trust: *Conservation Statement*, 1998]

Wheeler, Heneage: 'Brean Down – Memories of a Familiar Promontory'*; Weston Mercury*, 12 August 1955

Archive sources

Unpublished typescripts
Penny, John: 'The Portishead and Avonmouth Gun Batteries, 1643 to 1919'

Penny, John: 'The War Diary of the Severn Estuary Coastal Defences, 1939/45'

Interviews and correspondence
Hicks, Stuart: Interview – Brean and Berrow Home Guard; 1996

Patterson, Ray: Correspondence – Steep Holm and Brean Down in the Second World War; 1999

Sampson, Irene: Interview – Brean Down café; 1996

Stevens, Reginald: Interviews – Steep Holm and Brean Down in the Second World War; 1996–99

Walford, Joe: Correspondence and interview – Steep Holm and Brean Down in the Second World War; 1999

Public Record Office documents
ADM 277, Department of Miscellaneous Weapons Development

WO 166 1842, 365 Battery, Portishead

WO 166 3937, War Diary 930 Port Construction Coy, March–December 1941

WO 166 6029, HQ RA Western Command, January–December 1942

WO 166 6713, Area HQ Somerset and Bristol, January–December 1942

WO 166 7278, Fixed Defences in Severn

WO 166 8027, Movements Control, Bristol Channel Ports

WO 196 131, Ports and Harbours Western District, Revision of Coast Defences Armaments prior to June 1894

WO 199 523, Formation of Coast Batteries

WO 199 524, Coast Artillery Search Lights

WO 199 525/526, Home Guard Coast Batteries

WO 199 1175, Fixed Defences, Severn Area

Index

Bold type indicates illustrations. Due to the extensive use of local names, areas, rivers etc. references are only included for important events where appropriate.